D0744480

HISTORY OF THE ARCHBISHOPS OF
HAMBURG-BREMEN

RECORDS OF WESTERN CIVILIZATION

RECORDS OF WESTERN CIVILIZATION

HISTORY OF
THE ARCHBISHOPS OF
HAMBURG-BREMEN

ADAM OF BREMEN

TRANSLATED WITH AN INTRODUCTION AND NOTES
BY FRANCIS J. TSCHAN

WITH A NEW INTRODUCTION AND SELECTED BIBLIOGRAPHY
BY TIMOTHY REUTER

COLUMBIA UNIVERSITY PRESS
NEW YORK

Columbia University Press
Publishers Since 1893
New York   Chichester, West Sussex

Copyright © 2002 Columbia University Press
All rights reserved

Library of Congress Cataloging-in-Publication Data
Adam, von Bremen, 11th cent.
  [Gesta Hammaburgensis ecclesiae pontificum. English]
  History of the archbishops of Hamburg-Bremen / Adam of Bremen ;
  translated with an introduction and notes by Francis J. Tschan ; with
  a new introduction and bibliography by Timothy Reuter.
       p. cm. — (Records of Western civilization)
   Includes bibliographical references and index.
    ISBN 0–231–12574–7 (cloth)—ISBN 0–231–12575–5 (paper)
     1. Catholic Church. Archdiocese of Hamburg-Bremen—History—To
  1500.   2. Hamburg Region (Germany)—Church history.   3. Bremen Region
  (Germany)—Church history.   I. Tschan, Francis Joseph, 1881–1947.
  II. Reuter, Timothy.   III. Title.   IV. Series.

BX1538.H35 A3313 2002
282'.43515'0902—dc21   2001053731

Columbia University Press books are printed on permanent and durable acid-
free paper.
Printed in the United States of America
c 10 9 8 7 6 5 4 3 2 1
p 10 9 8 7 6 5 4 3 2 1

RECORDS OF WESTERN CIVILIZATION is a series published under the auspices of the Interdepartmental Committee on Medieval and Renaissance Studies of the Columbia University Graduate School. The Western Records are, in fact, a new incarnation of a venerable series, the Columbia Records of Civilization, which, for more than half a century, published sources and studies concerning great literary and historical landmarks. Many of the volumes of that series retain value, especially for their translations into English of primary sources, and the Medieval and Renaissance Studies Committee is pleased to cooperate with Columbia University Press in reissuing a selection of those works in paperback editions, especially suited for classroom use, and in limited clothbound editions.

Committee for the Records of Western Civilization

Caroline Walker Bynum

Joan M. Ferrante

Carmela Vircillo Franklin

Robert Hanning

Robert Somerville, editor

CONCORDIA UNIVERSITY LIBRARY
PORTLAND, OR 97211

*TO MY SON ROBERT AND
MY DAUGHTER MARGARET*

Contents

Introduction to the 2002 Edition

Timothy Reuter

Francis Tschan's translation of Adam of Bremen's *History of the Archbishops of Hamburg-Bremen* was published at a time when studies of Adam were about to experience a renaissance.[1] Adam's key position as the author of one of the earliest written sources for early Scandinavian history had by 1959 already been established for two generations, following the source-critical studies of the Weibulls in the early decades of the twentieth century, and it has been further reinforced by more recent work. Even if Adam's view of the ninth and tenth centuries must also be treated with some scepticism,[2] his importance as a writer, a biographer, and a church historian, as well as an ethnographer, now seems far more significant than it did in 1959. At the same time, our understanding of the complex thought patterns and working habits of medieval historians has also grown, and historians are now even more cautious than they were about reading texts as unmediated accounts of a past reality. Though Adam was exceptionally well informed—not least through conversations with King Sven Estridsen of Denmark—about Scandinavian history and contemporary Scandinavian politics, and his testimony about them is invaluable, he was nevertheless writing in the genre of the *gesta episcoporum*, or deeds of bishops:[3] his primary interests were the greatness of his archbishopric—its claims to primacy over the Scandinavian church and to direction of missionary work over the Slavs of the lower Elbe—and the importance of Hamburg. As we shall see, he was also writing at a time when the archbishopric was threatened by forces nearer to home: by its local rivals, the Billung dukes of Saxony; by the conflict between Henry IV and the lay and ecclesiastical magnates of Saxony, in which Adam's archbishop, Liemar, was among the small minority who supported Henry; and by the growing tendency of the papacy to subordinate episcopal and archiepiscopal churches to its own aims.

Adam's Work: Editions, Translations, and Manuscript Studies

Tschan translated the text as established by the last full edition of Adam's complex text, published by Bernhard Schmeidler with the Monumenta Germaniae Historica in 1917. Schmeidler divided all Adam manuscripts into three classes, of which one representative of class A, Vienna 521, transmitted the first version of Adam's work as completed probably in 1076 and presented to his patron, Archbishop Liemar of Bremen. The remaining manuscripts—all those of classes B and C (including derivatives found in late medieval and early modern transcripts and printed books) but also the remaining A-class manuscripts—were based on a copy that Adam retained and continued to work on by adding the so-called *scholia* (additional notes); however, some of the later scholia found only in class B and C manuscripts were the product of later editorial interventions by a Bremen colleague of Adam's after his death sometime in the early 1080s.

Schmeidler's text is unlikely to be changed substantially by any new edition, but his view of the manuscript tradition has been challenged in a number of ways. Not long after the appearance of his edition, Store Bolin, Eberhard Otto, and John Danstrup proposed corrections and changes to his detailed account of the relations between the various manuscripts.[4] Most recently, Anne Kristensen has argued plausibly that the Vienna manuscript is not derived from an early edition by Adam himself, but rather, like all of the other manuscripts, a later edition produced by a scribe who unusually sought to eliminate as many of the scholia as possible.[5] What we have, therefore, is a text transmitted to us by manuscripts that fall into three equal classes and are derived from early exemplars, none of which survive directly. The text itself was in a state of continual modification during Adam's own lifetime and possibly beyond it, but no surviving manuscript can be shown to represent a "definitive" dedication version that was presented to Archbishop Liemar, and indeed it is not clear that any such presentation took place, even though Adam was a canon of Bremen and his work is clearly dedicated to Liemar, as the prologue shows (p. 3).

A number of editions and translations have appeared since the Schmeidler edition, though none is based on a completely new collation of the manuscripts. Apart from those noted in Tschan's bibliography, we have a German-Latin edition by Werner Trillmilch,[6] a Danish-Latin edition of the fourth book with its extensive ethnographic material by Allan Lund,[7] a Swedish translation by Emanuel Svenberg[8] with very extensive commentary, and most recently an Italian-Latin edition by Ileana Pagani.[9]

The Church of Hamburg-Bremen

Adam's bishopric was not an ancient one going back to early Christian times. Bremen had been founded, like most of the other Saxon bishoprics, in Charlemagne's time; its first bishop, Willehad, was ordained in 787 and the cathedral consecrated in 789. It was not an archbishopric but a suffragan of the archbishopric of Cologne, like neighbouring Verden. Hamburg was founded as a bishopric in 831 by Louis the Pious, as a base for Ansgar's missionary work in the north, and became an archbishopric shortly afterward. Ansgar was driven from Hamburg in 845 and given the bishopric of Bremen when its holder died; in 848 the two sees were united, a move confirmed by Pope Nicholas I in 864.[10] The failure of the northern mission in the years following Ansgar's death in 864 led to attempts in the early 890s to remove archiepiscopal status from the double see and restore Bremen to the province of Cologne, attempts ended only by Pope Sergius III in the late 900s. The whole of this history is very difficult to reconstruct, not least because of the extensive forgeries conducted on behalf of the see in the eleventh and twelfth centuries; some historians have argued that the whole idea of an early "archbishopric of Hamburg" is a later invention, but the account just given is probably broadly correct.[11]

The missionary aspirations of the ninth century were revived in the tenth century following Henry I's victory over the Danes, probably in 934. Just as the archbishopric of Magdeburg, founded by Otto I in 967/968, claimed extensive missionary rights over the Slav lands to the east, so the archbishops of Hamburg-Bremen claimed similar rights over the Scandinavian north (as well as over the northernmost Slavs in Oldenburg and Mecklenburg, where suffragan bishoprics were set up for a time). However, the Danish rulers in particular, and to a lesser extent those in Norway and Sweden, were increasingly unhappy about such external control. They sought repeatedly to have their bishops consecrated elsewhere, and there are signs (some of which are noted by Adam) of missionary work by Anglo-Saxon and French clerics in the Scandinavian lands.[12] Adam's hero Adalbert tried to have Hamburg-Bremen turned into a patriarchate, that is an archbishopric with even higher status, in order to preserve his claims over the north,[13] but from the mid-eleventh century the writing was on the wall for Hamburg-Bremen's metropolitan claims. In spite of protests by the archbishops and their rulers, archbishoprics were established with papal support and approval in Denmark (Lund, 1103/1104), Norway (Trondheim/Nidaros, 1152) and finally Sweden (Uppsala, 1164).[14] Hamburg-Bremen, never a rich see even at the height of its prosperity between c. 950 and c. 1060, had already suffered severe material losses during the German civil war of 1073–1122, and it was reduced to the status of an impoverished archbishopric with a handful of still more impoverished suffragans; for much of the twelfth century it and they were largely under the control of the dukes of Saxony, especially following the defeat of the archbishops in the struggle for succession to the counts of Stade in the years 1144 to 1148.[15]

This external decline, whose beginnings Adam witnessed and feared, was matched by internal conflict: the constituent bishoprics of the joint archbishopric had both had cathedral chapters, and al-

though the Hamburg chapter disappeared for a time, it was re-
founded in 1020 by Archbishop Unwan, as Adam records (II 48, p.
89), only to be dispersed again following the disastrous fire of 1066
(III 51, p. 158). In the next one hundred and fifty years, the rights
of the Bremen chapter came to dominate over those of the Hamburg
chapter, a position confirmed by Pope Honorius III in 1224.[16] Adam
was a strong partisan of Hamburg, and some of his fiercest criticism
of past archbishops was directed against those who, as he saw it,
neglected Hamburg.[17] His narrative also records the beginnings of
"church reform" in the archbishopric and the attempts by successive
archbishops to impose a life according to a rule on the canons of
their two chapters (II 69, p. 105; III 30, p. 139).[18]

Church reform was a matter of acute concern at the time Adam
was writing. Archbishop Liemar (1073–1101), to whom Adam's
History is dedicated, like his fellow German archbishops, bitterly
resented the claims of Pope Gregory VII (1073–1085), complaining
in a famous letter to his colleague, Bishop Hezilo of Hildesheim,
that "this dangerous man wants to order us around as if we were his
bailiffs."[19] Expelled from his diocese by Henry IV's opponents following the outbreak of the Saxon revolt in 1073, Liemar refused to
obey Gregory's summons to Rome in 1075 and was excommunicated;[20] he was absolved along with Henry IV at Canossa in 1077
but remained a firm supporter of Henry thereafter, at a time when
Gregory and his successors were establishing independent communications with the rulers of Scandinavia. Henrik Janson has even
argued that the famous account in book IV of the temple at Uppsala
is not to be taken literally but is rather a satirical attack on the Gre-
gorians,[21] and though this probably goes too far, it is certainly true
that Adam and Liemar were fighting on a number of fronts in the
1070s.

The greatest threat came from local enemies, in particular the
Billung dukes of Saxony, who erected a rival fortification in Hamburg and raided Bremen, and the counts of Stade, whom Adalbert
sought to make his allies by granting them extensive fiefs. So long
as Adalbert could use his position at Henry IV's court to compensate
his local losses through the grant of monasteries and royal estates,

all was well, but with his fall from favour in 1066, which coincided with a devastating Slav uprising that led to the destruction of Hamburg, the material position of the archbishopric was seriously threatened: as Adam notes, its treasures accumulated over generations were rapidly dispersed (pp. 153–54).[22]

Adam as Biographer

In the first two books of the *History*, Adam reconstructs the history of the archbishopric of Hamburg-Bremen as it had evolved since the times of Willehad and Ansgar, stressing the importance of Hamburg within the joint archbishopric and of the claims to missionary supremacy over the lands of the north. The third book is devoted to the pontificate of Archbishop Adalbert, who had summoned Adam to Bremen and given him the post of *scholasticus* at the cathedral school. Adam greatly admired Adalbert, and yet he saw him as at least in part responsible for the decline in the greatness of the see because of his overexposure in the dangerous game of court politics; if he had been able to use his closeness to the king to good effect under Henry III and in the early years of Henry IV's minority, his fall from grace in 1066 led to the attacks on the see by its local aristocratic enemies, the devastation of Hamburg, and the subsequent loss of the "investments" he had made earlier on in his pontificate in order to secure rights of jurisdiction within his diocese. Adam's "biography" of Adalbert has long attracted attention from historians, not least because it is perhaps the earliest example of a medieval biography that records not development but decline.[23] Adalbert was a man of considerable ability, proud of his high-ranking family,[24] and conscious of his extensive learning;[25] and yet in seeking to do precisely what all bishops were supposed to do for their sees, namely to enhance their rights and wealth and to defend their prerogatives uncompromisingly, he risked too much and achieved the opposite of what he had intended. The account of Adalbert's pontificate is the longest section in Adam's work, and the most heartfelt.

Adam as Historian and Ethnographer of the Scandinavian World

Adam was not the first medieval writer to describe the manners and customs of neighboring peoples. Earlier missionary literature, including Bede's *Ecclesiastical History* and the biographies of Ansgar and Rimbert, had frequently done so, and there are substantial ethnographic digressions in the work of an earlier Saxon author, Thietmar of Merseburg's *Chronicon*, completed in 1018.[26] But the fourth book of the *History* is the first systematic ethnography of a region, though it is introduced by Adam as "background information" to Adalbert's claims to appoint bishops throughout the lands to the north of Hamburg-Bremen (p. 186). As such it marks the beginning of more systematic medieval ethnography, as developed by writers like Gerald of Wales and Helmold of Bosau in the twelfth century and by the medieval encyclopedists, from Gervase of Tilbury onward.[27]

It is from Adam's fourth book, and from his discrete references to Scandinavian history in the course of the first three books, that much of tenth- and eleventh-century Scandinavian history has to be written, though the study of both the archaeological remains and of runic inscriptions has substantially transformed our perspectives in the forty years since Tschan's translation was published.[28] Adam was writing at a time when the fluid Scandinavian empires based on overlordship and tribute-taking, which had characterized the period between 850 and 1050, were consolidating into west European–style kingdoms supported by bishoprics, administrative institutions, and taxation—a proccess of consolidation that would take a further hundred and fifty years to complete. Adam's work throws considerable light also on the processes of Christianization and the activities of rival missionaries, as well as on the forms of pre-Christian religion they encountered.

Adam as an Author and Thinker

Adam was much more than a mere compiler, though he drew extensively on a range of sources (see Tschan's introduction, pp. xvi–

xix, for details). As one might expect from someone who became *scholasticus* at a cathedral school in an era when such posts were the object of considerable competition, Adam was an author with considerable literary pretensions; he made extensive use of both the Bible and of classical writers, not simply to decorate his work with apposite quotations but to shape his style and his structure.[29] Karl Morrison has argued for seeing Adam as an early exponent of a kind of non-linear and complexly textured historical writing that was to become much more widespread in the twelfth century.[30] Recent scholarship has done much to elucidate his worldview: it has investigated the coherence of the terminology he used for peoples[31] and the way in which he viewed the political world around him,[32] as well as his legitimizing use of both law and memory to justify the claims of his see to greatness.[33]

Adam's Influence

Adam's work was drawn on by a number of later compilers, notably the great mid-twelfth-century compilation known as the *Annalista Saxo*.[34] Some of these works, indeed, can be used for reconstructing the manuscript tradition of Adam's own text. The *History* was far less influential as a model, however. This is partly because the genre in which Adam wrote was dying out in the eleventh and twelfth centuries; few new *gesta episcoporum* were begun in this period, and those which were continued had their agendas already defined. It is possible that Adam was used by the author of *Íslendingabók*, which is in effect a *gesta episcoporum* for the recently founded Icelandic bishopric.[35] His work was more influential locally; later medieval and early modern Bremen historical writing, and in particular his namesake and successor Adam Krantz, owed a good deal to Adam's work.[36] But unlike some medieval authors who were widely read in their own time or by subsequent generations, Adam's real influence did not emerge until the nineteenth and twentieth centuries: his work reveals the way in which the great churches of medieval Europe faced the complex and conflicting claims of missionary ambition, royal service, and preservation of their own rights, property, and traditions in a way which can hardly be matched by any other work of the high middle ages. Though it has often been used as a quarry from which to mine information about early Scandinavian history, its title has to be taken seriously: it is a history of the archbishops of Hamburg-Bremen, and of their aims and actions, written at a time when the decline of the see from its greatest heights was already clearly visible but not, as yet, evidently irreversible.[37]

Notes

1. Neither this introduction nor the additional bibliography provided with this reprint can hope to give a comprehensive account of recent work on early Scandinavian history, and it has not been possible to update Tschan's commentary. Useful guidance on many topics is provided by Pulsiano (ed.), *Encyclopedia of Medieval Scandinavia.* Fuller bibliographical details should be sought from the CD-ROM version of the *International Medieval Bibliography*, from the extensive commentary provided with the recent Swedish translation of Adam (see n. 8), and from the *Kulturhistorisk Leksikon for nordisk midelalder*; convenient English-language introductions to the subject are provided by Sawyer, *The Oxford Illustrated History of the Vikings*, and Sawyer and Sawyer, *Medieval Scandinavia*; I am grateful to Peter and Birgit Sawyer for commenting on an earlier draft of this introduction and the supplementary bibliography, though any errors which remain are my own.
   References to Adam's own text in what follows are given as page numbers to Tschan's translation.
2. Peter and Birgit Sawyer will set out the case against Adam's "reliability" in an appendix to their forthcoming survey of Viking-Age Scandinavia to be published by Siedler Verlag, and in a forthcoming article, "A Gormless History? The Jelling Dynasty Revisited." See also Lund, *Harald Blåtands død*, for Adam's account of Harald Bluetooth.
3. On this genre, ultimately derived from the example of the papal *Liber pontificalis* and diffused through Europe from the eighth century onward, see Sot, *Gesta episcoporum.*
4. Bolin, "Kring Mäster Adams text" and "Zum Cod; Otto, "Textgeschichte." Cf. also Bernhard Schmeidler, "Entstehung und zum Plane"; Danstrup, "Esgruserhaandskriftet" (important for the relationship of the B-class mss.).
5. Kristensen, *Studien zur Adam von Bremen Überlieferung*, pp. 11–56.
6. *Quellen des 9. und 11. Jahrhunderts.*
7. *Adam af Bremen, Beskrivelse af øerne i Norden.*
8. *Historien om Hamburgstiftet och dess biskopar. Adam av Bremen.*
9. *Storia degli arcivescovi della chiesa di Amburgo, di Adamo di Brema.*
10. On the foundation, see Wavra, *Salzburg und Hamburg*, and the con-

troversial literature cited in the following note; the sequence of bishops is established by Reinecke, "Hammaburgensis sive Bremensis ecclesia (Hamburg-Bremen)." An English translation of the *Life of Ansgar* can be found in Robinson, *Anskar*, a new edition is being prepared by Ian Wood. On Ansgar, see Drögereit, "Ansgar"; Haas, "Foris apostolus intus monachus"; Katholische Akademie (ed.), *Mit Ansgar beginnt Hamburg*; Reinecke, "Bischofsumsetzung und Bistumsvereinigung."

11. For a critique of the papal privileges for Hamburg-Bremen, see Seegrün, *Provincia Hammaburgo-Bremensis*, and his preparatory studies: *Das Papsttum und Skandinavien* and *Das Erzbistum Hamburg in seinen älteren Papsturkunden*. For the controversy, besides Wavra, *Salzburg und Hamburg*, see also Drögereit, "Hamburg-Bremen, Bardowiek-Verden," and "Erzbistum Hamburg"; Reinecke, "Das Erzbistum Hamburg-Bremen und Köln 890–893"; Seegrün, "Das Erzbistum Hamburg—eine Fiktion?." For (provisionally) concluding comments, see Schieffer, "Adnotationes"; Theuerkauf, "Urkundenfälschungen."

12. Abrams, "Eleventh-Century Missions" and "Anglo-Saxons and Christianization"; Birkeli, "Earliest Missionary Activities"; Johnsen, "Om misjonsbiskopen Grimkellus"; Nyberg, *Die Kirche in Skandinavien*; Skre, "Missionary Activity"; Staecker, "Bremen—Canterbury—Kiev—Konstantinopel?."

13. See pp. 140–41; on these plans, see Fuhrmann, "Studien zur Geschichte mittelalterlicher Patriarchate," and "Provincia constat duodecim episcopatibus." Fuhrmann shows that Adalbert was here influenced by canon law, especially the view of the nature of metropolitans and patriarchates established by the Pseudo-Isidorian decretals.

14. For these developments, see Seegrün, *Papsttum und Skandinavien*.

15. Glaeske, *Erzbischöfe*, summarises the development and decline of the archbishopric. On the events of 1144–1148, see Jordan, "Heinrich der Löwe und Bremen"; Hägermann, "Heinrich der Löwe und Bremen."

16. Seegrün, "Hamburg-Bremen."

17. See especially Johanek, "Erzbischöfe."

18. Adam, scholion 76, p. 139. See Fuhrmann, "Adalberts von Bremen Mahnung," who shows that Adalbert's warning should not be translated as "If you can't be good, be careful" but rather as "If you can't be chaste, at least be legal," that is, marry.

19. Robinson, *"Periculosus homo."*

20. Janson, *Templum Nobilissimum*, pp. 60–80, shows that Liemar did not travel to Rome in 1075. For Gregory's conflicts with the German episcopate, see Cowdrey, *Gregory VII*, pp. 89–129.

21. Janson, *Templum Nobilissimum*, pp. 257–320.

22. For the conflicts and power struggles at Henry's court in the 1060s,

see Glaeske, *Erzbischöfe*, pp. 60–97; Jenal, *Anno II*, pp. 155–356; Robinson, *Henry IV*, pp. 19–62.

23. Misch, "Bild des Erzbischofs Adalbert"; Bagge, "Decline and Fall."

24. On this family, that of the counts of Goseck, see their house chronicle, edited by Ahlfeld, "Gozecker Chronik"; Starke, "Pfalzgrafen von Sachsen."

25. See, for example, his use of canon law, nn. 13 and 18.

26. For the *Life of Ansgar*, see n. 10. For Thietmar, see Warner, *Ottonian Germany*.

27. For twelfth-century ethnography, see Bartlett, *Gerald of Wales*, and the papers in Bartlett and MacKay, *Medieval Frontier Societies*.

28. The additional bibliography provides a sample of recent research and synthesis on this period.

29. Buchner, "Geistige Anleihen"; Piltz, "Adam, Bibeln och auctores."

30. Morrison, *History as a Visual Art*, pp. 5–19.

31. Nowak, Johannes, *Untersuchungen*.

32. Buchner, "Vorstellungswelt"; Theuerkauf, "Hamburgische Kirchengeschichte."

33. Goetz, "Geschichtsschreibung und Recht"; Trommer, "Komposition und Tendenz."

34. See Nass, *Annalista Saxo*, pp. 122–31.

35. Christensen, "Aris Íslendingabók"; Mundal, "Íslendingabók."

36. Andermann, *Albert Krantz*.

37. This view of Adam is well expounded in Nyberg, "Stad, skrift och stift."

Foreword

To every author his own preface. Adam wrote one for his opus. A foreword by me would then seem uncalled for were it not for acknowledgments I should make for kindly assistance. Librarians are always helpful: Mrs. Margaret K. Spangler for promptly securing books on interlibrary loan; Miss Liberata Emmerich for confirming some surmises of mine about the *surtarbrand* off the Icelandic coast; and Miss Vera L. Moyer for verifying some references in the Bibliography. Dr. Frank J. Manno must be credited for a final check on a number of references in the Library of Congress. Deep is my gratitude to the Misses Emily Pikus and Marie C. Reilly for having generously expended time and effort to make my miserable script readable by the editor and the printers. Then, too, I must thank my fellow "retiree," Austin P. Evans, for his patience with my foibles, and the ladies and gentlemen of the Press for emendations even when I was loath to accept them. Good people all these who charitably did their best to spare me from what Adam also feared—the wrath of critics.

F. J. T.

State College, Pennsylvania
August 9, 1955

PUBLISHERS' NOTE

The publishers are grateful to Robert E. Tschan, of Pennsylvania State University, son of the late Francis J. Tschan, who assisted in the final stages of preparing the manuscript for the printer and who gave further invaluable aid in the proofreading.

Introduction

But for the chronicler Helmold, Adam of Bremen might today be known only as "A, the least of the canons of the holy Church at Bremen." This all but anonymous identification Helmold cleared up by citing "Master Adam, who eloquently recounted the deeds of the bishops of the Church of Hamburg," as authority for what he had said about the early prelates of the suffragan see of Oldenburg. Little more can be learned about Adam. His own pen vouchsafed the information that he came to Bremen in the twenty-fourth year of the archbishop Adalbert, that is to say, between the beginning of May, 1066, and the end of April, 1067. Adam was then or soon after made a canon of the cathedral chapter at Bremen, perhaps also given charge of its school, for an *Adam magister scolarum* wrote and signed a document for Adalbert, June 11, 1069.

Adam noted, too, that he came to Bremen "a proselyte and stranger," a remark which suggests the thought that his life as a member of the Saxon cathedral chapter, favored though he was by Adalbert, could not always have been pleasant. Sectional feelings in Germany ran high and, no doubt, the ways and politics of the archbishop whom he loved were not always agreeable to the clerics.

Whence Adam came and how he attracted the attention and won the favor of Adalbert can be fairly well surmised. The scribe who annotated the fourth book of the *Gesta* stated that its author had come from upper Germany. His scholium appears in a codex derived from one drawn about 1085 from the manuscript X, which Adam was revising when he died. At that time upper Germany was thought of as extending from the Alps to the Danube between the

Rhine on the west and the Elbe on the east. The forms of personal and place names employed by Adam point to this region. Of the early missionaries he mentions in the course of his narrative, three worked there: Gall in Alemannia, Emmeram in Bavaria, and Kilian in Franconia. Indeed, the language he uses in connection with these men is reminiscent of that of the first chapter of the *Passio altera Kiliani* and of the *Chronicon Suevicum.* Other particulars narrow the search for Adam's home to the vicinity of Würzburg, the country of the upper Main and Werra rivers on the southern slopes of the Thuringian Forest. From the region of the upper Werra and the stream called Kosten (*Quistina*), a confluent of the Main, came a man who at Adalbert's bidding perpetrated a forged document in the second half of the eleventh century—therefore, probably in Adam's time. Presumably influential in the archbishop's chancery, this cleric may have drawn Adam, if he was of those parts, to Bremen. Another possibility lies in the fact that in 1065 the clergy of Bamberg on the upper Main were in correspondence with Adalbert. The archbishop may thus have come to know Adam as a man of scholarly attainments, particularly in the classics, and, therefore, invited him to come to Bremen. The school at Bamberg, founded and well endowed by Emperor Henry II, was famous throughout the Empire for its scholarship. Adam may also have been drawn to Bremen from the little less noted school at nearby Würzburg, which had long enjoyed the patronage of the affluent and politically ambitious bishops of the city.

Domiciled at Bremen, Adam apparently lost no time in preparing for the writing of his *Gesta.* Modestly he says that he pondered long what he, "a proselyte and stranger," might do to show that he "was not ungrateful for having been favored with so important a post." It occurred to him that "since what was done is not remembered" and the history of the great deeds of the prelates of Hamburg-Bremen had not been written down, someone might sometime contend that these churchmen had not done anything worth noting. Therefore he determined to write the history of that diocese. Because the archbishops of Hamburg-Bremen were in his time also charged with the conversion of the Slavic and Scandinavian folk, and because some of the latter peoples had spread through the far reaches of the North Atlantic, Adam's interest in their exploits was aroused. Very soon after he came to Bremen, therefore, he sought out Svein Estrithson, king of the Danes, to get first-hand information about the missions.

But Adam was not one who would write Church history in a vacuum. He was not content with recounting the story of the movements and doings of prelates and priests. He was also interested in the movements and doings of the peoples whom they sought to convert; in other words, to write the history of the Church in the North against the backdrop of the contemporary milieu. To his history of the prelates of Hamburg-Bremen he therefore appended a geographical account of the Baltic, North Sea, and North Atlantic regions. For this task he was exceptionally well-placed in Bremen, a city visited by the northern merchants and sailors, men who could tell him things Svein Estrithson, with all his over-all knowledge and outlook, could not have known. Then, too, Adam had the advantage of access to the archives of his archbishops and to the books in their cathedral repositories.

Remarks dropped here and there in the *Gesta* make it possible to determine approximately in what years Adam wrote his history. In Chapter xxvi (24) of the second book he noted Svein Estrithson as living, and two chapters further on as reigning. In Chapter xliii (41), however, he refers to the king as one "ever to be remembered." Between the writing or revising of these chapters Adam had evidently heard of the king's death, April 28, 1074. Adam, then, must already have been at work on the second book in the summer and autumn of 1074, seven or eight years after he came to Bremen. In Chapter li (50) of the third book he noted that Butue and Henry, sons of the Slavic prince Gottschalk, had been born to the great destruction of their people. Since Butue met his end on August 8, 1074, or more probably 1075, Adam must then have been at work on the third book. If he wrote consecutively, progress was rapid thereafter, for in the epilogue (verse 54) there is reference to Archbishop Liemar's mediatory efforts in the Saxon war of 1075. These concluding verses, therefore, were probably composed in 1075 or 1076. Altogether, Adam must have been actively engaged in the writing of his work for some three or four years, from the time of Adalbert's death in March, 1072, to 1075 or 1076. After composing a new dedication to the third book, Adam presented his work to Archbishop Liemar in the form noted below as codex *a*. Between 1076 and about 1081, possibly even 1085, Adam was busy revising and annotating his original manuscript, codex *A,* thus producing the codex *X,* from which ultimately stem most of the extant versions.

After 1085 there is no trace of Adam's hand in the text or scholia of the *Gesta.* He must, then, have passed away that year or even as early as 1081. In the *Dyptichon Bremense* a *magister Adam* is noted as having died on October 12, but, as was the rule in such records, without mention of the year.

Many were the writers whose sayings Adam remembered and whose books he perused. That he was an indefatigable collector of materials, often widely scattered, no one can gainsay. That he used them with perhaps more circumspection and insight than many of his contemporaries often showed must be admitted. But he had his faults and they come most clearly to light in the first book because many of the sources he used for it are still extant. Next to his convictions regarding the truth of the religion he professed, those regarding the greatness and efficacy of the missions of the archbishops of Hamburg-Bremen were strongest in his mind and heart. Naturally, then, he was disposed to exaggerate the importance of Hamburg, even making it the locus of events when, as a result of a Norse incursion in 845, it could hardly have been an inhabited place. Not that Adam consciously misread or distorted his sources and combined statements from them which should not have been combined: as is evident from his history of the great Adalbert, his patron, he could be highly objective and critical. Nevertheless, Adam cannot be absolved from some carelessness and even from superficiality in the use of his materials. If haste may be alleged in excuse, certainly failing to check what he wrote cannot be offered in extenuation. Instances of his shortcomings may be noted in the footnotes accompanying the text and scholia.

At Adam's disposal were the biographies of early missionaries, such as those of Boniface, Ansgar, Liudger, Radbod, Rimbert, Willehad, and Willibrord. Indeed, he seems to have preferred what biographers had to say to what he could find recorded in annals and chronicles. Considering the penetrating study of Adalbert he presented in the third book, it may perhaps be said that Adam's mind ran to the personal in history. In addition to the *Vita Karoli,* he attributed to Einhard a work he cites as the *Gesta* (or *Bella*) *Saxonum.* His borrowings from it, however, correspond so often and so closely to the *Translatio S. Alexandri* that it is surmised Adam had a work mistakenly thought to be Einhard's, the first part of which was fairly identical with the first part of the *Translatio.* Adam also used the *Historia Francorum* of Gregory of Tours and the *Annales Fuldenses,* including their Regensburg continuation. These annals he likewise entitled *Historia Francorum,* quoting them at times verbatim and citing them twice as authority in matters about which there is no mention in the extant text. Possibly the version he used had been amplified from other sources. His text of the *Annales Corbienses* also was fuller than the one known today. No longer to be found are the *Annales Caesarum,* the *Gesta Francorum,* the *Gesta Anglorum,* and a writing of the abbot Bovo of Corvey. Here and there are suggestions of the *Chronicon Suevicum* and of Regino of Prüm.

Adam also mentioned letters and documents of popes and emperors, sometimes directly, sometimes without noting them as such. That he knew the Pseudo-Isidorian decretals and the *Decretum* of Burchard of Worms is clear. He had besides the *Liber fraternitatis*

Bremensis ecclesiae and the *Liber donationum Bremensis ecclesiae,* which Ansgar probably began to compile. That Adam failed to detect forgeries is not to his discredit, for the falsifications of papal and imperial documents relating to Hamburg are many and baffling. Oddly, Adam appears to have known little or nothing of the numerous documents Henry IV issued in Adalbert's favor. Did that astute prelate not trust his historian in his inner sanctum?

In the course of his work, then, Adam apparently came to realize more and more that a history dealing with the Church and her missions was like a chart without indication of the cardinal points of the compass unless it took account of geography and ethnography, not to mention the life of the times. Schmeidler's studies of how Adam developed the content of his work make it clear that even in the course of preparing his original draft for presentation to Archbishop Liemar he began to make substantial additions to the text and to annotate it with scholia. Of these additions and scholia, some 141 are quite certainly from Adam's pen, not the work of later scribes. Classified by subject matter, some twenty-eight deal with the personalities of the archbishops (except Adalbert) and with matters of local interest to Bremen; twelve deal with the activities of the Church in Bremen, in particular its missions; thirty-one deal with geographical and ethnographical matters; thirty-four with the history of the northern lands, England, Norway, Denmark, Sweden, and Russia; and nine with Saxon and north German affairs. Another twenty-seven are of a miscellaneous nature.

These statistics Schmeidler used to show that most of Adam's additions belong to contemporary or nearly contemporary times. Only fourteen additions were made to the first book, as compared with forty-six, forty-two, and thirty-nine to the second, third, and fourth books respectively. For nearly contemporary times he must have checked extensively with the older canons to emend his second book. For the period of Adalbert, Adam drew in part on his own knowledge and on that of those about him. The fourth book he also checked partly with the canons and partly with others, who could correct data about which he thought Svein Estrithson was either in error or too biased in his views. Making allowances in the distribution of the several classifications, Schmeidler arrives at totals: seventy-one additions of geographical, ethnographical, and local interest, and fifty-six of a miscellaneous nature. Of exceptional biographical interest are the remaining fourteen that relate to Adalbert. When the third book, dealing with Adalbert's character and fortunes, and the fourth, dealing with the geography, ethnography, life, and conditions in the mission lands, are considered along with the additions he made in the course of revising the *Gesta*, Adam's conception of the writing of Church history clearly is unique for his times.

His geographical sources were, as has been noted, by no means all "academic." Steeped in the classics, Adam naturally had recourse to the ancients for the wonders of unknown lands. And the ancients were sometimes not above adorning what they learned from travelers, merchants, sailors, and adventurers, who themselves were not above adorning what they related. Adam drew on Solinus, Martianus Capella, Macrobius, and Sallust as well as on later writers, such as Orosius and Bede, on poets—Horace, Lucan, Vergil—and on a commentary on Vergil by the so-called Servius. From one or another of these writers he culled the fantastic stories about Amazons, Cynocephali, Wizzi, Anthropophagi, Husi, Ymantopodes, and the other folk whom he distributes over little frequented or unknown regions much as early cartographers, abhorring blank spaces on their maps, used to picture monsters in places about which they knew little or nothing.

Adam did, however, enlarge the scope of geographical science by consulting people whom he had reason to trust. There was the Danish king, Svein Estrithson, who called Adam "son." The monarch was already of years when the historian-geographer visited him. The nephew of Canute the Great of English fame, Svein had seen twelve years of service in Sweden. He had warred, too, in Slavia, whither he sent his daughter in marriage to the Abodrite chieftain, Gottschalk. He was well acquainted with Saxony and England, besides knowing something of Courland, Estonia, Iceland, Greenland, and Vinland. All the king's geographical information was fortified by a knowledge, often first-hand, of the history of the northern lands. The data got from Svein Estrithson Adam tried to check and, if possible, to reconcile with what he could gather from memoranda on scattered sheets, papal and imperial documents, the ancient historians and geographers already mentioned, and other well-informed men. To some of the latter he referred indefinitely, as, for example, a certain Danish bishop, a nobleman of Nordalbingia, a number of Danes, and a Christian. The Danish bishop told Adam about Henry I's invasion of Denmark, the Nordalbingian about the warlike nature of the Circipani, the Danes about Vinland, and the Christian about the pagan sacrifices at Uppsala. Other sources Adam noted by name, as the Swedish bishop Adalward the Younger and Archbishop Adalbert. From the latter he learned much about the sees and bishops of the mission lands, about contemporaneous happenings in Sweden, and about the polar expedition of certain Frisian burghers. Adam says he could have written much more about the Atlantic Ocean and its islands but did not because it would have appeared too wonderful, even fabulous. Wondrous, indeed, but not altogether fabulous is the description of the far northern waters that rushed into an abyss only to surge forth again—tides, of course, of which Solinus and others also had heard.

Adam well merits being regarded as the earliest German, if not also the first mediaeval, geographer. He told what he knew frankly and in an orderly way. Nevertheless, he was not free of superstition. A comet heralded Adalbert's fall in 1066. Crucifixes perspired, wolves howled and owls screeched in the outskirts of the towns in anticipation of the prelate's demise.

These portents, significant to Adam, are not nearly so significant to us as are his delineation and analysis of that man's character and fortunes in the third book of the *Gesta*. Adam's literary ability is also to be judged by that book as it stands in manuscripts to be designated as of Class *A*. In manuscripts of classes *B* and *C* the book is broken up, disordered, and lacking in literary quality because of the many additions he made to the first draft. How Adam finally would have rewritten the book no one can tell.

As it stands, the story of Adalbert's episcopate falls into two nearly equal parts, the first relating his prosperous years, the second the unfortunate ones. Of the hierarch's background and career before he was named archbishop, Adam has as little to say as he has had about the prepontifical careers of the prelates whose doings he tells about in the first and second books of the *Gesta*. That Adalbert's selection for the see of Hamburg-Bremen had not been well received apparently concerned the biographer little. Gratitude as well as loyalty prompted him to begin with a recitation of Adalbert's good and praiseworthy qualities—not, however, without touching lightly upon his faults. What critics had to say about his subject's character Adam regards as said in the main without insight, exaggerated, in part even unjustifiably. But he would tell the truth about Adalbert. He had known the archbishop personally during the last five or six years of his life—the years, therefore, of his misfortunes—or had been able at least to study his personality and character at fairly close range. The two, the archbishop's misfortunes and his character and personality, Adam connected as he proceeded in his narrative. Indeed, a man of biographical instinct could hardly have considered them apart. Furthermore, events could historically not have been stated well and clearly except in the light of Adalbert's character and personality. Nevertheless, the archbishop's enemies had contributed as much to his undoing, both outward and inward, as he himself. Events in Slavia, Scandinavia, England, even in Saxony and the Empire, over which neither Adalbert nor his enemies had much if any control, provided Adam with the setting for his tragedy.

Adam, however, was not satisfied with telling about events as they were shaped by the prelate's character and personality or about his character and personality as they were affected by events. He tried to reduce Adalbert's faults to fundamentals—pride, inordinate ambition and the lust for worldly glory closely associated with it, and inability to comprehend actuality. Adalbert was proud of the Greek blood he thought flowed in his veins, of his noble birth, worth, and wealth. Hence, his wanting everything bigger and better and more splendid than anything others had, his extravagant hospitality, his grandiloquence, his tireless energy, and much else. Unable to comprehend actuality, he surrounded himself with flatterers, spurned men to whom the adulation he craved was nauseating, believed in prophecies that fitted in with his desires, in fables, in dreams, in the golden age he would bring about if he could direct affairs unhindered. And yet the archbishop was free of the failings and vices of which many of the ecclesiastics of the day were guilty. His devotion to his Church and diocese was exceptional, his loyalty to the Salian dynasty boundless. This character and personality, here only partially suggested, Adam reveals bit by bit in the events of Adalbert's years, noting causes and results as forces of many kinds and degrees of intensity interplayed. No study comparable to Adam's is to be found in the literature produced since Saint Augustine wrote his *Confessions*.

After two chapters of preliminary characterization, Adam tells of the archbishop's early efforts in Bremen, his entry into the politics of the Empire, and the first steps he took to advance his diocese as a whole. From this discussion Adam passes on to consider the missions in Adalbert's charge, both in the northern lands and in Slavia. The account of the archbishop's successes afield is followed by ten chapters (*III.* xxiv-xxxiii), on his successes at home. As failure began to look impossible to Adalbert, Adam has him formulate the grandiose idea of a northern patriarchate. The prelates of Hamburg-Bremen were to rule over the archbishops and bishops of Scandinavia and all the lands in which Scandinavians had established themselves. Blind to actuality, Adalbert did not realize that his see was historically and in many other respects not comparable with those of Jerusalem or Constantinople. Nor did he realize the import of the reform movement then under way in Rome, which was to enmesh Henry IV, for Leo IX's ideas lived on after his death in 1054.

Henry III, the ablest of the Salians, was succeeded in 1056 by a child, Henry IV. A regency had to be set up. Anno of Cologne and Adalbert, rivals, were made consuls of the Empire. At this point, the highest in Adalbert's career, Adam pauses further to characterize, with well-calculated restraint, the two prelates. Quietly he draws attention to Adalbert's passion for worldly glory, a passion that led him to consort more and more with worthless men who flattered him as they consumed the resources of his diocese. His vanity estranged friends and won him the enmity of worthy and influential men who might have been his friends. His good traits were overshadowed, if not wholly negatived. This inward decadence was matched by the misfortunes which overtook him from without. The Saxon duke Bernhard, with whom the prelate could at least get along, died, and the sons who succeeded him were bent on destroying the powerful archbishopric that limited their power. The child king could do little to save Adalbert. The ecclesiastic Anno of Cologne needed do little more than look on as Adalbert vainly spent the last resources of his see trying to conjure the mirage of power and glory into actuality.

Then fell the archbishop. All plans came to naught. All hopes were dashed. Misfortune followed misfortune not only in Hamburg and Bremen, but also in the Slavic country, in England, and in the northern lands. Undone, Adalbert sat in Bremen, *privatus, solitarius et quietus.* But inwardly he was as energetic as ever. Misfortune only drove him into a headlong and desperate attempt to save what was left of the substance of his see. Alas, the bad traits in his character also asserted themselves as he could not but see the ruin that had been wrought.

Then fortune smiled again, momentarily and deceptively. There was light before utter darkness fell all about him. Portents announced his death; he could not believe them. Inwardly his dissolution was such that Adam intimates he was no longer in command of his senses. The biographer would not say he had lost his reason. Nevertheless, neither Adam nor anyone else could tell what the prelate wanted or did not want. And still he was never at rest. His indomitable will and sacrificial energy drove him hither and thither until, abandoned by the swarm of flatterers and parasites, he died alone at Goslar, his head still lifted up. Adam even then has a kind, excusing word to say for him: Adalbert's undoing was at least in part the fault of those with whom he had surrounded himself and of those with whom he had worked for power and glory. As Adalbert is laid to rest at last and the mourners depart, Adam sadly turns once more, in retrospect, to the prelate's great days and ends his book.

That there was much interest in the Middle Ages and long after in what Adam had written—if not in his history of the prelates of Hamburg-Bremen, certainly in the geographical allusions in that narrative and especially in his fourth book—is attested by the complexity of the genealogy of the manuscripts of the *Gesta.* These manuscripts, and some printings, fall into three main classes, *A, B,* and *C,* that have been tabulated by Schmeidler after years of assiduous study.

The reasoning from which this tabulation is deduced was presented in some detail in the introduction to Schmeidler's edition of the text issued in the *Scriptores rerum Germanicarum* in 1917, and in greater detail in his *Hamburg-Bremen und Nordost Europa,* published the following year. Since these details will be of interest only to the special student, merely a summary is offered here to make clearer the accompanying table and the relationship of certain readings and scholia to what most probably was of Adam's own composition as presented in this translation.

As has been noted, the chronicler-geographer was received into the cathedral chapter at Bremen in 1066 or 1067, a "proselyte and stranger," as he put it. Apparently he set about collecting material for his story without delay, drawing as we have seen, upon earlier

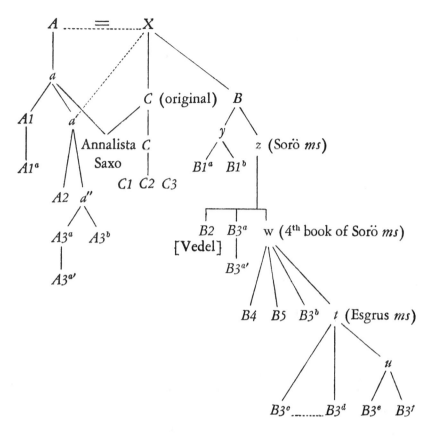

writers, the archives of the see, and conversations with important persons. The data thus assembled were roughly written up in a manuscript designated *A*, which is no longer extant. Adam labored over this text for years before he copied it, or had it copied, for presentation to Liemar, who was then archbishop of Hamburg-Bremen. This text, designated *a* by Schmeidler, has also been lost. While *a* was in the making and for years after, presumably until he died about 1081, Adam worked over *A*. The resultant text, designated *X*, was never completed so far as Adam was concerned, and, like *A* and *a*, it has been lost.

Although these three texts were prepared by Adam or by someone under his supervision, they differed from one another in details as represented both in readings and in annotations or scholia. These differences came about through additions and corrections he made in *A* as he copied or dictated *a*. Interlineations and marginal notes obviously are likely to produce as well as to eliminate errors. Adam, too, must have made changes in *a* that he did not enter in *A*. Doubtless he did not always clearly indicate where additions were to be placed or corrections made. Again, the transcriptions could not always have been perfectly intelligible. Scribes, furthermore, do not always read accurately or listen carefully to dictation. Words that had been omitted could be supplied in a manner that either disturbed the smooth structure of a sentence or even changed its sense. As for manuscript *X*, what with interlineations and deletions and marginal notations, even inter-leavings, its text could eventually have become difficult even for Adam to make out, besides containing additions and corrections and stylistic changes not in *A* or *a*.

The confusion that consequently reigned in the Adam manuscripts was heightened by the canons of Bremen who came into possession of them when he died. One of these ecclesiastics, no doubt Adam's successor as *magister scholarum*, reworked *X* and in doing so introduced errors through misunderstandings and probably also changed the meaning of some passages in trying to better the style. Paradoxically enough, all this confusion has made it possible to approximate the ancestry of other codices and printings and to determine the original texts with a fair degree of accuracy. Schmeidler's studies led him to the conclusions that class *A* texts were descended from *A* by way of *a*, and class *B* and *C* texts were ultimately derived from *X*. From the latter class of manuscripts the nature of *X* could be determined with some measure of certainty.

The manuscripts of class *A* are characterized by fewer additions to the text and fewer chapter divisions than the manuscripts of classes *B* and *C*. Some passages are common to all three classes, but those of class *A* often differ from those of classes *B* and *C*.

The most important of class *A* manuscripts, designated *A1* (Wiener Hofbibliothek No. 521) was copied almost entirely by one hand at the turn of the twelfth-thirteenth centuries and evidently from an older rendering of the *Gesta* than the manuscripts of classes *B* and *C*. *A1* is the only manuscript of class *A* that presents Adam's work in its entirety without scholia and without passages to be found in the manuscripts of classes *B* and *C*. Adam's literary talent may be appraised from *A1*. Its language is cruder than that of the manuscripts of classes *B* and *C,* and at times it is even ungrammatical. The third book, however, appears in *A1* clear and reasoned, even dramatic, whereas it is broken up in the manuscripts of classes *B* and *C* which were derived from the much belabored *X* text. From the latter classes, however, something may be learned about Adam's ability as a collector and evaluator of historical materials.

Codex *A1ᵃ*, copied from *A1* in 1451 and preserved in the Vatican (No. 2,010) presents little of interest. *A2*, known as the *Codex Vossianus Latinus* because it once belonged to an Isaac Voss, is now in the library of the University of Leiden (4° 123). It was copied about 1100 from a codex *a'* done in Bremen and no longer extant. Several persons, one of whom may have been a canon of Bremen, produced the Leiden manuscript. It comprises only seven chapters of the second book and the fourth. The interests of the copyists of *A2* appear to have been mainly geographical, for they included scholia of that nature found in *X*. There are, besides, seventeen other scholia that appear in no other codex and quite certainly did not originate with Adam. Still other scholia are also in manuscripts of classes *B* and *C* and in the *A3* group.

This last group is made up of three closely related texts of the fourth book for which there must be assumed a parent manuscript *a''* derived from *a'* and no longer extant. *A3ᵃ* may have been a true copy of *a''*. All three codices of this group are late : *A3ᵃ*, the Copenhagen codex (Old Royal Collection No. 718) was written in the fifteenth century; *A3ᵇ*, in the city library of Hamburg (JC folio), is a collection made by Heinrich Lindenbrog from some manuscript he did not designate and unreliably printed by Staphorst in his *Hamburgische Kirchengeschichte,* I, 363-70; and $A3^{a'}$, also in the city library of Hamburg, was immediately derived from $A3^{a}$ by Heinrich Lindenbrog. That the members of this group were late of production is evident not only from the influence of *B* on them, but also from the fact that nearly all references to Adam and his times were obliterated. Nevertheless, many passages and scholia in group *A3,* and also in *A2,* that likewise appear in manuscripts of classes *B* and *C* are from Adam's text *X.* Scholia found only in *A2* and in the *A3* group could have come from Adam; more probably, however, they come from others.

Class *B* is the most ramified of the versions. Its ancestor *B* was copied from *X* probably by Adam's successor as *magister scholarum* at Bremen. This editor misunderstood or misinterpreted not a few of Adam's statements, pardonably because Adam evidently had died before he could bring order out of the chaos his *X* had become. Far from satisfactory though *B* must have been, it for some reason got currency in Denmark, for all the known manuscripts of the class are either still in Denmark or betray their Danish origins in annotations, orthography, and other details.

The manuscripts and printings derived from the archetype *B* may be divided into two groups, the one from a text *y* that must be assumed because of the close relationship between the codices which Schmeidler tabulates as $B1^{a}$ and $B1^{b}$, the other derived from a codex *z* associated with the Cistercian monastery of Sorö on the island of Zeeland, the first abbot of which was a Saxon. The latter codex passed from the keeping of the monastery into that of the library of the University of Copenhagen and perished in a fire which devastated that depository in 1728. From this manuscript *z* were derived at least a dozen other versions, some extant, others lost.

However much one might be tempted to trace the relationship of one text of the *B* family to another, the patience of the reader must be considered. Suffice it to say that the second group, derived from the Sorö codex *z,* was, as is evident from the table, subjected to almost baffling changes, if not textually quite certainly in presentation. Copied some time between 1161 or 1162, when the monastery was founded, and about 1250, the fourth book was placed after the epilogue and divided into sections, each comprising a number of chapters, prominently titled to indicate what Adam had written about things Danish. That the other books of his *Gesta* were subjected to changes may be safely assumed.

According to Schmeidler, the texts of class *C* were copied from a manuscript prepared soon after Adam's death, between 1085 and 1090, by one of the older canons of the cathedral of Bremen. This manuscript, the archetype *C*, apparently was drawn from *X* with more than the usual respect for an author's work, although the canon added from his own knowledge some data which Adam either did not have or would not have offered. Of this text someone made a thoroughgoing revision, both grammatical and stylistic, toward the end of the twelfth century, producing a codex *C* from which the three extant versions, *C1*, *C2*, *C3*, of the class were derived. Among the liberties the copyist of *C* took may be mentioned the deletion of many of the observations Adam had made either about himself or about his times and the omission or alteration to positive form of such guarded expressions as *aiunt, ferunt,* and *ut dicitur.*

It was not until the first third of the thirteenth century that the earliest extant manuscript of the class *C1* was made. Its history can be traced back to a Joachim Moller of Hamburg, who died in 1558. From his chests it passed into those of two other families of the city, and in 1761 to one F. C. Sevel, a Dane. When he died twenty years later, the codex became the property of the Old Royal Collection at Copenhagen as No. 2,296. Despite some changes by the copyist, *C1* preserved many of Adam's grammatical peculiarities and errors better than any other text, excepting only *A1*. The division into chapters, however, was much disturbed: they were lengthened by combining several and were left unnumbered. *C2* was printed in 1595 by Erpold Lindenbrog from a manuscript then in the possession of Heinrich Rantzau of Breitenfeld but now lost. So close is the correspondence of *C2* and *C1* that a study of it might justify saying that it had been copied from that codex or from its exemplar. Close examination, however, reveals chapter divisions and a number of passages that have been contaminated from *B2*, the Vedel printing, and another manuscript, now lost, of class *B*. *C3* is a fragment preserved in the New Royal Collection (folio 1,463) in Copenhagen. It was found wrapped about the feudal accounts of Nyborg in Denmark for the year 1628. Its carefully written script, however, dates it early in the fourteenth century. Since it presents only six chapters of Adam's first book, relatively little can be said about its place in the family of *C* manuscripts, except that it has readings in common with *C1* and *C2*.

In 1948 C. A. Christensen published *C1* in lithography. In the preface to this book, Christensen amplified, but diverged somewhat from, Schmeidler's conclusions about the relationships of the later manuscripts of Class *C*. Basing his reasoning on a study of Albert of Stade's use of Adam in the first half of the thirteenth century and that of Albert Krantz about 1500, and on the readings of a number of passages and scholia, Christensen reached the conclusion that between the time Schmeidler's archetype was made and 1180 a manuscript of Adam's *Gesta* came into Denmark, possibly Schleswig, and that this manuscript was the stemmatic ancestor of a number of lost codices used by Albert of Stade, Albert Krantz, and the copyists of *C1*, *C2*, and *C3*.

The complexity and confusion which characterize the history and state of the extant texts may suggest the question: What after all is there left of Adam's own work, and why trouble to translate it? Wholly apart from the value of what is left for the history and geography of the North Atlantic lands, it may be observed that later generations of copyists and writers considered Adam's *Gesta* substantially correct and, consequently, well worth preserving or incorporating in their works. Where there is doubt, a few simple rules—simple, however, only in statement—lead to safe or fairly safe conclusions. Thus, passages and scholia in which the first person singular or plural appears, or in which words and expressions evidently peculiar to Adam occur, surely belong to him. Readings that are common to *A1*, *A2*, *A3*, and also to manuscripts of classes *B* and *C* are nearly all doubtless Adam's without changes by others. Some readings of class *A* not in texts of classes *B* and *C* or only in scholia are probably Adam's in that they go back to *a*. Additions to the text and scholia of the manuscripts of classes *B* and *C* quite certainly may be Adam's in respect of content, although others, too, may have made additions. Readings in a single manuscript or in a single group very probably are not Adam's. Scholia that appear only in *A2*, or only in *A2* and *A3*, or only in class *B*, or only in class *C* are not by Adam.

Writers of the centuries preceding the invention of printing drew on Adam's work in ways that lend support to the classifications and subclassifications worked out by Schmeidler. As might be expected, nearly all these writers took liberties, substantial or verbal, in their borrowings from the codices at their command and at times must have used manuscripts of which there is no longer any trace. Writing in the twelfth century, the Saxon Annalist relied on a manuscript that in the main presented a text of class *A*. Readings and a number of scholia, however, appear in his annals that savor of classes *B* and *C*. His version of the *Gesta*, therefore, must have been much contaminated. Also of the twelfth century was Helmold's *Chronicle of the Slavs*. That writer dealt so freely with the Adam text or texts at his disposal that little can be said with certainty about the versions that entered into his work. Apparently he used a codex which preserved an old version of class *A* that had been contaminated by later readings, some of which came from texts belonging to groups *B* and *C*. Since the *Annales Lundenses* were of Scandinavian origin, their writer more than likely had only a codex of class *B* at hand. Although the one he used was one of that group and in some places closely related to the Sorö version, it had in others the smooth reading of an *A* text not at all affected by the crude insertions to be found in manuscripts of classes *B* and *C*.

In the first half of the thirteenth century, Albert of Stade carefully followed a *C* text older than any of that class still extant but contaminated by versions of classes *A* and *B*. Some time later was compiled the *Historia episcoporum Bremensium*, which for part of the period it covers used a text manifesting readings to be found in all the three main classes and then made exclusive use of Albert of Stade.

Of the printings already noted, those of *B2* by Vedel in 1579 and of *C2* by Lindenbrog in 1595, only the latter was republished. Lindenbrog put out his earlier edition, without the scholia and with many errors, in his *Scriptores rerum septentrionalium* in 1609 and again in 1630. Forty years later Joachim Johannes Mader of Helmstadt repeated the errors in the last Lindenbrog printing and added many others. This edition was put out again by J. A. Fabricius at Hamburg in 1706. Adam's fourth book was printed a number of times; the first by Johannes Messinius, Stockholm, in 1615; then by Stephanus Johannes Stephanius of Leiden, Elzevier, in 1629; and a third time in 1629(?), with the same title page and preface but without data making it possible to tell whether it also emanated from Stephanius or from another source at another date.

With the exception of the Vedel and the first Lindenbrog printings these editions are of little value. The first critical edition was prepared in 1846 for the *Monumenta Germaniae Historica, Scriptores* (VII, 267-89) by J. M. Lappenberg. Taking account of all the available versions, he based his text on *A1*. That same year it was reprinted in the series *Scriptores rerum Germanicarum*, but without critical apparatus. This text was adopted by J. P. Migne for his *Patrologia Latina*, CXLVI, 451-662. In 1876 Weiland reworked the Lappenberg text and expanded the notes under the editorship of J. W. Waitz, also for the *Scriptores rerum Germanicarum*. With the exception of more or less extensive parts included in a number of non-German collections, the *Gesta* was not again critically treated until Schmeidler undertook his study of it in preparation for the edition published in 1917 in the *Scriptores rerum Germanicarum*.

This editor's careful evaluation of all the texts and printings that have come to light has resulted in the presentation of a version at which only minor criticisms have been leveled.

Of translations, there appear to be only one in Danish, by P. W. Christensen (Copenhagen, 1862), and three in German. C. Miesegaes published the first at Bremen in 1825, prior, therefore, to the first critical text that was used by J. C. M. Laurent in preparing the second German translation of the *Gesta* for the *Geschichtschreiber der deutschen Vorzeit* (Berlin, 1850). The Laurent rendering was republished in the same series (Leipzig, 1888), as revised by Wattenbach to accord with the Weiland-Waitz version. Lappenberg took an active interest in both of the Laurent translations. With the appearance of Schmeidler's edition of the text, further revisions in the translation were imperative. This work was undertaken by S. Steinberg in cooperation with Schmeidler and published in the *Geschichtschreiber* series (Leipzig, 1926). A Swedish rendering was contemplated by the Academy of Sciences of Stockholm. No trace of it has been found, however, by the present writer, whose translation is the first to appear complete in English.

The procedure, in the main, has been the same as that outlined for the translation of Helmold's *Chronicle of the Slavs*, published in 1935 as No. XXI of the present series. Only material considered helpful toward an understanding and appreciation of Adam's work, along with corrections of errors he made, has been included in the footnotes. That rule has also been followed in compiling the general bibliography. Well-known works, unless cited, and titles incidental in their application have been excluded. Since the original Douay translation of the Scriptures follows the Vulgate used by Adam more closely than the Authorized Version, the former has been preferred, including designations of chapters, verses, and even book titles, which, it should be recalled, differ in some particulars. To have done otherwise would have classified the author as another of Adam's many errant transmitters. The titles of familiar classical works have been Englished; others have been kept in the

Latin form their authors or editors gave them to facilitate consul-
tation by readers who would delve deeper into the study of Adam's
work. Not by any means all the scriptural and other borrowings
Adam made have been noted because their number is legion. The
double numbering of chapters also is intended, as in Schmeidler's
text, to facilitate reference to the earlier Weiland-Waitz edition of
1876. The lower-case roman numerals correspond to Schmeidler's
text; the arabic numerals, to the Weiland-Waitz edition.

HISTORY OF THE ARCHBISHOPS OF HAMBURG-BREMEN

Prologue

To the most blessed father Liemar, by heaven elected archbishop of Hamburg, Adam the least of the canons of the holy Church at Bremen, offers this slight token of his complete devotion.

When not long ago[1] your predecessor, evangelical pastor, admitted me to the number of your company, I was anxious to show that I, a proselyte and stranger,[2] did not appear ungrateful for having been granted so great a favor. As I saw and heard then that the ancient and honorable prerogatives of your Church had been gravely diminished and that the hands of many builders were needed, I pondered long by what muniment of my endeavor I might help a mother spent of strength. And, behold, there came to mind the many achievements of your predecessors. Their deeds, of which I had read and heard from time to time, appeared to be worth relating both because of their own importance and because of the exigencies of this Church. Since what was done is not remembered and the history of the prelates of this place has not been recorded in writing, someone may perhaps contend that they had in their days either not done anything worth recalling or that, if some of them did, they had lacked writers by whose diligence the facts might have been transmitted to posterity. Convinced of this need, I addressed myself to writing about the succession of prelates seated at Bremen and Hamburg. It was my belief that it would not be

---

[1] In 1066. Adam uses *nuper* and similar words loosely.
[2] Tob. 1:7; Ezech. 14:7. Adam draws expressions in this Prologue from the Scriptures, classical and postclassical writers, the Fathers and some medieval chroniclers: Ambrose, Cicero, Gregory the Great, Horace, Juvenal, Lucan, Orosius, Regino of Prüm, Sallust, Solinus, Sulpicius Severus, Terence, and Vergil.

inconsistent either with my bounden devotion or with the business of your mission if I, as a son of this Church, brought to mind again the deeds of the most holy fathers by whom the Church was raised up and the Christian religion spread among the pagans. For this undertaking, truly very difficult and surpassing my powers, I entreat the more indulgence because, since scarcely any predecessor has left a tread to follow, I did not fear, as if in the dark, to grope along an unknown way, preferring to bear the burden and heat of the day in the vineyard of the Lord rather than to stand idle outside the vineyard. To your consideration, then, I commit this bold undertaking, most holy prelate. I implore you to be its judge and at the same time also its advocate. I know that nothing worthy of your wisdom can be offered to you who, after running the course of earthly knowledge, have now risen with greater glory to the study of godly wisdom, disdaining the earthly and contemplating only the heavenly. And although you easily surpass many men in knowledge and truth, that is, by pastoral word and example, the humility which is preeminent among your virtues and which makes you gracious to all, has also given me courage to presume, though I speak as a child, to converse with a philosopher and to appear a Saul among prophets.[3] Nevertheless, I know that—as regularly happens with really novel works—I shall not lack critics. They will say that what I have written is fictitious and false, like Scipio's dreams as invented by Tully.[4] Let them, if they will, even say that my story has come out of the ivory portal of Maro.[5] It was my purpose to please not everybody but you, father, and your Church. To please the envious is very difficult. But because the ill will of my rivals thus constrains me, I shall make known to you in what meadows I have gathered this garland that I may not be said to have laid hold of falsehood in the guise of truth. Of that about which I write I collected some items from scattered records. I borrowed much from the histories

---

[3] Cf. I Kings 10:12.
[4] Cf. Macrobius *Somnium Scipionis.*
[5] Cf. Vergil *Aeneid* vi. 894ff.

and charters of the Romans. By far the greater part I learned from the tradition of older men who knew the facts. Truth is my witness that I prophesied nothing out of my own heart and made no statement without due consideration. Everything I am about to put down will be substantiated by sound authorities so that, if I am not believed, credit at least may be accorded my source. Let all know that for this work and for such a bold venture I neither desire to be praised as an historian nor fear to be condemned as a falsifier; in fact, that which I myself could not do well I left for others to write about better.

Beginning, then, with the advent of Saint Willehad, when all Saxony was both overcome by the arms of the Franks and delivered to the worship of God, I end this little book at your salutary installation. At the same time I supplicate Almighty God in His mercy to grant that, as He has constituted you pastor over His people, long in error and afflicted, He also may through your efforts and in your days make right what is wrong among us and keep it righted forever. Besides, may you, who hold an hereditary commission[6] to preach in all the length and breadth of the North, speedily accomplish that which of old your predecessors vigorously undertook in respect of the conversion of the heathens—this grant Jesus Christ, our Lord of whose kingdom there is no end, for ever and ever. Amen.

---

[6] Although Liemar had barely attained canonical age for episcopal office when Adam dedicated his history to him, the fulsome praise he heaped on the prelate in this Prologue, and also in the Epilogue, bespeaks his hopes and expectations after the debacle of Adalbert's episcopate described in the third book. Other writers also were generous in their praise of Liemar. Adam may have had documentary substantiation for his reference to a "hereditary commission"—hereditary, figuratively speaking, in the see, not in its incumbent. A charter was issued to Liemar by Pope Alexander II, February 2, 1073, but Curschmann, *Ältere Papsturkunden*, No. 25, declares it a forgery. This charter also appears in Lappenberg, *Hamburgisches Urkundenbuch*, Vol. I, No. 103. On the whole, however, the statement reflects Adam's disposition to exaggerate the importance of the see and its Slavic and Scandinavian mission. Cf. Manitius, *Geschichte der lateinischen Literatur*, II, 39-400; Meyer von Knonau, *Jahrbücher*, II, 156-58 and Notes 83-85; Schmeidler, *Adam*, p. 3, n. 5, and *Hamburg-Bremen*, pp. 109-14, 201-3.

Book One

i (1). Since Hamburg was once the noblest city of the Saxons, we think it neither unsuitable nor profitless, in setting out to write the history of the Church at Hamburg, to state first what the most learned man Einhard[a] and other well-known authors left in their writings about the Saxon people and the nature of its country. "Saxony,"[1] they say, "is no small portion of Germany. It is reckoned to be twice as broad as the part inhabited by the Franks; at the same time it may possibly be as long." Rightly surveyed, Saxony appears to be triangular in shape,[2] with the first leg of the triangle reaching southward as far as the River Rhine. The second leg, which begins in the coastal region of Hadeln, extends a great distance along the Elbe eastward to the Saale River. At this point is the third angle. From angle to angle it is an eight-day journey, except for the part of Saxony across the Elbe of which the upper portion is inhabited by the Sorbs[3] and the lower by the Nordalbingians. Saxony is noted for its men, arms, and crops. Except for an occasional hill, the country, looked at closely, is nearly all a sloping plain. Only the sweetness of wine is wanting; it produces all else that is needful.

[a] Schol. 1. Einhard, one of the chaplains of the Emperor Charles, wrote an account of his life and of his Saxon wars.

---

[1] Einhard *Vita Karoli* xv, with some unimportant changes. Adam distinguished between the *Vita* and a *Gesta* (*Bellum Saxonicum*) associated with Einhard. Cf. Manitius, *Geschichte der lateinischen Literatur,* I, 645-46.

[2] Suggestive of Orosius' delineation of Spain, *Hist. adv. Paganos* I.ii.25 (Migne, *PL,* XXXI, 688). Cf. II.xxi(18), below, for similar phrasings.

[3] The Sorbs between the Elbe and Saale are the best-known of the several divisions of the Slavic people. Cf. *Annales Fuldenses, an.* 806; Einhard, *Annales, an.* 782; Schulze, *Die Kolonisierung und Germanisierung der Gebiete zwischen Saale und Elbe,* p. 19; Tschan, *Helmold,* p. 45 n. 3; Zeuss, *Die Deutschen und die Nachbarstämme,* p. 642.

The land is everywhere fertile, abounding in common pasturage and woodland. Where it touches Thuringia or the Saale or Rhine rivers it is especially rich. On the other hand, it is somewhat less fruitful along the border of Frisia, where the ground is marshy, and near the Elbe, where it is dry. Copious streams everywhere pleasantly and no less opportunely water the country.

ii (2). The principal rivers of Saxony are the Elbe, the Saale, and the *Wisera,* which is now called the Weichsel or the Weser.[4] This river, like the Saale, has its source in the wooded highlands of Thuringia. After coursing thence through mid-Saxony it comes to an end in the vicinity of the Frisians. But the largest river, reported even by Roman authorities, is the *Albia,* now called the Elbe.[5] With its source, they say, beyond Bohemia, early in its course it separates the Slavs from the Saxons. Near Magdeburg it receives the Saale River, and not far from Hamburg the Elbe itself empties into the Ocean. The fourth of the large rivers of Saxony is the Ems, which divides the Westphalians from the other peoples of that region. It rises in the wooded hills about Paderborn[6] but flows through the heart of the Frisian country into the British Ocean.

iii (3). It may be asked what mortals first inhabited Saxony and from what region this folk first came forth. We have learned from much reading of the ancients that this people, like nearly all the peoples in the world, had by a hidden judgment of God been passed more than once from one kingdom to another people,[7] and that their territories had also been named from the names of their conquerors. If, then, the Roman writers are to be believed, the Suevi were the first to live along the Elbe and in the rest of Germany, and their neighbors were those called Druids, Bardi, Sicambri, Huns, Vandals, Sarmatians, Lombards, Heruli, Dacians,

---

[4] Adam mistook Einhard's reference to the Weichsel (*Vistula*) for another name of the Weser (*Visurgis*). *Vita Karoli* xv. Cf. Schröder, "Zur Heimat des Adam von Bremen," *Hansische Geschichtsblätter,* XXIII (1917), 351-66.

[5] Cf. Lucan *Civil War* ii. 51-52. Adam also refers this verse to the Göta älv in iv. xxi below.

[6] The Teutoburg Forest.

[7] I Paral. 104:13; Ps. 16:20.

Marcomanni, Goths, Northmen, and Slavs.[8] On account of the barrenness of their native soil and of domestic strife or, as it is said, because of the need of reducing their numbers, these peoples left their homes and together overran all Europe as well as Africa. Gregory of Tours and Orosius give this account of the Saxons of antiquity: "The Saxons," the latter says "are a very warlike people, terrible in their valor and agility. They live on the seacoast, inaccessible because of impassable swamps. When at one time they meditated a hazardous incursion into the Roman territories, they were subdued by the Emperor Valentinian."[9] Later, when the Saxons took possession of the Gallic country, they were vanquished by the Roman commander, Syagrius, and their islands were seized.[10] Accordingly, the Saxons were first settled along the Rhine and were called Angles;[11] part of them then went to Britain and expelled the Romans from that island. Another part conquered Thuringia and occupied that region. After briefly relating these events, Einhard enters upon his history as follows:

iv (4). "According to an ancient tradition," he says,[12] "the Saxon people sprang from the Angles, the inhabitants of Britain, and sailed over the ocean to the coast of Germany, intending, as was necessary, to seek a place in which to settle. They landed in a region called Hadeln at the very time when Theodoric, the king of the Franks, was at war with his brother-in-law, Irminfrid, the duke of the Thuringians, and was cruelly devastating their land with fire and sword.

---

[8] Several of these peoples have not been identified. Adam may have thought that the *bardi* and *dryadae* mentioned by Lucan, *Civil War* I. 447, 451, were peoples. The poet, however, thought of the former as bards and of the latter as priests. Adam's confusion about the *bardi* may be the result of association with the *Bardi,* whose name survives in Bardengau, the *vicus* of which was Bardowick. Cf. Tschan, *Helmold,* p. 85, n. 13. Herodotus, IV.cx-cxvii, associates the Sarmatae with the Amazons. Cf. Zeuss, *Die Deutschen und die Nachbarstämme, passim.*

[9] Orosius *Hist. adv. Paganos* VII.xxxii (Migne, *PL,* XXXII, 1, 143).

[10] Gregory of Tours *Hist. Franc.* II.xviii-xix, xxvii (Migne, *PL,* LXXI, 215-16, 222). Adam misread these chapters, for the Frankish Clovis defeated Syagrius at Soissons in 486. Cf. Brehaut, tr., *Hist. of the Franks,* pp. 35-38.

[11] For a detailed account of the early homes and movements of the Angles and Saxons, see Schmidt, *Geschichte der deutschen Stämme,* pp. 52-74.

[12] Chaps. iv-vii are taken from the *Translatio S. Alexandri* by Meginhard and Rudolf, monks of St. Gall, Chaps. i-iii (*MGH, SS,* II, 674-76).

But when after two engagements, in which he suffered grievous losses, the fighting was still indecisive and victory hung in the balance, Theodoric, his hope of conquering frustrated, sent messengers to the Saxons whose leader was Hadugato. On learning the reason for their coming, Theodoric induced them to aid him by promising them a place in which to settle in the event of victory. And since they fought valiantly with him as if their own liberty and country were at stake, he overcame his adversaries and, after having plundered and almost exterminated the natives, assigned their territory to the victors as he had promised. When on dividing the land by lot they could not occupy it all themselves, because many of them had been killed in battle and because their numbers were small, they turned over part of it, in particular that which lay to the east, to individual settlers who were to work it under tribute, each one according to his lot. The other parts, however, the Saxons themselves possessed.

v (5). "South of the Saxons lived the Franks and that part of the Thuringians which had not been touched by the preceding storm of war, with the channel of the River Unstrut between them. On the north there were the Northmen, a very ferocious folk. On the east lived the Abodrites and on the west the Frisians. These peoples had constantly to secure their borderlands either by treaties or by wars against the Saxons who, though peaceful at home and benignly mindful of the welfare of their tribesmen, were excessively restless and troublesome to the settlements of their neighbors.

vi (6). "Since they also have the most scrupulous regard for their stock and for the nobility of their blood, they did not readily taint[13] themselves by any intermarriage with other peoples or with inferior persons but tried to make of themselves a people peculiar, pure, and like none but itself. Hence, their appearance as well as their stature and the color of their hair are as nearly identical as is possible in so large a number of men. Now that folk consists of four different classes, namely, of nobles, freemen, freedmen, and

[13] The *translatio* here excerpted is Tacitus *Germania* iv.

bondsmen. And it is fixed by law that in marital unions no class may transgress the bounds of its own estate, but that a nobleman must take a noblewoman and a freeman a free woman, that a freedman must join with a freedwoman and a bondsman with a bondswoman. If any of them takes unto himself a wife that is not of his own but of more distinguished rank, he pays the penalty with his life. They also have in force excellent laws for the punishment of misdeeds. And in the interest of upright morals they strove to have many useful and, according to the natural law, honorable regulations, which could be very helpful to them in meriting true happiness if they were not ignorant of their Creator and strangers to the truth of His worship.

vii (7). "For they worshiped those who, by nature, were not gods.[14] Among them[15] they especially venerated Mercury, whom they were wont on certain days to propitiate, even with human sacrifices. They deemed it incompatible with the greatness and dignity of heavenly beings either to confine their gods in temples or to mold them in any likeness of the human form. They consecrated groves and coppices and called by the names of the gods that mysterious something which alone they contemplated with reverence. To the flight of birds and the lots they paid the utmost attention. The rite of casting lots was simple. A twig was cut from a fruit-bearing tree and divided into slips, which they distinguished by certain marks and spread casually and at random over a white cloth. Then, if the inquiry was public, the priest of the people, if private, the father of the family in person, after praying to the gods with eyes turned toward heaven, picked up three slips, one at a time, and interpreted the ones he had taken up according to the marks which had previously been impressed on them. If the answer was negative, no more inquiry about the same matter was made on that day; if the answer was favorable, further confirmation of the results was required.

[14] Gal. 4:8.
[15] The *translatio* draws on Tacitus *Germania* ix-xi and on Einhard *Vita Karoli* vii for the greater part of this chapter.

(8). "To inquire of the cries and flight of birds was characteristic of this folk; also to make trial of the presentiments and movements of horses and to observe their neighing and snorting. On
no other auspices was more reliance placed, not merely by the
common people but also by their betters. They also had another
method of taking auspices, by means of which they were wont to
probe the issue of serious wars. This was the method: a member
of the tribe with which there was to be war was somehow or other
captured and pitted against one selected from their own countrymen.
Each fought with his own tribal weapons. The victory of one or the
other was taken as conclusive. I forbear to tell how they regarded it
as most auspicious to enter upon the transaction of business on certain days, when the moon is either new or at the full, and how they
respected innumerable other kinds of vain superstition in which they
were involved. These particulars, however, I have mentioned that
the thoughtful reader may know from what darkness of error they
were freed through the grace and mercy of God when He conde-
scended to bring them by the light of the true faith to a knowledge
of His name. For they were, like nearly all the inhabitants of
Germany, both fierce by nature and given to the worship of demons.
Hostile to the true religion, they thought it no disgrace either to
dishonor or to transgress the laws of God and man. For they even
regarded with reverence leafy trees and springs. They worshiped,
too, a stock of wood, of no small size, set up in the open. In native
language, it was called Irminsul, which in Latin means universal
column, as if it sustained everything." These excerpts about the
advent, the customs, and the superstitions of the Saxons (which
superstitions the Slavs and the Swedes still appear to observe in
their pagan rites)[16] we have taken from the writings of Einhard.

viii (9). How the rude Saxon folk came to a knowledge of
God's name or from what preachers it received the precepts of
the Christian religion it will be in order to explain after we have
made mention of the war which Charles long waged with the

---

[16] Cf. IV.xxvi-xxvii below; Zoepfl, *Deutsche Kulturgeschichte*, I, 30-38.

Saxons and at the same time have related the causes of the war. The Thuringians and Saxons, and likewise the other nations who lived along the Rhine, we read,[17] had from antiquity been tributary to the Franks. When these peoples withdrew from their rule, Pippin, the father of Charles, made war on them. This war, however, his son brought to an end with greater success. About this war the same writer, Einhard, recorded in a short epilogue: "So war was declared against the Saxons and was fought for thirty-three years continuously with great ferocity on both sides; at greater loss to the Saxons, however, than to the Franks. It could, indeed, have been ended sooner but for the faithlessness of the Saxons." [18]

ix (10). When all who were hardened to resistance had thus been overcome and brought under his power, this condition was proposed by the king and accepted by them, that, renouncing the worship of devils and abandoning their ancestral rites, they should receive the sacraments of the Christian faith and, joined to the Franks, make one people with them. And so it appears that this war, protracted through so many years, was in this manner ended.[19] And now, girded to write about spiritual triumphs over men's souls, we shall begin as follows about the preachers who brought the fiercest peoples of Germany to the divine religion.

x (11). Winfrid, by birth an Angle, a true philosopher of Christ, later bynamed Boniface because of his virtue, first of all brought the knowledge of the divine and Christian religion to the southern parts of Germany, which were given over to the worship of idols. And although other writers assert that either Gall in Alemannia, or Emmeram in Bavaria, or Kilian in Francia, or certainly Willibrord in Frisia had preached the Word of God earlier, he, like Paul the Apostle,[20] nevertheless excelled all others in the zeal and assiduity of his preaching. For, as we read in his

---

[17] Gregory of Tours *Hist. Franc.* II.xxvii, IV.xiv (Migne, *PL,* LXXI, 223, 279-80); *Annales Fuldenses, an.* 737, 740, 742, 748, 758.

[18] *Vita Karoli* vii.

[19] 772-804: *Vita Karoli* vii.

[20] Cf. I Cor. 15:10.

Gesta,[21] with the support of the authority of the Apostolic See, he undertook a mission to the pagans and made the German peoples, among whom there now flourishes vigorously the greatest reverence for both the Roman Empire and the worship of God, renowned for their churches, their knowledge of the divine, and their virtues. He also organized their provinces as dioceses, namely, those of the Franks on this side of the Rhine and those of the Hessians and Thuringians, who are the neighbors of the Saxons, uniting them with Christ and the Church as the first fruits of his labor, so to speak. And, finally, he was crowned with glorious martyrdom by the Frisians, whom he had earlier converted to the faith. His deeds have been fully set forth by his disciples, who say that he suffered death with fifty or more fellow warriors in the thirty-seventh year of his consecration, that is, the seven hundred and fifty-fifth year after the incarnation of our Lord,[a] the fourteenth of the younger Pippin.

xi (12). Willehad,[22] also a native Angle, inflamed with a desire for martyrdom hastened into Frisia after the passion of Saint Boniface. While he tarried at the sepulcher of the blessed martyr[23] he received the pagans who repented the deed and baptized many thousands of believers. Then he is said to have made the rounds of the whole province with his disciples, breaking up idols and receiving the people unto the worship of the true God. Because of

---

[a] Schol. 2. Paul I then held the papal chair.*

* This scholium appears in codex *C2*. Boniface died on June 5, 754, before Paul I (757-67) came to the papal throne. The datings in the text were compounded from the Annals of Fulda, but the date of Boniface's death was derived from the first *vita* by Willibald. The Annals correctly put Boniface's death in 754, the 36th year of his episcopate. Cf. *Acta SS. Boll.*, June 5; Oelsner, *Jahrbücher unter König Pippin*, Chap. xi.

---

[21] In the following Adam drew on several *vitae* of Boniface, notably the first (Chaps. vii, viii) and third (Chaps. v, xii), and to some extent on the *Annales Fuldenses, an.* 719, 746.

[22] This chapter is so compounded of borrowings that to avoid confusing the text no attempt is here made to distinguish them. Adam's enthusiasm for the missions led him to use his sources in a manner that savors of tendentious writing. His errors can be checked against *Annales Fuldenses, an.* 778, 783; *Vita Liudgeri prima* xviii-xix (*MGH, SS,* II, 410-11); *Vita Willehadi* i-viii (*MGH, SS,* II, 380-83).

[23] Boniface was entombed at Fulda.

the rage of the pagans, we read then, he was both beaten with cudgels and condemned to have his throat cut with the sword. Although the grace of God designed him for greater honors, yet his will and desire were none the less bent on martyrdom. A while later he was sent into Saxony by King Charles and was the first of all the preachers who called the maritime and northern parts of Saxony and the Transalbingian peoples to the Christian faith. For seven years he is said to have preached in that region, until the twelfth year of the Saxon rebellion,[24] when Widukind, stirring up a persecution against the Christians, devastated the territory of the Franks as far as the Rhine. In that persecution some disciples of Saint Willehad, one reads, suffered at Bremen, many in Frisia, others across the Elbe. On this account the confessor of God, hopeful of still greater advantages from the conversion of multitudes, is said in the words of the Gospel[25] to have fled from city to city and, after sending forth his associates to preach, to have himself gone to Rome with Liudger. When they had there been encouraged by the consolation offered by the most holy Pope Hadrian, Liudger withdrew to the tomb of Saint Benedict at Monte Cassino, Willehad turned back into Gaul to the tomb of Saint Willibrord.[26] And so for a period of two years each of them devoted himself in retirement to the contemplative life, praying above all for the persecutors and the Saxon people that the enemy might not with cockle entirely choke the seed of the Word of God which had been sown among them.[27] And in them was fulfilled the Scriptural saying, "The continual prayer of a righteous man availeth much."[28] These excerpts, selected according to their sense, we took out of his *Vita*. Now, at the end of the two years, that is in the eighteenth year of Charles, Widukind, the instigator of the rebellion, came into

[24] In trying to reconcile the dating of the rebellion in the Annals of Fulda with that in the *Vita Willehadi*, Adam made the mistake of transferring the event from 778 to 783. This misreckoning also affects other datings in this chapter.

[25] Cf. II Macc. 5:8; Matt. 10:23, 23:34.

[26] At Echternach.

[27] Cf. Matt. 13:25.

[28] Jas. 5:16.

Charles's obedience and was baptized, he and other magnates of the Saxons. Then Saxony was conquered at long last and reduced to a province. At the same time it was divided into eight dioceses subject to the archbishops of Mainz and Cologne. The charter[29] establishing this division at the king's command is preserved in the church at Bremen and can be understood from these words:

xii (13). "In the name of the Lord God and of our Savior Jesus Christ. Charles by the dispensation of divine providence king. If with the help of the Lord God of hosts we have achieved victory in battle, we glory in Him and not in ourselves, and trust that we may merit in this life peace and prosperity and in the life to come the everlasting reward of mercy. Wherefore let all the faithful of Christ know what we have devoutly declared in the case of the Saxons, who because of their treacherous obstinacy always resisted conquest by our forebears and were for a long time rebellious against both God Himself and ourselves, until by His might and not our own we both overcame them in battle and through God's favor brought them to the grace of baptism. They are hereby granted their pristine liberties and are absolved of every payment due us for the love of Him who accorded us victory, and are tributary and subject to Him. Let it be known, then, that those who hitherto refused to bear the yoke of our overlordship, but are now, thanks be to God, overcome both by arms and by faith, are, rich and poor, legally bound to pay to our Lord and Savior Jesus Christ and to His priests tithes of all their beasts and fruits and of all their fields and income. Further, we have reduced all their land, according to ancient Roman practice, to a province and partitioned it with fixed boundaries among bishops. The northern part of the province, which is considered both the richest in respect of the abundance of fish and the best adapted for the raising of cattle,

---

[29] A forgery probably done at Adalbert's bidding by a cleric who doubtless was partially responsible for Adam's coming into the archbishop's company. The connection established by Schmeidler in Steinberg, tr., *Adam von Bremen*, pp. viii-xvi, explains Adam's attitude in the Saxon-Salian struggles of his time. Cf. Lappenberg, *Hamburgisches Urkundenbuch*, Vol. I, No. 2; Schröder, "Zur Heimat des Adam von Bremen," *Hansische Geschichtsblätter*, XXIII (1917), 351-66.

we have in thanksgiving devoutly bestowed upon the blessed Christ and the chief of His apostles, Peter. For him we have also appointed a church and episcopal see in a place in Wigmodia called Bremen, on the Weser River. To this diocese we have subjected ten districts which, discarding their ancient names and boundaries, we have furthermore constituted two provinces, naming them Wigmodia and Largau.[30] Moreover, in presenting seventy hides with their peasants in the districts noted above for the construction of the aforementioned church, we by this our majesty's charter command, grant, and confirm that the inhabitants of the whole of this diocese faithfully pay their tithes to the church and to its provisor. Furthermore, by the precept of the supreme and universal pontiff, Pope Hadrian, as well as by that of Bishop Lull, of Mainz, and on the advice of all the bishops who were present, we have in the presence of God and of His saints also committed that same church at Bremen with all its appurtenances to Willehad, a man of approved life. We have on the third day before the Ides of July also caused him to be consecrated[31] the first bishop of this same church to the end that, by faithfully dispensing to the people the seed of the divine word according to the wisdom given him and by profitably administering this new church according to canonical order and monastic competence, he may plant and water the while until Almighty God is moved by the prayers of His saints to give increase.[32] The same venerable man also has made known to our serenity that the diocese which we have mentioned can by no means suffice, because of the danger from hostile barbarians and of the diverse incidents which habitually take place in it, for the subsistence and support of the servants of God laboring therein for God. Wherefore, since Almighty God has opened the door of faith[33] unto the Frisian nation as well as unto the Saxon, we have assigned to the

---

[30] Place names have been modernized wherever they could be identified.
[31] Adam omitted "at Worms" Cf. *Vita Willehadi* viii (*MGH, SS,* II, 383).
[32] Cf. I Cor. 3:6-7.
[33] Cf. Acts 14:26.

same church of Bremen and to its provisor, the bishop Willehad, and to his successors possession in perpetuity of the part of the aforementioned region, namely of Frisia,[a] which is known to be adjacent to this diocese. And since what has occurred in the past makes us cautious for the future, we have caused this territory to be fixed by definite bounds that no one may seize for himself any power in that diocese contrary to our desire. These are the bounds, firm and inviolable, by which we have ordered it circumscribed: the ocean sea, the Elbe River,[34] the Lüne, the Steinbach, the Harsehla, the Wimarch, the Sneidbach, the Oste, the Alpeshausener Mühlenbach, the Mede, the marsh called Sigfridsmoor, the Twiste, the Twistermoor, the Ascbroch, the Wissebroch, the Bever, the Otter, and again the Oste; from the Oste to the place at which one comes to the marsh called Chaltenbach, thence to the marsh itself, to the Wumme River; from the Wumme to the Wieste, the Faristina to the Weser River, thence on the eastern bank of this same river the highway, called the Hesseweg, which divides Sturmgau from Largau, the Schipse-Graben, the Alpe, the Aue, the Chaldowa, and again the Weser; from its western bank the highway called Folwech which divides Derve from Largau, as far as the Hunte River, thence that river and the Haarenbach, the woodland which the inhabitants of the place call the Wildloch, the Vehne, the Hochmoor, the Barkenbusch, the Endiriad marsh dividing Emsgau from Ostergau, the Dobbe-Meer, the Sandwater-See, and again the sea. And that the charter of this donation and circumscription may with the protection of God endure firm in our own and future times we have

---

[a] Schol. 3.* Frisia is a coastal region, inaccessible because of impassable swamps, and comprises seventeen districts, of which a third part belongs to the bishopric of Bremen. They are distinguished by the following names: Ostergau, Rustringen, Wanga, Triesmer, Harlingerland, Norden, Morseti. And these seven districts comprehend about fifty churches. This part of Frisia is separated from Saxony by the marsh called Waplinga and the mouth of the Weser River, and from the rest of Frisia by the Emsgau marsh and the ocean sea.

* Repeated as Schol. 118 (3) below.

[34] On the names of rivers see Witt, *Flussnamen Nordwestdeutschlands.*

signed it with our own hand and ordered it sealed with the impression of our ring.

"The seal of the Lord Charles, emperor[35] and most invincible king. I, Hildebald, archbishop of Cologne and chaplain of the sacred palace, authenticate. Given the day before the Ides of July in the seven hundred and eighty-eighth year of our Lord's Incarnation, the twelfth Indiction, the twenty-first year of the reign of the Lord Charles. Done in the palace at Speyer; felicitously. Amen."

xiii (14). Our lord and father Willehad, then, held the chair for two years, three months, and twenty-six days after his consecration, and he preached both to the Frisians and to the Saxons thirty-five years in all after the martyrdom of Saint Boniface.[36] He died, "old and full of days,"[37] in Frisia at a villa called Blexen, situated in Rustringen. His body was brought to Bremen and placed in a sepulcher in the Basilica of Saint Peter, which he himself had built. His passing is celebrated with joyous festivities on the sixth day before the Ides of November, his consecration on the third day before the Ides of July. There is a notable book about his life and deeds, trustworthily written by Ansgar,[38] his fourth successor. We recommend it for perusal to him who desires to know more because we are hastening to other matters.

xiv (15). We read that after the saintly Willehad one of his disciples, Willeric (whom others call Willeharius), presided over the Church in Bremen. And he occupied the see for fifty years, until the next to the last year of the elder Louis. Since, however, it is written in the Book of Donations or Traditions of the Church at Bremen that Willeric presided from the thirty-seventh year of Charles to the twenty-fifth year of Louis, the number of years is

---

[35] Charles was still king of the Franks at the time alleged as the date of this charter, 788. Cf. Lappenberg, *Hamburgisches Urkundenbuch*, Vol. I, No. 2. The monogram also is a fabrication. Cf. Schmeidler, *Hamburg-Bremen*, pp. 204-6.

[36] Correctly only thirty-four years and five months. Adam counted full years of mission activity for Willehad, 755-89. Much of this chapter is drawn verbatim from Vita Willehadi viii, x (*MGH, SS*, II, 382-84).

[37] I Paral. 23:1. Cf. Job 42:16.

[38] Ansgar wrote only the *Miracula*.

found to be twelve less than that we have given.[39] That the bishopric of Bremen was vacant for so long a time, as others also were, is credible because the Saxon people, recently converted, would not as yet let themselves be ruled by episcopal authority; especially since, with barely a year free from warfare, the Saxons are recorded to have become at length so exhausted that of those who lived along both sides of the Elbe River ten thousand men with their women and children were transported into Francia. And that was the thirty-third year of the long Saxon war, the one that historians of the Franks count as memorable, namely, the thirty-seventh of the emperor Charles. Since at that time the Slavic tribes also were subjected to the rule of the Franks, Charles is said to have committed Hamburg,[a] the city of the Nordalbingians, to the governance of a certain saintly man, Heridag, and to have designated him as bishop of the place after he had built a church there.[40] On account of the barbarian raids Charles also gave him the monastery Rodnach in Gaul at which to stay for their duration. This same church at Hamburg he designed to establish as the metropolitan see for all the Slavic and Danish peoples. The death of the priest Heridag and the cares of the realm prevented the emperor Charles from realizing his desires and carrying this project to completion. We read in the Book of Donations of the Church of Bremen that Willeric, the bishop of Bremen, had preached to the Transalbingians even before Ansgar[41] and had frequently visited the church in Meldorf even up to the time when Hamburg was made the metropolitan see.

[a] Schol. 4 (5). This is recorded in the *Gesta* of Saint Ansgar and the privileges of the Roman pontiffs.*

* *Vita Anskarii* xii. The papal privileges do not mention the transfer of the Saxons into Francia.

---

[39] Perhaps in the document printed by Lappenberg, *Hamburgisches Urkundenbuch*, No. 102. In this chapter Adam drew on *Annales Fuldenses, an.* 804-6, 808-12, 814; Einhard *Vita Karoli* vii-viii, xii, xiv, xxx; *Transl. S. Alexandri* iii (*MGH, SS,* II, 676); *Vita Anskarii* xii; *Vita Willehadi* viii (*MGH, SS,* II, 383).

[40] Louis the Pious, not Charles, issued the charter Adam used. The charter notes only that Charles planned to establish a bishopric *in ultima parte Saxoniae.* Louis fixed the see at Hamburg. There is no reference to a bishop Heridag in papal documents.

[41] He was in Denmark with Ebbo in 823. *Annales Xantenses, an.* 823.

(16).   And because we have mentioned the Danes once, it seems worthy of mention that the most victorious emperor Charles, who had conquered all the kingdoms of Europe, is reported to have undertaken last of all a war with the Danes. Now, the Danes and the other peoples who live beyond Denmark are all called Northmen by the historians of the Franks. After their king, Gotafrid, had subjected the Frisians and likewise the Nordalbingians, the Abodrites, and other Slavic peoples to tribute, he threatened even Charles with war. This strife very seriously retarded the emperor's purpose with respect to Hamburg. When at length, by the dispensation of Heaven, Gotafrid died, Hemming, his cousin, succeeded and soon made peace with the emperor, accepting the Eider River as the boundary of the kingdom.[42] The most illustrious emperor Charles died not long after, leaving his son Louis the heir of the empire. His passing on high took place in the twenty-fifth year of Willeric, the fifth day before the Kalends of February.

xv (17).   Forgetful of his father's wishes, Louis commended the Transalbingian province to the bishops of Bremen and Verden. At this time begin the *Gesta* of Saint Ansgar.[43] And because the history of the northern peoples in part concerns our Church (that

---

[42] Gotafrid died in 810. The Annals of Fulda, *an.* 811, merely state that peace was made on the Eider River, not that that river was made the boundary of the kingdom. On the use of the expression Danish kings, often so-called, see Kendrick, *History of the Vikings,* pp. 92-93; Vogel, *Die Normannen,* pp. 404-5. The early rulers of the Scandinavian countries were, like the Indian chiefs of our early days, often called kings by their contemporaries in more advanced cultures. Some of these "kings" were merely rulers of parts of the country, struggling for primacy with other "kings" of Denmark. A genealogical table in this period would be marked by gaps and uncertainties. Thus Gotafrid's father remains unknown. Hemming, who came to power after him (810-12), apparently was the son of one of the latter's four brothers, none of whose names is known. Horic I, who succeeded Hemming in 813 and died fighting Gudorm in 854, was one of Gotafrid's three other sons, whose names are also not known. Since Gudorm died in this fight, the scepter was said to have passed to Horic II. His father, too, is unknown. He may not even have been related to the Gotafrid family, unless remotely. Mentioned as king in 854, he passed from the scene some time between 864 and 873, apparently without a known heir of his own immediate kin.

[43] Adam drew, at times verbatim, on *Annales Corbienses, an.* 822 (*MGH, SS,* III, 3); *Annales Fuldenses, an,* 812, 826, 850; *Annales regni Franc., an.* 813-14; *Vita Anskarii* vi-xiii; *Vita Willibrordi* ix (Jaffé, *Bibliotheca rerum Germanicarum,* VI, 47). He errs at times in his datings and tends to exaggerate the success of Ansgar's missions.

is, the Church of Bremen), I intend, in my opinion not uselessly, to touch at times upon the deeds of the Danes as they occur. In the course of this same time, on the death of Hemming, the king of the Danes, Gotafrid's nephews Sigefrid and Anulo[44] disrupted the kingdom by a war because they could not come to agreement between themselves over the primacy in the government. Eleven thousand men lost their lives in the conflict, and both kings were killed. After winning a bloody victory, Anulo's faction set Reginfrid and Harold upon the throne. But Harold soon drove out Reginfrid, who with a fleet resorted to piracy; Harold entered into an alliance with the emperor. The history of the Franks relates more fully what took place. It is written that at that time Ebbo of Rheims, aglow with religious zeal for the salvation of the heathen, received with Halitgar[45] from Pope Paschal a legateship to the heathen, which commission our Ansgar with the help of divine grace later happily carried out. In the thirty-third year of Willeric the emperor Louis founded New Corvey in Saxony, congregating in that monastery the most religious monks of Francia.[46] Especially distinguished among them, one reads, was our most holy father and philosopher of Christ, Ansgar, deservedly renowned for his life and learning and accepted by the whole Saxon people. At that very time the king of the Danes, Harold, despoiled of his kingdom by the sons of Gotafrid, came to Louis a suppliant. And on being instructed thereupon in the doctrine of the Christian faith, he was baptized at Mainz with his wife and brother and a great multitude of Danes. The emperor lifted him from the sacred font and, resolved to restore him to the kingdom, gave him a fief across the

[44] Sigefrid was the son of one of Gotafrid I's brothers. Anulo, however, was the son of a Halfdan (fl. 807?) who was the brother of a Harold I (d. before 804). Their father remains unknown but may have been related to the house of Gotafrid I. When Sigefrid and Anulo died in their war, two of the latter's brothers were set up: Reginfrid, who died in 814, and Harold II, who, baptized in 826, lived until about 845. Cf. Note 42 above; Vogel, *Die Normannen,* pp. 405-9.

[45] Bishop of Cambrai. For Ebbo's activities, see Lappenberg, *Hamburgisches Urkundenbuch,* Vol. I, No. 6; Reuter, "Ebbo von Reims und Ansgar," *Historische Zeitschrift,* CV (1910), 237-84.

[46] In 822.

Elbe, and, to withstand the pirates, granted his brother Horuch a part of Frisia. This territory the Danes still claim as if it were legitimately their own. Since, however, there could not readily be found a preacher who would go with them to the Danes because of their barbarous cruelty—on account of which everyone shuns that people—the blessed Ansgar, inspired, as we believe, by the Holy Spirit and desirous of obtaining martyrdom in whatever way he could, of his own accord presented himself with his associate Autbert, as being ready to go not only among the barbarians but also "both into prison and to death"[47] for Christ. And so they spent two years[48] in the kingdom of the Danes and converted many of the heathen to the Christian faith. And when, on their return thence, the emperor asked them a second time to make trial of the grace of the Gospel with the remotest peoples, the Swedes,[49] the dauntless champion of Christ, Ansgar, gladly set out for Denmark, taking with him as preachers the brethren Gislemar and Witmar. Leaving Gislemar there with Harold, he himself and Witmar sailed across to Sweden where they were kindly received by King Björn and were permitted publicly to preach the Word of God. And so in the course of one year they won many to the Lord Jesus Christ, among them the prefect of the town of Björkö, Herigar, who, they say, was himself distinguished for his miracles and wonder-working powers. Rejoicing over the success of their mission, the new apostles returned to Corvey with two peoples for their triumph. O, the wonderful providence of the omnipotent God for the calling of the heathen, which the Maker orders as He wills and when He wills and by whom He wills! Behold, we read that what Willebrord as well as Ebbo and others had wished long ago to do but could not, our Ansgar has now marvelously both desired and accomplished, saying with the Apostle, "It is not of him that willeth, nor of him that runneth, but of God that sheweth mercy .... Therefore," says

---

[47] Luke 22:33.
[48] 826-28. Ansgar was in Sweden probably in 830.
[49] On Ansgar's Swedish mission see Bugge, "Altschwedische Gilden" *Vierteljahrschrift für Sozial- und Wirtschaftsgeschichte,* xi (1913), 129-56.

the Apostle, "He hath mercy on whom He will; and whom He will, He hardeneth." [50]

xvi (18). The emperor[51] and his great nobles then felicitated Saint Ansgar on the deliverance of the heathen and rendered great thanks to Christ. In a general council of clerics which he held, the pious Caesar, desirous of fulfilling his parent's will, appointed Hamburg, the city of the Transalbingians, as the metropolitan see for all the barbarous nations of the Danes, the Swedes, and likewise the Slavs and the other peoples living round about. And he had Ansgar consecrated as first archbishop of this see. This was done in the year of our Lord eight hundred and thirty-two, which was the eighteenth of the emperor Louis, the forty-third of Bishop Willeric of Bremen. Ansgar was consecrated by Drogo, bishop of Metz, Caesar's own brother, in the presence and with the approval of Otgar of Mainz, Ebbo of Rheims, Hetti of Trier, and others, also with the consent of Willeric of Bremen and Helmgaud of Verden, the bishops to whom this diocese had previously been commended. Pope Gregory IV confirmed the actions by his apostolic authority and by the bestowal of the pallium.

The precepts of the emperor and the privileges the pope gave Saint Ansgar are preserved in the church at Bremen.[52] In these documents there also is contained a statement that Caesar granted him a certain monastery in Gaul, called Turholz,[53] in aid of his mission. This was done in the year of our Lord eight hundred and thirty-four, the twelfth Indiction, which was the twenty-first year of Louis.

[50] Rom. 9:16, 18.

[51] Adam drew, sometimes verbatim, on *Vita Anskarii* xii-xiii and on papal privileges for this chapter.

[52] Adam distinguishes between the date of the founding of the archbishopric (correctly the latter part of 831) and that of the papal and imperial documents (834). For the chronology see Dehio, *Hamburg-Bremen*, Vol. I, App., p. 54. There is a considerable number of studies about the genuineness of the documents, and the last word on the subject has apparently not yet been written. Schmeidler, *Hamburg-Bremen*, pp. 125-287; Tamm, *Anfänge des Erzbistums Hamburg-Bremen*. For the nature of the early German papal legateships, see Ruess, *Rechtliche Stellung der päpstlichen Legaten*, pp. 59-63.

[53] Today Thorout, southeast of Ostend between Bruges and Ypres.

xvii (19).[54]   Visiting now the Danes, now the Transalbingians, Ansgar drew to the faith an innumerable multitude of both peoples. When at times his zeal in preaching was checked by a persecution of the barbarians, he retired to Turholz with his disciples. To aid him in his preaching he was assigned Ebbo of Rheims, of whom we have previously spoken. When the latter was detained either by the fatigue of a journey or by weakness of body or by the greater pleasure he found in worldly activities, he gave Ansgar his nephew Gauzbert to act in his stead.[55] These two consecrated him bishop, called him Simon, and, having commended him to divine grace, sent him to Sweden. Since these events are related in detail in the *Vita* of Saint Ansgar, we may here deal with them briefly. But because chronological points are there obscure, we have taken much that is in accord with chronology from other writings. We shall return now to the other matters with which we began.

xviii (20).[56]   In the meantime Bishop Willeric of Bremen, by going sedulously about his diocese, baptizing the heathen and strengthening the faithful in Christ, performed the duty of a strenuous preacher. Everywhere throughout the bishopric he erected churches in appropriate places; three, indeed, in Bremen, the first of which, that is to say the Cathedral of Saint Peter, he made over from wood into stone. And he translated the body of Saint Wille-had from that church, entombing it in the south oratory, which he built. This fact the author of his *Vita* also did not wish to overlook. Later writers relate, too, that it was done for fear of the pirates, who would gladly have carried off the body because of the miracle-working power of our confessor. At that same time the Blessed

---

[54] Adam drew on *Vita Anskarii* xiv-xv, at times verbatim, for this chapter, and exaggerated some statements he read, e.g., the number of conversions.

[55] Adam either misunderstood *Vita Anskarii* xiv or more probably wrote tendentiously. Ebbo was commissioned to carry on missionary work in Denmark before and independently of Ansgar and never was his helper. Gauzbert also worked independently of Ansgar. For a keen characterization of the latter and his work, see Hauck, *Kirchengeschichte Deutschlands*, II, 617-29. Cf. Lappenberg, *Hamburgisches Urkundenbuch*, Vol. I, No. 6; Reuter, "Ebbo von Reims und Ansgar," *Historische Zeitschrift*, CV (1910), 237-84.

[56] Adam drew on *Vita Willehadi* xi (*MGH, SS*, II, 384).

Ansgar is said to have moved across the Elbe the bodies of the saints which he had received in gift from Archbishop Ebbo. He deposited, thus, the body of Saint Maternianus at Heiligenstedten; but those of Sixtus and Sinnicius, together with other relics of martyrs, he placed in the city of Hamburg. The reliquary of the blessed Remi, however, he reserved at Bremen with fitting honor. Now Willeric brought together a very large body of clerics; he acquired a large heritage from the people for the Church of Bremen. In those days[57] Charles made the Savior at the Church of Bremen the beneficiary of a hundred hides. This is recorded in the third Book of Donations, the first chapter. In this book there also frequently occurs the line, "To the most holy basilica which was built in honor of Saint Peter the Apostle in the place or public estate called Bremen, where Willeric, the servant of the servants of God, presides as bishop." And he died, "old and full of days,"[58] in the year of our Lord eight hundred and thirty-seven, which is the twenty-sixth and next to the last of Louis, and was entombed in the Cathedral of Saint Peter on the north side of the altar on the fourth day before the Nones of May.

xix (21). Leuderic, the third in succession, held the see for eight years. Although we could not ascertain his years exactly, we did learn from the same Book of Traditions, in the fifty-eighth chapter, that he had been Willeric's deacon and that he had occupied the chair until the sixth year of the younger Louis.[59] He was proud, they also say. From this statement it may be inferred that he gloried in having been at one time custodian, at another pastor, of the Church of Bremen.

xx (22). In those days[60] our holy father Ansgar vigorously administered the mission entrusted to him, toiling for the new

[57] 837-38? Charles the Bald, who acquired Frisia in 837 and so could endow Bremen.

[58] I Paral. 23:1; Job 42:16. Willeric died in 838, which was not the next to the last year of Louis the Pious. This dating no doubt was a copyist's error. Cf. *Annales Corbienses, an.* 838 (*MGH, SS,* III, 3).

[59] Louis the German.

[60] Adam drew on *Vita Anskarii* xv and on *Vita Rimberti* iii, v-vi.

plantation at Hamburg, fostering the Church by word of mouth and work of hand. He also frequently visited the monastery in Gaul, Turholz, which he held by Caesar's donation, by word and example pointing out the way of the salutary rule to the brethren striving there for God. In their noble company Rimbert already shone out for his sanctity, though he was then but a child. Adopting him as his son, the holy father Ansgar in the spirit of prophecy, with which he was filled, predicted far in advance that he would rival him in virtue, succeed him on the episcopal throne, and by the grace of his merits share his lot in the heavenly Kingdom. In this matter the providence of the almighty God, which of old put Elisha in the place of Elijah,[61] did not fail Ansgar with respect to Rimbert.

xxi (23). In the meantime the Northmen,[62] making piratical forays in every direction, subjected the Frisians to tribute. Sailing up the Rhine at this time, they besieged Cologne and, up the Elbe, set fire to Hamburg. The celebrated city was utterly ruined by the pillage and the fire. The church, the monastery, the library collected with the utmost effort, were destroyed. The saintly Ansgar, as it is written, escaped all but naked with the relics of the holy martyrs. The history of the Franks does not pass over the destruction of Hamburg in silence; nor do the privileges of the Romans. This calamity, as they say, took place in the last year of the elder Louis.[63]

At that time[64] Bishop Gauzbert also was driven from Sweden by the fury of the heathen, and Nithard, his chaplain, and several

[61] Cf. IV Kings 2:1-15.

[62] For this chapter, Adam drew on *Annales Bertiniani, an.* 837; *Annales Fuldenses, an.* 836-37; *Vita Anskarii* xvi-xvii, xix.

[63] Hamburg was destroyed in 845 by Horic I. No other source mentions the siege of Cologne. An incident that may have led to such an event is noted in *Annales Colonienses brevissimi, an.* 836 (*MGH, SS,* I, 97); *Annales Bertiniani, an.* 837; *Annales Fuldenses, an.* 845. Cf. Kendrick, *History of the Vikings,* p. 136; Vogel, *Die Normannen,* p. 74, n. 4.

[64] What follows is not entirely in accord with the sources Adam used and is exaggerated. For instance, Hergeier may not have been a Christian, although he promoted the spread of Christianity, and Anund's raid was not in the nature of a persecution. Cf. Schmeidler, *Hamburg-Bremen,* p. 110.

others were crowned with martyrdom. And Sweden after that lacked the presence of a priest for a period of seven years. Although he had been expelled from the kingdom, Anund[65] at that time carried on a persecution of the Christians. Alone Hergeier, the prefect of Björkö, upheld there the Christian religion. So much grace also did he merit for his faith that he saved many thousands of pagans through his miraculous power and religious exhortation. This is written in the *Acta* of the blessed Ansgar.

xxii (24). In the third year of Bishop Leuderic of Bremen the death of the emperor Louis[66] left the kingdom in turmoil. There ensued much discord among the brothers, a mighty war in which, as the historians testify, all the strength of the Franks was consumed. The inciter of this discord, Ebbo,[67] who had previously stirred up the sons against their father and now was spurring on the brothers in their domestic dissension, was therefore accused of conspiracy and deposed by Pope Gregory. But since some uphold this charge and others maintain that he had acted rightly, we shall not attempt to decide on the truth, especially because the love which our holy father Ansgar had for him at the beginning of their association endured to the very end. Read in his *Vita* and in a writing of Hrabanus[68] about Ebbo's ambiguous reputation. At length, through the mediation of Pope Sergius,[69] a peace was agreed upon among the brothers, and the kingdom was divided into three parts in such wise that Lothair, the eldest, should possess Rome with Italy and Lotharingia with Burgundy; Louis should rule the Rhine with Germany; Charles, Gaul; Pippin, Aquitaine.[70] In this division of the kingdom among the brothers, the monastery of

[65] King of Sweden, brother and coregent of Björn, who in alliance with Louis the Pious had invited missionaries to preach in Sweden. Ansgar responded to this call. Cf. i.xv (17) above. When Björn expelled Anund, the latter sought revenge with the help of Horic I of Denmark. Cf. Kendrick, *History of the Vikings*, p. 135.

[66] In 840. Adam drew on *Annales Fuldenses, an.* 841, 843, but betrays the influence of Regino of Prüm, *Chronicon, an.* 841, and of *Vita Anskarii* xxi.

[67] The sources disagree. The *Annales Fuldenses, an.* 843, mention a Count Adalbert as the inciter. Cf. *Annales Bertiniani, an.* 833.

[68] Perhaps his letter to Heribald, Chap. xxxiv (*MGH, Epp.,* V, 410-14).

[69] Gregory IV. Sergius did not become pope until 844.

[70] Pippin the Younger was ignored in the partition.

Turholz passed into Charles's portion and so was withdrawn from Saint Ansgar's jurisdiction.[a]

xxiii (25).   But, glorifying God in his poverty, Ansgar indefatigably disseminated the Word of God among both his own people and others in the performance of his legateship. Whence it also happened that he received from a certain venerable matron, named Ikia, the property called Ramelsloh.[71] This place, situated in the diocese of Verden, is about three stages distant from Hamburg. There the saint of God founded a monastery in which he deposited the remains of the holy confessors, Sixtus and Sinnicius, and the other relics which he had carried off in his flight from Hamburg. There he assembled his fugitive flock and in that haven kept his associates who had been driven out by the heathen. From that place he visited the Church at Hamburg and restored the faith among the Nordalbingians who had wavered before as a result of the persecution. Then also, that his mission to the heathen might not be numbed by any sluggishness on his part, he sent preachers into Denmark; the hermit Hartgar, however, he directed to go into Sweden. It is said also that Ansgar went to Bremen but was driven off by the bishop of the place, who envied him for his learning and virtues. Bishop Leuderic of Bremen died[72] after that and was buried in the Church of Saint Peter at the south side of the altar. He died on the ninth day before the Kalends of September and the Church remained widowed for a long time.

xxiv (26).   Louis the Pious,[73] the illustrious Caesar, then took

---

[a] Schol. 5 (6). Turholz is a very celebrated monastery in Flanders and distinguished for its monks. To recover this monastery, the archbishops of our Church were involved in a dispute of long duration. Archbishop Adalbert, however, made an end to the controversy by effecting an exchange, which was approved by Caesar and by the duke of Flanders.*

* Henry III and probably Count Baldwin V, in 1049 or 1050.

---

[71] The documents which Adam may have seen originated early in the eleventh century and have been found spurious.

[72] Correctly, August 25, 845. Bremen apparently became Ansgar's seat after the destruction of Hamburg. Schmeidler, *Hamburg-Bremen,* p. 112.

[73] Louis the German. In this chapter Adam quoted or drew on *Vita Anskarii* xxii, xxiv.

pity on the desolation of the Church at Hamburg and gave the bishopric of Bremen to the venerable Ansgar. Although he was not unaware of the canonical decrees which provide that a bishop who, as a result of persecution, is expelled from his city, may be received in another where the see is vacant,[74] Ansgar nevertheless did not for a long time yield to Caesar in respect of this proposal in order that others might not through envy be scandalized. Finally he consented, but only on condition that it could be done without complaint on the part of the brethren. These proceedings are very fully recounted in the *Vita* of our bishop, but the chronology is not clearly noted.[75] This the Book of Donations indicates more plainly; namely, that the lord Ansgar was inducted into the bishopric by Caesar's representatives, the priest Aldrich and the count Reginbald in the ninth year of the second Louis.[76] These things are written in the third book, the twentieth chapter; and in his *Vita* there is the following statement: "A long time passed," it reads, "after the Blessed Ansgar assumed the bishopric of Bremen before Pope Nicholas confirmed the action."[77]

xxv (27). And so the saintly Ansgar was bishop for eighteen years after he received Bremen. Now, he had previously presided over the see of Hamburg for sixteen years. Taken together this makes thirty-four years.[78] Rejoicing greatly over this gift of royal munificence, the confessor of God hastened into Denmark. There he found Horic,[79] king of the Danes, and made a Christian of him. The latter forthwith erected a church in the seaport at Schleswig, at the same time granting anyone in his kingdom liberty to become a Christian if he wished. A countless multitude of heathen accepted

[74] Cf. Burchard *Decretum* i.*cxxiii* (Migne, *PL, CXL,* 585-86); Gregory the Great *Epistulae* II.xxv, xxxvii (*ibid.,* LXXVII, 561, 575).

[75] In 848. Cf. *Vita Anskarii* xxii, xxxvi; Dümmler, *Geschichte des ostfränkischen Reichs,* I, 309.

[76] Nothing is known about these men.

[77] *Vita Anskarii* xx.

[78] Ansgar presided at Hamburg 832-47 and over the two sees 848-65. Adam drew on *Vita Anskarii* xxiv almost verbatim in his account of the Danish mission, but he exaggerated its results.

[79] Horic I, son of Gotafrid I. Cf. i.xiv (16), Note 42, above and i.xxix (31) below.

the faith. Record is left in books about these conversions, and that a great many were freed from every bodily infirmity on being washed by the water of baptism.

xxvi (28). The saint of God[80] still cherished a longing for the Swedish people. After fulfilling this mission, then, according to his desire, he counseled with Bishop Gauzbert as to which of them should for the sake of Christ undergo the praiseworthy hazard. But the latter of his own accord declined the perilous enterprise, saying that he would rather have Ansgar go. Without delay the intrepid champion asked King Horic for an escort and safe-conduct[81] and, putting off from the Danish shore, came to Sweden. There King Olaf was then holding a general assembly of his people at Björkö. Anticipated by the mercy of God, Ansgar found the king so favorably disposed that at his bidding and with the consent of the people and according to the casting of the lots and the response of the idol, he was permitted to build a church there and everyone was given leave to be baptized. When these matters also had been settled to his satisfaction, our evangelist commended the Swedish church to the priest Erimbert and returned. In our zeal for brevity we have abridged what is related at great length about his deeds in the *Vita* of Saint Ansgar. And unless I am mistaken in my opinion, the prophecy of Ezechiel about Gog and Magog here appears to have been very aptly fulfilled. "And I will send," says the Lord, "a fire on Magog, and on them that dwell confidently in the islands."[82] Some think that this and similar sayings were spoken about the Goths who captured Rome.[83] When, however, we consider the fact that the Gothic peoples rule in Sweden and that all this region is dispersed in islands scattered far and wide, we are of

[80] Adam drew on *Vita Anskarii* xxv-xxviii, quoting and paraphrasing not always correctly, sometimes tendentiously.

[81] Horic I perhaps gave him a piece of wood marked by runic letters. The King Olaf who received Ansgar apparently has not been identified. He is not mentioned in the Icelandic series of Swedish kings.

[82] Ezech. 39:6; cf. Isa. 49:1. Ansgar also seems to have thought the Isaiah verse referred to the Swedes. *Vita Anskarii* xxv.

[83] In 410 by the Visigoths under Alaric.

the opinion that the prophecy can be applied to them, especially since the prophets made many predictions which as yet do not appear to have been fulfilled.

xxvii (29). In the meantime[84] there arose in the Frankish kingdom great controversy about the bishopric of Bremen, stirred up in envy of Ansgar. The contention was carried on for a long time throughout the realm in serious and indecisive disputes and brought the partisans into hot-tempered collision. The orthodox Caesar, Louis, at length reconciled the discordant minds of the disputants, in particular that of Gunther, archbishop of Cologne, whose suffragan Bremen previously had been, and laid the matter before the most holy Pope Nicholas in Rome. The latter readily gave his approval to what ecclesiastical necessity required and to what had been sanctioned in councils of the fathers as something that could reasonably be done. By virtue of his apostolic authority, therefore, he decreed that the bishopric of Bremen be joined with that of Hamburg and that the two be henceforth considered as one.[a] The documents concerning this action are to this day carefully preserved in the church at Bremen. In them is also the added statement that this same Pope Nicholas constituted the same Ansgar, as well as his successors, legates and vicars of the Apostolic See for all the Swedish, Danish, and Slavic peoples.[85] This grant also had previously been made by Pope Gregory. In the last days of Saint Ansgar, then, was effected the union of the dioceses of Bremen and Hamburg.[86] His *Vita* does not give the year, but the royal decree fixes it as the twenty-first of the reign; the papal privilege notes it as the year of the Lord eight hundred and fifty-eight, which is

---

[a] Schol. 6 (7). As the privilege manifests, the council by which the union was effected took place at Worms in the presence of Caesar and of the bishops.

---

[84] Adam drew on *Vita Anskarii* xxii-xxiii and on the papal and imperial documents there noted, but with some changes. Cf. Dehio, *Hamburg-Bremen*, Vol. I, App., pp. 54-55.

[85] Cf. Ruess, *Rechtliche Stellung der päpstlichen Legaten*, pp. 62-63; Schmeidler, *Hamburg-Bremen*, pp. 198-203.

[86] In 864. The dating at the end of the chapter is confused and not wholly in accord with that given in Chap. xvi above.

the twenty-ninth as reckoned from the consecration of the archbishop.

xxviii (30).   After this, it is written in the *Vita* of the blessed
bishop[87] that he went into Denmark, where he found the younger
Horic[88] on the throne.   To this time the History of the Franks
assigns the following account about the Danes: that the Northmen, going up the Loire, set fire to Tours, and going up the Seine,
besieged Paris; that the terror-stricken Charles gave them a land
in which to live.   Then, it says, with Lotharingia devastated and
Frisia overcome, "they turned their victorious right hands against
their own vitals."[89]   For, now disputing with each other, Gudorm,
the Northman chief, fought with his uncle, namely, Horic, the king
of the Danes.   So great was the slaughter on both sides that the
whole people perished.   Of all the royal stock not one remained,
save only a boy named Horic.[90]   As soon as he took over the kingdom of the Danes he raged with an inborn ferocity against the
Christians, expelling the priests of God and ordering the churches
to be closed.

xxix (31).   The holy confessor[91] of God, Ansgar, did not fear
to go to him and, because he was attended by divine grace, so far
placated the grim tyrant that he himself accepted the Christian faith
and by edict ordered all his followers to become Christians.   In
addition, he erected in another port of his realm, at Ribe, the second
church in Denmark.   When he had set these matters aright according to ecclesiastical prescriptions, our blessed pastor entrusted
that church to the priest Rimbert and returned to Hamburg.   There
he corrected the Nordalbingians with respect to the sale of Chris-

[87] Adam drew on *Vita Anskarii,* xxxi-xxxii and *Annales Fuldenses, an.* 850, 853-
54, but confused their data. Thus, Ansgar could hardly have gone to Denmark after
855, and there is no mention of a siege of Paris in other sources of this time.
[88] Horic I. He perished with his nephew Gudorm in 854.
[89] Lucan *Civil War* 1.3.
[90] Horic II. It is not known how he was related to Horic I or Gudorm.
[91] Adam drew on *Vita Anskarii* xxxii*f* and xxxvii*f* but altered some of the statements; thus, Horic II did not become a Christian, Ansgar placed Rimbert in charge
of the Swedish mission and not of the church at Ribe, Hamburg was still in ruins
and remained so for another half century, Ansgar's reproval of the Frisians preceded
that of the Nordalbingians.

tians. Going thence to the Frisians, he reproved them for working on the Lord's day; those who were more persistent he punished with celestial fire. And we read in his *Vita* of his doing other things which are not unlike the miracles worked of old.

xxx (32). And, since every endeavor of his was for the salvation of souls, he was concerned about his congregations at home whenever he was free from preaching to the heathen without. Of these he moved the first, as we have said before,[92] to Ramelsloh at the time when the community was driven from Hamburg by the barbarian incursion. The second, maintained in Bremen, consisted of holy men who, although they wore the habit of canons, lived according to the monastic rule almost down to our own age. He organized the third congregation, of holy virgins, at Bassum. There Liutgart, a matron devoted to Christ, presented the Heavenly Spouse with all her patrimony, supporting under his guidance a great company of nuns. He provided also in many places hospices for the care of the poor and the reception of strangers. One, the most important indeed, he maintained at Bremen. To it he himself went daily, and he was not ashamed to minister to the infirm, of whom he is said to have healed a very great number by word or touch.

xxxi (33). He retranslated[93] the body of Saint Willehad to the mother church of Saint Peter the Apostle from the south oratory to which Willeric had borne it. And at this time were wrought the miracles which through the merits of Saint Willehad have been declared to the people from the eight hundred and sixty-first year of our Lord, which is the thirtieth year following the archbishop's consecration. In fact, he who moved the remains recounted both Willehad's life and miracles, each in a separate book.[94]

xxxii (34). And, if we take careful account of the course of events, this is the time at which the translation of Saint Alexander

---

[92] Chap. xxiii above. Adam drew on *Vita Anskarii* xxxvf, xxxix, with slight changes.

[93] Adam drew on *Miracula S. Willehadi* xxxviii (*MGH, SS,* II, 38), with changes of lesser importance.

[94] Ansgar wrote only the *Miracula.*

into Saxony took place. In this connection it appears worth noting that our confessor vied with the foreign martyr as to "which of them should seem to be the greater"[95] and the more acceptable to the people in regard to the grace of healing.[96] On these matters Einhard has descanted with a kindly pen in his *Gesta* of the Saxons.[97]

xxxiii (35). In the meanwhile,[98] ransoming captives, encouraging those in tribulation, instructing his own people at home, evangelizing the barbarians, the blessed Ansgar, outwardly an apostle but inwardly a monk, was, as we read, never idle. He was solicitous not only as to how his own people lived but also as to how others did. Of his bishops also he reproved one and exhorted another by word as well as letters to be watchful over the Lord's flock. He also addressed himself frequently to the kings of the Romans in behalf of his mission, and to the kings of the Danes in behalf of the Christian faith. Many such letters of his are extant. In particular, one that he wrote to all the bishops about his mission, which he asserts began with Ebbo, closes as follows:[99] "I beg you," he wrote, "to intercede with God that this mission may deserve to grow and to fructify in the Lord. For by God's favor the Church of Christ was established both among the Danes and among the Swedes, and priests are functioning unhindered in their proper office. May the omnipotent God make you all with pious benevolence participators in this work and joint heirs with Christ,[100] in heavenly glory."

xxxiv (36). Ansgar survived the plenary union of Hamburg and Bremen seven years. He held the see thirty-four years in all. His

[95] Mark 9:33; Luke 22:24.

[96] Cf. I Cor. 12:9.

[97] Since the translation of St. Alexander took place in 851, Einhard, who died in 840, could not have recorded the event. Adam must have had some work attributed to Einhard which contained a part of the *Translatio* by Rudolf and Meginhard of Fulda and the *Miracula S. Willehadi*. Cf. *Annales Xantenses, an.* 851; Schmeidler, *Hamburg-Bremen*, pp. lviii-lix.

[98] Adam drew only a few words in this chapter from *Vita Anskarii* xxxv.

[99] Lappenberg, *Hamburgisches Urkundenbuch*, Vol I, No. 17.

[100] Rom. 8:17.

interment is observed with the greatest reverence on the third day before the Nones of February. He died[101] in the year of our Lord eight hundred and sixty-five, the thirteenth Indiction, which is the twenty-sixth year of the second Louis, and he was entombed in the Basilica of Saint Peter before the altar of the Blessed Mary, Mother of God. Rimbert, his deacon, was elected by the clergy as well as by the people the same day on which he was committed. Rimbert, furthermore, composed a faithful account of the life of the most holy father. Writing in the manner of Saint John,[102] as if about another person, he intimated that he, the most trusted of Ansgar's disciples, was giving testimony to the sanctity he had perceived in the man of God. This book he addressed to the brethren of the monastery of New Corvey,[103] blessing them for having sent forth such a man and congratulating us for having merited such a pastor.

xxxv (37). Saint Rimbert held the see for twenty-three years. His years and the time of the death of his predecessor we found in a certain *computus* which was brought from Corvey.[104] Besides, his *Vita,* in which is briefly and clearly stated who he was and how he lived, was given to our brethren by the brethren of that monastery. "As soon as he was elected," it reads,[105] "he was on Caesar's order conducted to Mainz by Thiadrich, bishop of Minden, and Adalgar, abbot of Corvey. When he had been consecrated there by the illustrious bishop Liubert, he came to Corvey, where he made his monastic profession and received the habit. The abbot Adalgar entrusted to him his own brother of the same name, Adalgar, who later was both his associate in preaching and merited being the heir of his dignity." Rimbert, as can be learned from the privileges, received the pontifical pallium from Pope Nicholas, the pastoral

---

[101] February 3, 865. *Annales Corbienses, an.* 865 (*MGH, SS,* III, 3). Adam drew on *Vita Rimberti* ix, xi, for this chapter.
[102] John 19:26-27; cf. *ibid.,* 18:33, 37.
[103] Correctly, its mother house, Corbie, on the Somme.
[104] *Annales Corbienses, an.* 865, 888 (*MGH, SS,* III, 3).
[105] *Vita Rimberti* xi-xii.

staff from the Caesar Louis.[106] What follows we have taken from the book of his *Vita*, the sixteenth chapter.

xxxvi (38).[107] "He actively discharged, besides, the duty of preaching the word of God to the heathen, the legateship which first he received from his predecessor and which later came to him as a heritage by right of succession. He, indeed, personally pressed this mission vigorously as often as his other work permitted. Always, however, he had at hand priests from whom the heathen might hear the Word of God and Christian captives receive solace, and by whom were administered churches situated afar off among the heathen and which, a most serious consideration, had to be reached by way of dangerous seas. He himself very frequently underwent perils of this kind, like the Apostle often suffering ship-wreck,[108] and many times also undergoing other hazards. In the hope of the blessedness to come he made light of all the hardships of the present life, in continual meditation recurring to the apostolic saying: 'The sufferings of this time are not worthy to be compared with the glory to come that shall be revealed in us.'"[109]

xxxvii (39). The names of the Danish kings in his time are not recorded in his *Gesta*. In the History of the Franks we read that Sigefrid ruled with his brother Halfdan. They also sent gifts to the Caesar Louis, namely, a sword with a golden hilt and other things, and asked for peace. And when mediators had been sent by both parties to the Eider River, they swore to a firm peace on their arms, according to the usage of the folk.[110] There were also other kings over the Danes and Northmen, who at this time harassed Gaul with piratical incursions. Of these tyrants the most important were Horic, Orwig, Gotafrid, Rudolf, and Ingvar.[111]

---

[106] This document is lost. Cf. Lappenberg, *Hamburgisches Urkundenbuch*, Vol. I, Nos. 19, 22.

[107] *Vita Rimberti* xvi.

[108] Cf. II Cor. 11:25.

[109] Rom. 8:18.

[110] *Annales Fuldenses, an.* 873, which, however, have the emissaries go to the Eider River and have the treaty sworn to at Metz.

[111] Little is known with certainty about these men. Some of them mentioned in

The most cruel of them all was Ingvar, the son of Lodbrok, who everywhere tortured Christians to death. This is written in the *Gesta* of the Franks.

xxxviii (40). In the twelfth year of the lord Rimbert, the great Caesar, Louis the Pious, died.[112] He had so far prevailed over the Bohemians, Sorbs, Susi, and other Slavic peoples that he made them tributary. The Northmen, checked by treaties and wars, he also restrained to the extent that, although they devastated all Francia, they did not in the least harm his kingdom. However, after the emperor's death, wild barbarism ruled without restraint. And because the Danes and Northmen had been subjected to the pastoral care of the Church at Hamburg, I cannot pass over the enormities which the Lord at that time permitted them to perpetrate, and how widely the pagans established their power over the Christians. All the facts are mournfully recorded in the History of the Franks and in other books. Then was Saxony laid waste by the Danes and Northmen. Duke Bruno was killed with twelve other counts and bishops Diethard and Markward were slain. At that time Frisia was depopulated and the city of Utrecht razed.[113] Saint Radbod, bishop of the town, retired before the persecution, fixed his see at Deventer and, taking his stand there, took vengeance on the pagans with the sword of anathema. Then the pirates set fire to Cologne and Trier. They stabled their horses in the palace at

the Sagas have been dubiously identified. Ivar may be the Viking called "The Bone-less." He was the son of Halfdan, also known as Ragnar Lodbrok, who was the son of Halfdan, the brother of Harold I. The elder Halfdan may have died about 807, the younger either in 845 or about 860. The latter doubtless was a brother of Anulo, Reginfrid, Rorik, and Harold II, who was baptized in 826. Brothers of Ivar were a Sigurd or Sigefrid, Ubbe, and a Halfdan. Sigefrid and Halfdan may have been kings of Denmark about 873, the latter also of Northumberland from about 875 to about 880. Ivar the Boneless, who flourished approximately between 855 and 871, and his brother Ubbe, who flourished from 855 until after 878, captured and martyred the English Edmund according to a notation in Codex BIb. Cf. *Passio Edmundi auctore Abbone Floriacensi* x-xi (Migne, *PL*, cxxxix, 514-15); Kendrick, *History of the Vikings*, p. 233; Vogel, *Die Normannen*, pp. 244-47, 261-372, 407-12. Rudolf may have been the son of Harold II noted above.

[112] Correctly, Louis the German, who died in 876. Adam drew on *Annales Fuldenses, an.* 880-82; *Vita Radbodi* v, vii (*MGH, SS*, XVa, 571).

[113] Correctly, Maastricht. Cf. Vogel, *Die Normannen*, pp. 279, n. 3, 280-94, 308-9.

Aachen.[a] The people of Mainz began to erect fortifications for fear of the barbarians. Why say more? Cities with their inhabitants, bishops with their whole flocks were struck down at one time. Stately churches were burned with the faithful. Our Louis was victorious in his battles with the pagans, but soon died. Louis of Francia died, after having been both victorious and vanquished.[114] These things, written with tragical lamentation in the Annals of the Caesars, we have touched upon because of our mention of the Danes.

xxxix (41). What, however, do we say our archbishop did in this time? Search in his *Gesta,* the twentieth chapter.[115] After having spent nearly everything he had in ransoming captives, it states, he did not hesitate even to sell the vessels of the altar, as he had to see the miseries of the many that still were detained by the pagans. With the Blessed Ambrose he said: "It is better to save souls for God than gold. Precious, therefore, are the vessels that redeem souls from death." [116]

In view of what we have said about the persecution which then raged far and wide against the churches, it seems not improper to touch upon a great miracle manifested to the Frisians through the merits of Saint Rimbert. I do not know why the author of his *Gesta* passed over this wonder, but Bovo, the abbot of Corvey, in writing of what happened in his times did not keep silence.[117] He wrote: "When in recent times a distressing irruption of barbarians

---

[a] Schol. 7 (8). The palace at Aachen, which the chief Orwig had destroyed, remained in ruins for eighty years until the time of Otto.*

* The account of the destruction wrought at Aachen must be exaggerated, for the palace is mentioned in sources in 887-88, 896, and 930. Cf. Kessel and Rhoen, "Beschreibung und Geschichte der karolingischen Pfalz zu Aachen," *Zeitschrift des aachener Geschichtsvereins,* III (1881), 1-96; Vogel, *Die Normannen,* pp. 280-94.

---

[114] Adam apparently attributed the fortunes of Louis the Younger, son of Louis the German, to Louis III of France.

[115] *Vita Rimberti* xvii.

[116] *De officiis ministrorum* II.xxviii. 137-38 (Migne, *PL,* XVI, 148-49).

[117] This work, probably by Bovo (879-90), is no longer extant. Cf. Manitius, *Geschichte der lateinischen Literatur,* I, 528.

raged savagely in nearly every kingdom of the Franks, it happened also that by the judgment of God they were routed in a certain Frisian district. Situated in a remote region and close to the great sea, it is called Norden. This district, then, they undertook to destroy. The venerable bishop Rimbert was there at that time and, encouraged and prepared by his exhortations and instructions, the Christians joined battle with the enemy and laid low ten thousand three hundred and seventy-seven of them, over and above the many who were slain crossing the streams as they sought safety in flight."[118] These facts Bovo recorded in writing. By reason of this miraculous occurrence the merits of Saint Rimbert are to this day most highly regarded among the Frisians, and his name is cherished with a certain singular affection by the people, so much so that even the hill on which the saint prayed while the battle was in progress is noted for its perpetually green turf. The Northmen proceeded to take vengeance on the whole empire for the blow they had received in Frisia. With their kings, Sigefrid and Gotafrid,[119] they invaded Gaul by way of the Rhine and the Meuse and the Scheldt rivers, slaughtering Christians in woeful carnage, and, attacking King Charles himself, made sport of our people. To England they also sent one of their number, Halfdan, and when he was killed by the Angles, the Danes put Gudröd[120] in his place. The latter conquered Northumbria. And from that time Frisia and England are said to have been subject to the Danes. This is written in the *Gesta* of the Angles.

xl (42). It is vain to look to the saints for signs and wonders which evil men also can perform, because on the authority of the holy Fathers it is a greater miracle to convert from sin a soul, which is to live for eternity, than to raise up from death a body, which is

---

[118] Cf. *Annales Fuldenses, an.* 884; Vogel, *Die Normannen,* pp. 294-311.

[119] Adam exaggerated the statements in *Annales Fuldenses, Cont. Ratisbon., an.* 882.

[120] Cf. Symeon of Durham *Historia regum,* ed. Thomas Arnold (Vol. 2, Symeon's *Opera omnia* in Rerum britannicarum medii aevi scriptores, no. 75), 86, 99, 377, 391.

to die again.[121] That, however, we may know Saint Rimbert did not lack this power, it is said that he worked some miracles in the manner of the ancient saints; namely, while on his way to Sweden, he often stilled stormy seas by his prayer, and gave sight to a blind man by the benediction he administered to him according to the episcopal rite. He is even said to have freed a king's son from a devil. On this occasion the unclean spirit repeatedly cried out of the mouth of the vexed boy to the many bishops who were standing nearby that Rimbert was the only one among them who worthily discharged the office committed to him and thereby made him suffer. See in the book of his *Vita,* the twentieth chapter.[122] We think this boy was Charles, the son of King Louis.[123] When he was deposed from the throne in the archbishop's last days, his brother's son, Arnulf, succeeded. The History of the Franks truthfully relates that this was done in Frankfurt in the thirty-fourth year of the Caesar Louis.[124]

xli (43). Now Saint Rimbert, like Moses,[125] was a man exceedingly meek, as says the Apostle,[126] one who had compassion on the infirmities of all; but especially was he concerned about relieving the poor and ransoming captives. And so at one time when he went into the Danish country, where he had a church built for the young Christendom in a place called Schleswig, he saw a multitude of Christians dragged captive by a chain. Why say more? There he worked a twofold miracle: for he both broke the chain by his prayer and redeemed the captives[127] with his horse. See the eighteenth chapter of his *Gesta.*

---

[121] Cf. Gregory the Great *Homilia in Evang.* II.xxix (Migne, *PL,* LXXVI, 1216) and *Dialog.* III.xvii *(ibid.,* LXXVII, 265).

[122] *Vita Rimberti* xx.

[123] Charles III, the Fat. Cf. *Annales Fuldenses, an.* 873; *Annales Xantenses, an.* 873.

[124] Arnulf succeeded Charles the Fat in 887. Cf. *Annales Fuldenses, an.* 887.

[125] Adam compiled this chapter from *Vita Rimberti* xvii-xix. For the reference to Moses, see Numb. 12:3.

[126] Adam refers what he said to Heb. 4:15, whereas the *Vita* refers it to II Tim. 2:24. Rimbert's concern for the poor is noted in *Vita Rimberti* xiv.

[127] The *Vita* (Chap. xviii) mentions only a woman captive.

xlii (44). And because the desolation brought about by the Northmen and Danes exceeded all belief, one may wonder the more that the holy confessors of God, Ansgar and Rimbert, should have gone undaunted through such great perils by sea and land and preached to peoples before whose onslaughts neither armed kings nor the mighty Frankish tribes could stand. But "there is now no saint: truths are decayed from among the children of men."[128]

A lazy crew that delights in shelter and shade,[129] we find it scarcely possible to believe that anyone, even an apostle, should in a time of such fierce persecution dare to go to a people so ferocious that it is hardly human, in a region so very remote, I say, from our world. We do not know that what the Savior said to the apostles is daily addressed also to us: "Go ye into the whole world. And behold, I am with you all days, even to the consummation of the world."[130]

xliii (45). Many other things are narrated at length about our saint in his book. Among them the most remarkable is that by fasting forty days on bread and water he released from torment the soul of a dead priest who had implored his help in a vision.[131] His predecessor had founded four monasteries. Rimbert added to them a fifth in the wilderness of Bücken. For the rest, although he paid meticulous attention to everything, he was especially solicitous for the see of Hamburg, affording both the brethren and the poor meet solace.[132]

xliv (46).[133] The xenodochium at Bremen, which Saint Ansgar had established for the support of the poor, he enlarged to an

---

[128] Ps. 11:2. A few lines are here taken from *Vita Rimberti* xx.

[129] Juvenal *Satires* VII.105, which reads, however, *lecto*, "lounging," not *tecto* as Adam has it.

[130] Matt. 28:19-20; Mark 16:15.

[131] Adam drew on *Vita Rimberti* viii for the notice about the priest.

[132] Cf. Chap. xxx (32) above. The charter of foundation for Bücken was tampered with, if not entirely forged, at the beginning of the 12th century. Cf. Lappenberg, *Hamburgisches Urkundenbuch*, Vol. I, No. 48. Hamburg may by this time have been partially restored.

[133] For this chapter, Adam drew on *Vita Rimberti* xiv-xv, xxi, xxiv, and on *Annales Corbienses, an.* 888 (*MGH, SS*, III, 3).

imposing extent, and he provided with all diligence for the mainte-
nance of the needy, not only in his bishopric but wherever he was.
To posterity he left noble words of exhortation when he said, "We
must not be slow in coming to the help of all the poor, because
we do not know who is Christ or when He will come to us."[134] The
alms of the word he ministered to all without ceasing. For this
purpose he had sayings of Saint Gregory selected, and these he also
copied with his own hand. Various letters of his were directed to
many people. Especially noteworthy is one adressed to nuns in
which, although he extols the virginity of the body, he declares
that many women mentally become harlots. Spent at length with
sickness and old age, he comforted those whom he himself could
not see through Adalgar, his coadjutor in the Lord. Him also he
commended to the hands of the king. He died in the year of our
Lord eight hundred and eighty-eight, the sixth Indiction. His death
took place on the third day before the Ides of June. He was buried
outside the Basilica of Saint Peter on the east side, as he himself
had requested.

xlv (47). Archbishop Adalgar held the see for twenty years.
His years we learned from the *computus* on which we drew above;[135]
his life from the book of Saint Rimbert, the twelfth chapter.[136]
Immediately after the statement that "Saint Rimbert made his
monastic profession and received the habit," there follows: "In
addition, it was thought proper to give him the assistance of a man
named Adalgar, of diaconal rank and distinguished for his way of
life. This man, they say, who was venerable in the imitation of Rimbert's bearing and also as to the dignity of being his successor, is
today still alive and with many others testifies that the holy bishop
Rimbert lost nothing of monastic perfection by reason of his
pastoral cares," and so on. Again, in the twenty-first chapter we
read: "Now, when Saint Rimbert was burdened with age, he also

---

[134] Cf. Matt. 25:35-40.
[135] *Annales Corbienses, an.* 889, 909 (*MGH, SS,* III, 3-4).
[136] *Vita Rimberti* xii, xxi.

was constantly troubled by pains in his feet. On this account he obtained of the most glorious king Louis and his sons, that the distinguished man, Adalgar, the monk, namely, of Corvey, should be confirmed as his aide, so that when he himself was hampered by his infirmity he might in the person of Adalgar have the consolation of making the rounds of the diocese, of attending diets, and, whenever necessary, of going with his company either on expeditions or to the palace. He procured also the ratification of Adalgar's election as his successor and his enrollment among the king's counselors. All these measures were assented to by the brethren and abbot of his monastery and confirmed in holy synod."

xlvi (48). Adalgar received the pastoral staff from King Arnulf, the pallium from Pope Stephen.[137] Sundarold, archbishop of Mainz, consecrated him, and his pontificate came in a hard time of barbarian devastation. Nevertheless he did not, as is evident in the privileges, yield in his endeavor for his mission to the heathen. Indeed, like his predecessors, he himself took care to have priests appointed to this work.

xlvii (49). I have not seen[138] anything further written about the history of the Danes nor have I learned that anyone else has. The reason for this may be, as I suppose, that King Arnulf in hardfought battles at that time overwhelmed the Northmen or Danes even to the point of utter destruction. The war was directed from on High, since, indeed, although a hundred thousand pagans were killed, scarcely a Christian was found to have fallen.[a] In such wise was an end made of the persecution of the Northmen. The Lord

a Schol. 8 (9). Kings Gotafrid and Sigefrid were killed there.

---

[137] The document Adam used was a forgery and is no longer extant. Its original, issued by Sergius III, did not confer the pallium. Cf. Lappenberg, *Hamburgisches Urkundenbuch,* Vol. I, No. 24; Schmeidler, *Hamburg-Bremen,* pp. 110-11.

[138] Adam misunderstood his source in respect of the casualties in the battle upon the Dyle at Louvain: *Annales Fuldenses, an.* 891. Cf. Vogel, *Die Normannen,* pp. 359-72.

revenged the blood which His servants had shed for seventy years.[139] These facts are narrated in the History of the Franks.

xlviii (50). But I have heard from the mouth of the most veracious king of the Danes, Svein,[140] when at our request he named over his forefathers: "After the overthrow of the Northmen," he said, "I have learned that Norway was ruled by Helge, a man beloved by the people for his justice and sanctity. He was succeeded by Olaf, who, coming from Sweden, obtained the Danish kingdom by force of arms, and he had many sons, of whom Chnuba and Gurd possessed the realm after their father's death." [141]

xlix (51). In Adalgar's seventh year Hermann, archbishop of Cologne, troubled our Adalgar with grave wrongs in an effort to subject Bremen to Cologne. A synod, assembled at Tribur[142] under the presidency of Hatto of Mainz, voided the privileges of the Apostolic See and annulled the precepts of the glorious princes in accord with iniquitous decrees issued, as they say, by Pope Formosus and King Arnulf.[a] Next, when they came to the signing, Archbishop Adalgar's name was entered at the end of the conciliar signatures. Then there is the noted story[143] about Adelin and Widger, who by their disputing made a spectacle of the synod. Mournfully tragic was it that Widger, the pleader for our party,

---

a Schol. 9 (10). Both, the king as well as the pope, came to a miserable end, for after Pope Formosus was dead his successor deposed him and cast his body out of its sepulcher.* King Arnulf was eaten alive by worms and by the mighty vengeance of God finally met death by poisoning.†

* Stephen VI (VII). The *Annales Fuldenses, an.* 896, state that he had Formosus reinterred after the desecration.

† Cf. Liutprand *Antapodosis* I.xxxvi.

---

139 Cf. Ps. 78:10; Apoc. 19:2. Adam uses "seventy" in a general way to denote a large number.

140 Svein Estrithson, king of Denmark (1047-74), was the son of Ulf and of Estrith, daughter of King Canute of England and Denmark. He was Adam's friend and his informant about the history of the northern peoples. For the date of Svein's death, see Schmeidler, *Hamburg-Bremen*, pp. 288-305. For his ancestry, see George, *Genealogical Tables*, No. 2.

141 In Chap. lii (54) below, Adam states that the sons ruled with their father and that Sigeric succeeded to the Danish throne. Widukind *Gesta Saxonum* I.xl notes that Otto the Great had Chnuba, the Danish king, receive baptism in 934.

142 Some of the documents are not genuine. Cf. Lappenberg, *Hamburgisches Urkundenbuch*, Vol. I, Nos. 22-26.

143 Evidently traditional.

lost and died the next day. And furthermore they say that under Adalgar and Hoger Bremen remained all the time a suffragan of Cologne. Because we found these statements in the records of that synod, we shall not pronounce them either true or false.

1 (52).   Pope Formosus died two years later, and King Arnulf four. There followed an invasion of the Hungarians, a persecution of the churches. Our archbishop, a very old man, was unable either to oppose his enemies or to direct what there was to be done. For this reason, they say, he was given an aide, Hoger, of the monastery of Corvey, with whose support, help, and ministrations he could know the leisure of a deserving old age. As the omnipotent God sometimes suffers the just to be tempted that they may become better, so also had He temptation come to our archbishop that he might be able to bear it.[144] For Pope Sergius, who was the seventh[145] after Formosus and ruled for nearly the same number of years, deplored the calumnies Adalgar had suffered and renewed the privileges in respect of the Church of Bremen and confirmed all the concessions made to Ansgar and Rimbert by Gregory and Nicholas, his predecessors.[a] Because, moreover, Archbishop Adalgar, weighed down by the burden of old age, was not equal to the discharge of his pastoral office, the pope gave him as assistants in the duties of visitation, preaching, and consecrating bishops, the five bishops who were his neighbors, Sigismund of Halberstadt, Wigbert of Verden, Biso of Paderborn, and the two Bernars of Minden and Osnabrück,[146] with whose help he might bear up in his old age. The privileges of

---

[a] Schol. 10 (11). Pope Stephen,* who held the see for six years, ordered Archbishop Hermann of Cologne and Archbishop Adalgar of Hamburg, who were in contention over the Church at Bremen, to attend a synod at Worms, and he commissioned Fulk, archbishop of Rheims, whom he appointed to act in his stead, to investigate their cause.

* Stephen V (VI), 885-91. This scholium is not Adam's but derives from Pseudo-Liutprand cxii (Migne, *PL,* CXXIX, 1, 255).

---

[144] Cf. I Cor. 10:13.

[145] Sergius III was the ninth pope after Formosus. Adam quotes his privilege. Lappenberg, *Hamburgisches Urkundenbuch,* Vol. I, No. 26.

[146] One of the Bernars must have been of Verden, not of Osnabrück. These assistant bishops are not mentioned in the privilege.

Pope Sergius to each of them, containing the facts as stated, are at hand. Still it is strange; nor is it satisfactorily known to us whether any bishops were consecrated for the heathen by Adalgar, as the privilege suggests, or whether this consecration of bishops was carried out only in the days of Adaldag, as we prefer to believe especially because the violence of the barbarians scarcely admitted of priests staying among them. "For as yet the iniquities of the Amorites are not at the full," nor had the time to favor them come yet.[147] The archbishop passed away after this in the year of our Lord nine hundred and seven,[148] the day before the Ides of May, and was entombed in the Basilica of Saint Michael, which out of love for his master he had built over his sepulcher.

li (53). Hoger was archbishop for seven years. His years we also found in the book before mentioned;[149] also the statement that he was consecrated by the archbishop of Cologne[150] while the controversy was in progress. He received the pallium from Pope Sergius, the pastoral staff from King Louis. Whence he came and how he lived is known only to God. However, we have found written in the older books of the Church a verse about him which runs as follows:

Holy and elect was Hoger, the seventh hero.

Testimony to his sanctity is given by an ancient tradition which narrates that, being most scrupulous in matters of ecclesiastical discipline, he according to custom frequently made the rounds of the monasteries of his diocese. Hence also, when he was in Hamburg,[151] he would, in order to find out what the brethren were doing, hasten to Ramelsloh for the matin vigils no matter how stormy the night. He was, I say, the faithful and wise steward who himself spent the night watching and kept his household from

---

147 Gen. 15:16; cf. Ps. 101:14.
148 May 9, 909(?). *Annales necrol. Fuldenses* (*MGH, SS,* XIII, 190) note his death in 910. *Chronicon breve Bremense* (*MGH, SS,* VII, 390-91) makes the date May 13, probably 908.
149 I.xxxv (37), Note 104 above. Hoger held the see from 909 to 915.
150 Hermann.
151 Adam, the only authority for the existence of the city at this time, may have depended on tradition. Cf. Schmeidler, *Hamburg-Bremen,* pp. 112-13.

sleeping and, when the bridegroom came,[152] gladly met him with the words, "Behold, I and my children, whom God hath given me."[153]

lii (54). In the second year of the lord Hoger, Louis the Child was buried and Conrad, the duke of the Franconians, raised to the throne. In this Louis the ancient stock of Charles came to an end.[154] To this point also extends the History of the Franks. What we shall henceforth relate we have found in various books which are by no means untrustworthy. Some things, too, the illustrious king of the Danes told us when we asked. He said that after Olaf, the Swedish prince who ruled in Denmark with his sons, Sigeric was put in his place. And after he had reigned a short time, Harthacanute,[155] the son of Svein, came from Normandy[156] and deprived him of the kingdom. How many Danish kings, or rather tyrants, there were indeed, and whether some of them ruled at the same time or lived for a short time one after the other, is uncertain. It is enough for us to know that to this day they all were pagans and that, in spite of so many changes in rulers and so many barbarian inroads, there was left in Denmark a little of the Christianity which Ansgar had planted and which did not entirely disappear. In those days Saxony was overwhelmed by a most frightful persecution, as from one direction the Danes and Slavs, from the other the Bohemians and Hungarians wrought havoc with the churches. At that time the diocese of Hamburg was laid waste by an attack of the Slavs, and that of Bremen by an attack of the Hungarians.[157] In the meantime the confessor of God, Hoger, died and was buried by the side of his predecessor in the Church of Saint Michael in the

---

[152] Luke 12:42; cf. Matt. 25:6.

[153] Isa. 8:18. The Vulgate has it *pueri mei.*

[154] In 911. Adam may have had a version of the *Annales Fuldenses,* with its continuation, that extended beyond 897, at which point the extant version ends.

[155] Generally identified with Harthacanute Gorm (Gorm the Old) of i.lv (57), lix (61) below, or his father. On the state of Denmark at this time, see Liliencron, *Beziehungen des deutschen Reichs zu Dänemark,* pp. 77-78.

[156] Perhaps Norway, although Adam has "Nortmannia." Cf. Kendrick, *History of the Vikings,* pp. 98-99.

[157] Cf. *Annales Corbienses, an.* 906, 915 (*MGH, SS,* III, 4).

year of our Lord nine hundred and fifteen.[158] The day of his death is commemorated on the thirteenth day before the Kalends of January. When, after a hundred and twenty years, the bishop's body was sought in the little chapel, which had fallen to ruin through its age, nothing but the crosses of the pallium and the pontifical cervical could be found. And we believe that his resurrection was accomplished, as is said by others to have truly happened in the case of David and of Saint John the Evangelist.

liii (55). Reginward held the see barely a year. Of his life nothing has come to hand but his name. Since, however, I have learned that his successor attended the synod of Altheim, which was held in the fifth year of King Conrad, the year also in which our Hoger died, I have concluded that Reginward, coming between them, died within less than a year. I have not been able to find a document concerning him anywhere. Those who lived later say that a great miracle took place at Bremen in those days. The Hungarians, indeed, were burning churches, butchering priests before the altars, and with impunity were slaying clerics and layman indiscriminately or leading them into captivity. At that time, too, crosses were mutilated and derided by the pagans. Signs of this frenzy have endured even to our age. But a jealous God, Whose passion was there held to ridicule, did not suffer the unbelievers to go away unpunished. For a sudden and amazing storm lifted the shingles from the half-burned church roofs and whirled them into the faces and mouths of the pagans until, seeking refuge in flight, they either had to cast themselves headlong into the river or let themselves be taken captive by the burghers. Not long after this the prostrated flock was overtaken by the sudden death of its good shepherd. He died on the Kalends of October[159] and was laid to rest along with his predecessors in the Basilica of Saint Michael.

liv (56). Archbishop Unni held the see for eighteen years. His

---

[158] The date is disputed: December 20, between 915 and 917. Cf. Dehio, *Hamburg-Bremen,* Vol. I, App., pp. 59-60.

[159] October 1, 918(?). Cf. Dehio, *Hamburg-Bremen,* Vol. I, App., pp. 59-60.

years and the time of his death I know from the source mentioned above.[160] The brethren have a tradition that when Reginward passed away, Leidrad, the provost of the chapter at Bremen, was elected by the clergy and the people. With Unni in his service as chaplain he went to court. Inspired, it is believed, by the Holy Ghost, King Conrad, however, looked with disfavor upon Leidrad's appearance and, seeing the slight Unni standing behind him, gave the pastoral staff to him. Pope John X, as the privilege indicates,[161] also conferred the pallium on him. As can be seen in his election and his death, he was a very holy man. Because of this sanctity he continually enjoyed the confidence and respect of the kings Conrad and Henry. For this reason, too, he is thus described in the verse:

Esteemed by the princes, Unni was the ninth of the line.

lv (57). In his days the Hungarians devastated not only our Saxony and the other provinces on this side of the Rhine but also Lotharingia and Francia across the Rhine.[162] The Danes, too, with the Slavs as allies, plundering first of all the Transalbingian Saxons and then ravaging the country this side of the Elbe, made Saxony tremble in great terror.[163] Over the Danes there ruled at that time Harthacanute Gorm, a savage worm,[164] I say, and not moderately hostile to the Christian people. He set about completely to destroy Christianity in Denmark, driving the priests of God from its bounds and also torturing very many of them to death.

lvi (58). But then King Henry, who feared God even from his boyhood and placed all trust in His mercy, triumphed over the Hun-

---

[160] *Annales Corbienses, an.* 917, 936. Cf. i.xxxv (37), li (53), above. Adam arrived at eighteen years for Unni's episcopate, 919-36, by allowing a year for Reginward's without making other allowances.

[161] Adam's source is no longer extant and those now at hand are not genuine. Cf. Lappenberg, *Hamburgisches Urkundenbuch*, Vol. I, No. 29.

[162] Cf. *Annales Corbienses, an.* 919 (*MGH, SS,* III, 4); *Annales Augienses, an.* 907-10, 913-17 (*MGH, SS,* I, 68).

[163] Cf. Vogel, *Die Normannen*, pp. 294-311; Waitz, *Jahrbücher*, pp. 41-42, 76-78, 150-58.

[164] Adam reads, "Hardecnudth Vurm . . . inquam vermis." The alliteration is lost in translation. Although unyielding pagans, this Gorm, called the Old, and his queen, Thyra, may be said to have laid the foundations of a consolidated Denmark, and the conversion of his son Harold furthered this consolidation. Cf. i.lii (54) above; Kendrick, *History of the Vikings*, pp. 100-3; Waitz, *Jahrbücher*, pp. 159-63.

garians in many and mighty battles. Likewise he struck down the Bohemians and the Sorbs, who had been subdued by other kings, and the other Slavic peoples, with such force in one great encounter[165] that the rest—and just a few were left—of their own accord promised the king that they would pay tribute, and God that they would be Christians.

lvii (59). Then he invaded Denmark with an army and in the first battle so thoroughly terrified King Gorm[166] that the latter pledged himself to obey his commands and, as a suppliant, sued for peace. The victorious Henry then set the bounds of the kingdom at Schleswig, which is now called Haddeby,[167] appointed a margrave, and ordered a colony of Saxons to settle there. All these facts, related by a certain Danish bishop,[168] a prudent man, we transmit to our Church as faithfully as we have truthfully received them.

lviii (60). When our most blessed archbishop Unni saw that the door of the faith had been opened to the gentiles,[169] he gave thanks to God for the salvation of the pagans, and more especially because the mission of the Church of Hamburg, long neglected on account of the adverse times, had with the help of God's mercy and through the valor of King Henry been given occasion and opportunity for its work. Deeming nothing hard and laborious if undertaken for Christ, he determined to go in person through the length and breadth of his diocese. The entire flock of the Church of Bremen followed him, as they say, saddened by the absence of its good shepherd and ready to go with him both into prison and to death.[170]

---

[165] At Lenzen, in 929. Much in this and the following chapter is open to question, especially the statement that the Bohemians and Sorbs accepted Christianity.

[166] In 934. Widukind *Gesta Saxonum* i.xl has Henry fight Chnuba, one of the then independent chieftains of Schleswig, but Gorm may, without fighting, have made peace with Henry as a result of Chnuba's defeat. Cf. Liliencron, *Beziehungen des deutschen Reichs zu Dänemark*, pp. 10-22.

[167] Schleswig lay north and Haddeby south of the Schlei River, across from Schleswig. Cf. II.xxxv and IV.i below for like errors.

[168] Possibly Ratolf of Schleswig. Cf. Liliencron, *ibid.*, p. 19.

[169] Cf. Acts 14:26; II Cor. 2:12.

[170] Luke 22:33.

lix (61). Thereafter the confessor of God came to the Danes over whom, as we have said, the most cruel Gorm then held sway. The latter, indeed, he could not win over on account of his inborn savagery, but he is said by his preaching to have won the king's son, Harold.[171] Unni made him so faithful to Christ that, although he himself had not yet received the sacrament of baptism, he permitted the public profession of Christianity which his father always hated.

And so, after the saint of God had ordained priests for the several churches in the kingdom of the Danes, he is said to have commended the multitude of believers to Harold. Seconded also by his aid and by a legate, Unni went into all the islands of the Danes, preaching the Word of God[172] to the heathen and comforting in Christ the faithful whom he found captive there.

lx (62). Following in the footsteps of the great preacher Ansgar, he then crossed the Baltic Sea and not without difficulty came to Björkö. Thither no teacher had dared to go in the seventy years since the death of Saint Ansgar save only Rimbert, as we read.[173] To such an extent did the persecution hold back our missionaries. Björkö[174] is a town of the Goths situated in the middle of Sweden not far from the temple called Uppsala, which the Swedes consider the most eminent in the cult of their gods. At that place a bight of the sea[175] which is called the Baltic or Barbarian Sea by extending northward forms a desirable, but to the unwary and those unacquainted with places of this kind a very dangerous, port for the barbarous tribes that lie spread about this sea. For the people of Björkö, very often assailed by the inroads of pirates, who are numerous there, have set about deceiving by cunning artifices the enemies whom they could not resist by force of arms. They have blocked that bight of the restless sea for a

---

[171] Harold Bluetooth, in 935 or 936. Cf. i.lv (57) above.
[172] Acts 8:4; 15:35.
[173] From 865 to 935. Cf. *Vita Rimberti* xx.
[174] Cf. iv.xx, Schol. 126-27, below.
[175] Lake Mälar.

hundred or more stadia by masses of hidden rocks,[176] making its passage as perilous for themselves as for the pirates. In this haven, the most secure in the maritime regions of Sweden, all the ships of the Danes and Northmen, as well as those of the Slavs and Sembi[177] and the other Scythian people, are wont to meet at stated times for the diverse necessities of trade.

lxi (63). Landing at this port, the confessor of God began to approach the people with his unfamiliar mission. The Swedes and the Goths—or, if this name is preferable, the Northmen—had, indeed, entirely forgotten the Christian religion and could by no means be easily persuaded to believe, because they had lived through the period of barbarian invasion when in a few years many kings had held bloody sway over them. We have it on the authority of Svein, the Danish king to whom we have often referred, that at that time a certain Ring and his sons Eric and Emund governed the Swedes, and that before this Ring there had been Anund, Björn, Olaf, of whom we read in the *Gesta* of Saint Ansgar,[178] and others, of whom no mention occurs. It is credible that the champion of God, Unni, approached those kings even though they did not believe and with their permission preached the Word of God throughout Sweden. As it seems useless, in my judgment, to scrutinize the doings of those who did not believe, so it is impious to pass over the deliverance of those who first believed and to leave unmentioned those through whom they did believe. Now the Swedes and the Goths, who were first grounded in the faith by Saint Ansgar and relapsed again into paganism, were recalled by the holy father Unni. This it is enough to know; if

[176] Several explanations for the obstruction of the channel have been advanced. Kohlmann, *Adam von Bremen*, p. 73, was of the opinion that nature rather than the people of Björkö was responsible for the hidden rocks. Henning "Zur Verkehrsgeschichte Ost- und Nordeuropas im 8. bis 12. Jahrhundert," *Historische Zeitschrift*, CXV (1916), 1-30, held that the town of Adam's age is not to be identified with the modern Björkö. This theory is untenable when the draught of ships of earlier times and the element of security are considered. Demmin lay upstream (II.xxii below); so also Hamburg and Lübeck. Cf. Häpke, "Hansische Umschau," *Hansische Geschichtsblätter*, XXVII (1922), 273-97.

[177] Prussians.

[178] *Vita Ansharii* xi, xix, xxvi, xxx. Cf. Kendrick, *History of the Vikings*, pp. 130-31.

we said more, we should be charged with a lying disposition. "For it is better," as the Blessed Jerome puts it, "to say what is true crudely than to proffer what is false elegantly."[179]

lxii (64). When the evangelist of God had completed the ministry of his mission and at length was arranging for his return, he fell ill at Björkö and there laid down the burden of his wearied body.[180] But his soul, attended by a great triumphal procession of souls, ascended the heights of the heavenly fatherland to rejoice forever. Then the bishop's disciples conducted his obsequies in tears and in joy. They buried all his members but the head in that town of Björkö. His head they brought home to Bremen, committing it with due honor before the altar in the Church of Saint Peter. When he had fought the good fight,[181] Unni died in Sweden, as stated above, in the year of our Lord's Incarnation nine hundred and thirty-six, the ninth Indiction, about the middle of September. This is the first year of Otto the Great and the hundred and forty-eighth after the passing of Saint Willehad, the first bishop of Bremen.[182]

lxiii (65). Lo, ye bishops who, sitting at home, make the short-lived pleasures of honor, of lucre, of the belly, and of sleeping the first considerations of episcopal office! Look back, I say, upon this man, poor and lowly in worldly respect but praiseworthy and a great priest of God. He who lately was rewarded with so noble an end gave posterity such an example that your indolence cannot be excused by any harsh condition of time and place. Undergoing such perils by sea and by land, he went among the fierce peoples of the north and with such zeal discharged the ministry of his mission that he died at the confines of the earth, laying down his life for Christ.

---

[179] *Ep.* xviii. 4 (Migne, *PL*, XXII, 363).
[180] Cf. I Pet. 1:13-14.
[181] Cf. I Tim. 6:12; II Tim. 4:7; *Vita Willehadi* xi (*MGH, SS*, II, 384).
[182] September 17, 936. The 148th year if 789 is included. Cf. *Annales Corbienses, an.* 936 (*MGH, SS*, III, 4).

Book Two

Here, reader, you may learn about the deeds
well done recorded in this second book.

i (1). Archbishop Adaldag held the see for fifty-three years. He it is who is said to have restored for us the state.[1] Illustrious of family, youthful of age, he was noble in appearance, nobler yet in the probity of his ways. He was chosen from the chapter of Hildesheim and was a relative and disciple of the blessed Adalward, bishop of Verden, whose uprightness of life, unblemished reputation, and fidelity were then highly recognized in the palace. It is said that he, celebrated also for his learning and miracles, had preached to the Slavic peoples at the time our Unni was on his mission to the Swedes.[2] Commended at court, doubtless because of his deeds and reputation,[3] Adaldag received the pastoral staff from Otto the Great and the episcopal pallium from Pope Leo VII and, like his predecessors, was consecrated by the archbishop of Mainz.[4] The see of Hamburg, however, had as yet no suffragans. These it acquired through the zeal of this Adaldag.

ii (2). And so, as soon as Adaldag entered upon the episcopate,

---

[1] Vergil *Aeneid* vi.846. Adalgag's episcopate lasted from 937 to 988.

[2] Adaldag must have been active among the Slavs at an earlier time because Unni died at Björkö on October 27, 933. Cf. Hauck, *Kirchengeschichte Deutschlands*, III, 986.

[3] He enjoyed the favor of Queen Matilda and was active in the chancery of Otto I. Cf. *Vita Mathildis altera* viii (*MGH, SS*, IV, 288).

[4] Probably Hildibert, who died on May 31, 937, or Frederick, who was consecrated on June 9. Adaldag's investiture took place between February 4 and June 30 that year. Cf. Lappenberg, *Hamburgisches Urkundenbuch*, Vol. I, Nos. 21, 33.

he caused Bremen, which for a long time previously had been controlled by royal officers and judges, to be set free by an edict of the king and given equality with other cities in respect of its immunities as well as its freedom. The precepts of the king containing these provisions and other documents are at hand. Next he turned his attention to the legateship, which his predecessors had first received for the salvation of the heathen and which came to him in such good order that what others had sowed in tears, he might reap in joy.[5] His soul was all aglow, I say, with a burning desire somehow to accomplish that which from a feeling of pious duty he had set himself to do. And because all things work together unto good to them that love God,[6] the Lord granted him the success he wished, both propitious times and the favor of the king. With the latter he enjoyed such intimacy that he could scarcely ever tear himself away from his side;[7] for all that he never lost sight of the needs of his diocese or neglected the care of his legateship. On the contrary, he did not cease to urge the will of the most victorious and just king in everything that is of God,[8] because he perceived that the king at that time was especially well disposed toward the conversion of the pagans. And this also turned out as he desired, since God worked with and confirmed the right hand of the most pious king in all things.[9]

iii (3). As soon as he was freed from the plots of his brothers, King Otto with the support of divine help executed judgment and justice unto his people. Thereupon, after he had brought into subjection to his empire nearly all the kingdoms which had seceded after the death of Charles, he took up arms against the Danes, whom his father had previously subdued by war. Bent upon

---

[5] Cf. Ps. 125:5.

[6] Rom. 8:28.

[7] Adaldag was royal chancellor from September 3, 936, to February 4, 937, and issued documents from June 30, 937, to August 10, 965. Cf. Lappenberg, *Hamburgisches Urkundenbuch,* Vol. I, Nos. 31, 32, 43; Schmeidler, *Hamburg-Bremen,* pp.196-97.

[8] Matt. 16:23.

[9] Cf. Mark 16:20.

fighting, they had murdered at Haddeby Otto's legates and the margrave and had utterly wiped out the whole colony of Saxons. To avenge this deed the king at once invaded Denmark with an army. Crossing the Danish frontier, which had formerly been fixed at Schleswig, he devastated the whole region with fire and sword, even unto the furthermost sea[10] which separates the Northmen from the Danes and which to this very day is called the Ottensond for the victory of the king.[11] As he was leaving, Harold met him at Schleswig and offered battle. In this conflict, manfully contested on both sides, the Saxons gained the victory, and the vanquished Danes retreated to their ships. When conditions were at length favorable for peace, Harold submitted to Otto and, on getting back his kingdom from the latter, promised to receive Christianity into Denmark. Not long after Harold himself was baptized together with his wife, Gunnhild, and his little son, whom our king raised up from the sacred font and named Svein Otto.[12] At that time Denmark on this side of the sea, which is called Jutland by the inhabitants, was divided into three dioceses and subjected to the bishopric of Hamburg. In the church at Bremen are preserved the royal edicts which prove that King Otto held the Danish kingdom in his jurisdiction, so much so that he would even bestow the bishoprics.[13] And it can be seen in the privileges of the Roman See that Pope Agapetus, in congratulating the Church of Hamburg upon the salvation of the heathen, also conceded to Adaldag everything that had been granted to the archbishopric of Bremen by his predecessors, Gregory, Nicholas, Sergius, and others.[14] To him also was conceded by virtue of apostolic authority the right to consecrate

[10] Doubtless the Kattegat. Cf Deut. 34:2; Joel 2:20; Zach. 14:8.

[11] Adam here attributes to Otto I the campaign Otto II made against Denmark in 974, which expedition he therefore does not mention in II.xxiv below. The *B* and *C* versions also falsely connect Otto's name with the Oddesund in the Limfjord at the northern tip of the Danish mainland. *Odde,* meaning a point or tongue of land, easily lent itself to the erroneous connection. Cf. Kohlmann, *Adam von Bremen,* p. 110; Liliencron, *Beziehungen des deutschen Reichs zu Dänemark,* pp. 30-39.

[12] Cf. Schol. 20 (21) below.

[13] Cf. iv.i below; Lappenberg, *Hamburgisches Urkundenbuch,* Vol. I, No. 41.

[14] Cf. Liliencron, *Beziehungen des deutschen Reichs zu Dänemark,* pp. 2-10.

bishops as papal legates to Denmark as well as to the other peoples of the north.

iv (4). Our most blessed father, then, was the first to consecrate bishops for Denmark: Hored for Schleswig, Liafdag for Ribe, Reginbrund for Aarhus. To them he also commended the churches across the sea in Fyn, Zealand, and Scania and in Sweden. This was done in the archbishop's twelfth year.[15] And indeed, such increase followed these beginnings of heavenly mercy, God working with them, that the churches of the Danes are seen to abound in the manifold fruits of the northern peoples from that time even to this day.

v (5). They say also that the most valorous king Otto at that time subjected to his sway all the Slavic peoples. Those whom his father had overcome in one great battle he now pressed with such might that for the sake of their lives as well as of their fatherland they willingly proffered the victor both tribute and their conversion to Christianity. The whole of the pagan folk was baptized. Then were churches first built in Slavia. About these things we shall more fitly say something toward the end,[16] as they occurred.

vi (5). I have also found in the archives of our Church that the archbishop of Cologne, then the illustrious Bruno, renewed the old-time dispute about Bremen, after he saw that our Hamburg had suffragans, in the hope that because he was King Otto's brother he would the more easily obtain what he desired. Although he put forth every kind of effort he labored in vain. He is said neither to have gained the pope's consent nor won his brother's help. Easily overcome by Archbishop Adaldag's repute, that noble and at the same time wise man, it is written,[17] then returned into the favor of our church making full amends. He declared that the church of Hamburg, established amid so much danger from the heathen, should suffer harm from no one, but rather was worthy of being

---

[15] In 948. Cf. Liliencron, *Beziehungen des deutschen Reichs zu Dänemark*, pp. 25-29.

[16] II.xx (17)—xxv (22), xxvi (24) below.

[17] The document is no longer extant.

fostered with all affection and consolation and of being honored everywhere by all the churches. Posterity still remembers that the king gave the bishopric of Verden to a certain Erp, Bishop Adaldag's deacon, because he had faithfully stood by him in the aforesaid controversy.[18] At the same time, also, others of the brethren who had zealously worked with the archbishop in preaching to the Danes and the Slavs were, they say, installed in greater sees for their labors.

vii (6.)   The zeal of the father Adaldag was in truth entirely directed to the conversion of the heathen, to the exaltation of the churches, and to the salvation of souls. For his masterful conduct of this cause this man, beloved of God and men,[19] merited being held in reverence by all, even by his enemies.

viii (7).   When, after these events, the most victorious king Otto was called into Italy to set free the Apostolic See, he is said to have taken counsel as to whom he should leave behind him as regent to render justice in the lands which lay along the barbarian frontier. For since the time of Charles, Saxony had not had any duke except Caesar himself, because of the ancient rebelliousness of its people. Persuaded by necessity, the king for the first time delegated his power in Saxony to Hermann. Of this man and his progeny[20] I think it necessary to give a fuller account, because they seem to have set up for the utter ruin of the Church of Bremen as well as of other churches.

ix (8).   This man[21] was of lowly birth and, they say, at first content with his paternal inheritance of seven hides and as many tenants. Then, because he was shrewd of mind and prepossessing in appearance as well as trustworthy and humble in his bearing toward his superiors and peers, he quickly attracted notice at court

---

[18] Actually by Otto II in 976. Cf. Thietmar *Chronicon* III.vi (4); Uhlirz, *Jahrbücher*, p. 731.

[19] Ecclus. 45:1.

[20] Adam had in mind only Hermann Billung's progeny, Bernhard II (Benno), Ordulf, and Magnus.

[21] This account of Hermann is generally questioned. Cf. Köpke-Dümmler, *Otto der Grosse*, Exkurs III.

and won the confidence of the king himself. On discovering the assiduity of the young man, he enrolled him among his aides. Later he appointed him tutor of his sons and soon, as things prospered, even committed high official posts to him. In the energetic administration of these offices it is said that when tenants of his own were accused of theft in his court, he rendered a decision condemning them one and all to death. The novelty of this extreme act at the time endeared him to the people and soon distinguished him at court. And when he later merited the duchy of Saxony, he governed the province with judgment and justice and to the end of his life remained zealous in the defense of the holy churches. For he was faithful and devoted both to the Church at Bremen and to the mother (Church) at Hamburg, doing the brethren[22] and all the communities of Saxony many favors.

x (9). On having, then, entrusted their authority in this region to such a man, the most pious king and our archbishop departed into Italy. There the king held a council[23] of the bishops and brought about the deposition of Pope John, named Octavian, who stood accused of many crimes. This he did notwithstanding the pope's absence—for he had fled to escape judgment—and had the *protoscriniarius* Leo consecrated in his stead. Soon afterward he himself was crowned emperor by Leo and was hailed as emperor and Augustus by the Roman people in the twenty-eighth year of his reign, one hundred and fifty-three years after Charles was crowned at Rome.[24]

xi (9). At this time the emperor and his son spent five years[25] in Italy fighting the sons of Berengar[26] and restoring Rome to her ancient freedom. Our archbishop, on whom depended the most

---

[22] The canons of Hamburg and Bremen.

[23] August, 961; but Otto was crowned emperor on February 2, 962, by John XII, who was then deposed. Leo VIII was elected on December 6, 963.

[24] Correctly, the 26th year of Otto's reign, 162 years after the coronation of Charlemagne.

[25] Otto II went to Italy for the first time in October, 967, his father's third expedition. Otto I spent only three years and four months in Italy on this, the first expedition, August, 961, to January, 965.

[26] Adalbert, Wido, and Cono.

important decisions,[27] spent all these days and years in the kingdom of Italy; not of his own accord, I say, but because he could not be torn from the king's side. Immense gain accrued to the Church at Bremen from his sojourn, for at this time, it is related, he collected the relics of the saints in which this our bishopric exults now and for all time. Impatient at the good shepherd's long absence, his people are said by their messengers and letters to have at length so disquieted him that he deigned to visit his flock. They also say that when he came, his people and strangers too went a three-day journey to meet him, weeping for joy and, as if he were another John, crying out, saying, "Blessed is he that cometh in the name of the Lord."[28]

xii (10). When he returned to his fatherland, the archbishop as, "we have heard and known, and our fathers have told us,"[29] brought in his company Pope Benedict who, though consecrated, had at that time been deposed by Otto.[30] And the latter commanded that he be kept in custody in Hamburg. The archbishop, however, detained him in great honor until his death. For he is said to have been a holy and learned man and apparently worthy of the apostolic chair, except for the fact that the Roman people had turbulently elected him after they had expelled the one whom the emperor had ordered to be consecrated. He lived, then, among us in holy conversation[31] and taught others to live holily and, when the emperor on the request of the Romans[32] would have restored him, he died at peace in Hamburg. His death is recorded to have taken place the fourth day before the Nones of July.[33] At this time the provost Eilhard was distinguished at Bremen as a man illustrious

---

[27] Otto I spoke highly of Adaldag in at least two documents between 962 and 965.
[28] The salutation was, of course, of Jesus and not of John. Matt. 21:9; Luke 19:38. Cf. Ps. 117:26.
[29] Ps. 77:3.
[30] In 965. Cf. Köpke-Dümmler, *Otto der Grosse*, pp. 361-65.
[31] Tob. 14:17. Benedict was called the Grammarian in Rome. Cf. Thietmar *Chronicon* II.xxviii (18), IV.xviii (12), lxii (40), VII.xxviii (VI.53).
[32] Perhaps after the death of John XIII in September, 972. Cf. Köpke-Dümmler, *Otto der Grosse*, pp. 379, 383, 506.
[33] July 4, 965. Cf. Lappenberg, *Hamburgisches Urkundenbuch*, I, 42, n. 2.

for his voluntary poverty and observance of the canonical rule. The schools belonging to our Church were then also directed with abounding zeal by Thiadhelm, who was one of the disciples of the great Ohtric of Magdeburg.[34]

xiii (11). With great care the archbishop now distributed among his parishes the relics of the holy martyrs that he had brought from the city of Rome. His predecessors are said to have founded five monasteries for souls who serve God. To this number he added a sixth at Heeslingen, where the most noble virgin of Christ, Wendilgart, and her father, named Hed,[35] offering their entire patrimony to God and the holy martyr Vitus, gathered a large company of nuns. At Reepsholt in Frisia he established a seventh congregation of saintly men, from the estate and the offering of the devout matrons Reingerd and Wendila. There he deposited the relics of saints. These[36] are the relics of the saints that the lord Adaldag brought from Italy: the bodies of Quiriacus and Cesarius, of Victor and Corona, of Felix and Felician, of Cosmas and Damian.

xiv (12). Although the holy archbishop exercised, as is evident, paternal solicitude for all his churches, he is said to have had great concern for the xenodochium at Bremen. This he enriched with incomes so much greater than had been bestowed by his predecessors that, beside the strangers who were frequently received, twenty-four paupers were daily fed in the hospice. In its administration Lievizo, whom the archbishop had brought with him from Italy,[37] proved most faithful.

xv (13). When in those days Otto the Great had subjugated the

[34] Ohtric died bishop-elect in 981. His scholarly reputation was widely acknowledged. Cf. iii.xii(8), iv.xxviii(19), vi.xxxvi(26) below; Richer *Historia* iii.lv-lxv.

[35] Count Hed. Thietmar *Chronicon* ii.xlii (26) mentions two sisters, Wendilgart and Reingerd, but not Hed. Cf. Lappenberg, *Hamburgisches Urkundenbuch*, Vol. I, No. 46, which associates Reingerd with Wendila.

[36] This reading occurs in *A*1, another in the *B* and *C* versions. The latter is given here because it includes the former. Cf. Schmeidler, *Hamburg-Bremen*, p. 76, n.1.

[37] Lievizo, known also as Libentius, came from southern Germany, *in confinio Alpium et Suevorum*, apparently also the homeland of Pope Benedict, whose exile he shared at Hamburg. Thietmar *Chronicon* iv.xviii (12), vii.xxviii (vi.53).

Slavic peoples and bound them to the Christian faith, he built on the banks of the Elbe River the renowned city of Magdeburg and, designating it as the metropolitan see for the Slavs, had Adalbert, a man of the greatest sanctity, consecrated as its archbishop. This man was the first prelate to be consecrated in Magdeburg, and he administered his episcopal office with untiring energy for twelve years.[38] By his preaching he converted many of the Slavic peoples. His consecration took place in the thirty-fifth year of the emperor and of our archbishop, and one hundred and thirty-seven years had passed since the consecration of Saint Ansgar.[39]

xvi (14).   To the archbishopric of Magdeburg was subjected all Slavia as far as the Peene River. There were five suffragan bishoprics. Of these Merseburg and Zeitz[40] were established on the Saale River, Meissen on the Elbe, Brandenburg and Havelberg farther inland. The sixth bishopric of Slavia is Oldenburg. Because it is nearer to us, the emperor put it under the jurisdiction of the archbishopric of Hamburg. For it our archbishop consecrated as the first bishop Ebrachar or Egward, whom in Latin we call Evagrius.[41]

xvii (15).   And because occasion has presented itself here, it seems proper to set forth what peoples across the Elbe belong to the diocese of Hamburg. The diocese is bounded on the west by the British Ocean; on the south by the Elbe River; on the east by the Peene River, which flows into the Barbarian Sea; on the north by the Eider River, which divides the Danes from the Saxons. There are three Transalbingian Saxon peoples. The first, along the ocean, are the Ditmarshians and their mother church is at Meldorf. The second are the Holzatians, named from the woods near which they

---

[38] 968-81; therefore, thirteen years.

[39] Since Adam fixed the year 832 as that of Ansgar's consecration, he should have arrived at the year 969 for that of Adalbert's consecration. Cf. i.xvi (18).

[40] On the Weisse Elster, not on the Saale. Since the see was transferred to Naumburg in 1032, it may in Adam's time still have been referred to as of Zeitz. Cf. Kretschmer, *Historische Geographie von Mitteleuropa*, pp. 428-32.

[41] The bishopric of Oldenburg was probably founded in 948, and Marco, its first incumbent, was consecrated by the archbishop of Mainz. Oldenburg continued as suffragan to Mainz until its transfer to Hamburg-Bremen in 968 or soon after, along with Aarhus, Ribe, and Schleswig. Cf. Annalista Saxo, *an.* 972 (*MGH, SS*, VI, 624). *Helmold* i.xi (Tschan, tr.).

dwell. The Stör River flows through their midst. Their church is at Schenefeld. The third and best-known are called Sturmarians[a] because they are a folk frequently stirred up by dissension.[42] Among them the metropolis Hamburg lifts up its head,[43] at one time mighty in men and arms,[44] happy in its fields and crops; but now, suffering vengeance for its sins, turned into a wilderness. Although this metropolis has lost its urban attraction, it still retains its strength, consoled for the misfortune of its widowhood by the progress of its sons, whom it sees daily enlarging its mission throughout the length and breadth of the north. They seem to justify one in crying out with much joy: "I have declared and I have spoken; they are multiplied above number."[45]

xviii (15). We have also found that the boundaries of Saxony across the Elbe were drawn by Charles and other emperors as follows: The first extends from the east bank of the Elbe up to the rivulet which the Slavs call Boize.[46] From that stream the line runs through the Delvunder wood up to the Delvenau River. And so it goes on to the Hornbecker Mühlen-Bach and to the source of the Bille, thence to Liudwinestein and Weisbirken and Barkhorst. Then it passes on through Süderbeste to the Trave[b] woods and again through this forest to Blunk. Next it goes to the Tensfelder Au and ascends directly up to the ford called Agrimeswidil. At that place, too, Burwid fought a duel with a Slavic champion and slew him; and a memorial stone has been put in that spot. Thence the line runs up, going to the Stocksee, and thus on to the Zwentifeld

---

a Schol. 11 (12). The Bille River flows by the Sturmarians on the east. Like the stream mentioned above, it empties into the Elbe River.

b Schol. 12 (13). The Trave is the river that flows through the midst of the Wagiri into the Barbarian Sea. On this river are situated a lone mountain, the Kalberg, and the city of Lübeck.

---

42 In other words, a stormy folk, from *Sturm*.

43 Cf. Ps. 82:3.

44 Cf. Vergil *Aeneid*, I, 531, III, 164.

45 Ps. 39:6.

46 Some of the place names in this chapter and its scholia have been identified with only fair certainty. Adam's Scythian Lake, Barbarian Sea, and Eastern Sea are other names for the Baltic.

lying to the east as far as the Schwentine River itself.[a] Along the latter stream the Saxon boundary goes down to the Scythian Lake and to the sea they call the Eastern Sea.

(16). Of the nature of this body of water Einhard made brief mention in his Gesta of Charles when he wrote of the Slavic war.

xix (16). "There is a gulf," he says,[47] "that stretches from the Western Sea toward the east, of unknown length, but nowhere more than a hundred miles in breadth, and in many places much narrower. Many nations live along the shores of this sea. The Danes and the Swedes, whom we call Northmen, hold both its northern shore and all the islands off it. The Slavs and various other nations dwell along the eastern shore. Among them by far the most important are the Wilzi,[48] against whom the king at that time waged war. He so broke and subdued them in a single campaign, which he himself conducted, that they no longer thought it wise to refuse to obey his commands."

xx (17). Thus far Einhard: but since the Slavs are mentioned so many times we do not think it improper to say something about the nature and peoples of Slavia by way of an historical survey, especially since it is related that nearly all the Slavs were at that time[49] converted to the Christian religion through the efforts of our archbishop Adaldag.

xxi (18). Slavia is a very large province of Germany[50] inhabited by the Winuli who at one time were called Vandals.[51] It is said to be ten times larger than our Saxony, especially if you count as

---

a Schol. 13 (14). The Schwentine River flows out of the lake on which the city of Plön is situated. Thence it courses through the wooded highland Isarnho and empties into the Scythian Sea.

---

47 Einhard *Vita Karoli* xii.

48 Einhard calls them Welatabi in this passage. They referred to themselves as Wilzi. Cf. Tschan, *Helmold*, p. 48, n. 3.

49 After the erection of the see of Magdeburg, about 970.

50 Cf. Thorpe, ed., Alfred the Great's translation of Orosius, in *The Life of Alfred the Great*, by R. Pauli, tr. by Thorpe, p. 247; Zeuss, *Die Deutschen und die Nachbarstämme*, pp. 600-666, especially pp. 642-66, for particulars about the Slavic tribes.

51 An error, for Paul the Deacon *Hist. Langobard.* I.i.7-9, refers them to the Lombards, and Helmold I.xv.19 (Tschan, tr.) calls them Winithi. Adam may have meant the Wends. Cf. Schmeidler, *Hamburg-Bremen*, p. 217.

part of Slavia Bohemia and the expanses across the Oder,[a] the Poles, because they differ neither in appearance nor in language. Although this region is very rich in arms, men, and crops, it is shut in on all sides by fast barriers of wooded mountains and rivers. In breadth it extends from south to north, that is, from the Elbe River to the Scythian Sea. And in length it appears to stretch from our diocese of Hamburg, where it begins, toward the east and, spread in boundless expanses, reaches clear to Bavaria, Hungary, and Greece. There are many Slavic peoples, of whom the first, beginning in the west, are the Wagiri, neighbors of the Transalbingians. Their city is Oldenburg by the sea.[52][b] Then come the Abodrites, who now are called Reregi,[53] and their city is Mecklenburg.[54] In our direction, too, are the Polabingi, whose city is Ratzeburg. Beyond them live the Linguones[55] and Warnavi.[56] Farther on dwell the Chizzini[57] and Circipani,[58] whom the Peene River separates from the Tholenzi[59] and from the Retharii[60][c] and their city of Demmin. There is the end of the diocese of Hamburg. There also are other Slavic peoples, who live between the Elbe and the Oder; such as the Heveldi, who are seated by the Havel River,

---

[a] Schol. 14 (15).* Across the Oder River the first people are the Pomeranians, next the Poles who are flanked here by the Prussians, there by the Bohemians, on the east by the Russians.

* This scholium, repeated as 29(29), is attached to this passage only in the *A2* version.

[b] Schol. 15 (16). Oldenburg, a large city of the Slavs that are named Wagiri, is situated on the sea called the Baltic or Barbarian, a day's journey from Hamburg.

[c] Schol. 16 (17). The Chizzini and Circipani live on the hither side of the Peene River, the Tholenzi and Retharii on the other side of the Peene River. Because of their bravery these four peoples are called Wilzi or Leutici.†

† Perhaps from *Ljut,* meaning strenuous, ferocious.

---

[52] Oldenburg is not on the sea. Cf. Schol. 15(16), 29.

[53] Mentioned nowhere else. Einhard, *Annales, an.* 808-9, speaks of a trading place, Reric, from which Adam may have concluded there was a tribe in the Abodrite country associated with it.

[54] South of Wismar, not the modern Mecklenburg.

[55] Near Puttlitz.

[56] On the River Warnow.

[57] Their name lives on in Kessin, near Rostock, and elsewhere.

[58] On the west bank of the Peene River.

[59] On the border of Schwerin and Strelitz, by the river and lake, Tollensee.

[60] In Mecklenburg-Strelitz.

and the Doxani,[61] Leubuzi,[62] Wilini,[63] and Stoderani,[64] besides many others. Among them the Retharii, centrally located, are the mightiest of all. Their city, very widely known as Rethra,[65] is a seat of idolatry. There a great temple was erected to the demons, the chief of whom is Redigast. His image is of gold, his bower bedecked with purple. The city itself has nine gates and is surrounded on all sides by a deep lake. A wooden bridge, over which approach is allowed only to those who would make sacrifices or seek oracular advice, affords a means of crossing. For this there is, I believe, a meaningful explanation: fitly the

"Styx imprisons with its ninefold circles" [66]

the lost souls of those who serve idols. This temple they say is a four-day journey from the city of Hamburg.

xxii (19).   Beyond the Leutici, who are also called Wilzi, one comes to the Oder River, the largest stream in the Slavic region. At its mouth, where it feeds the Scythian marshes, Jumne,[67] a most noble city, affords a very widely known trading center for the barbarians and Greeks who live round about. Because great and scarcely credible things are said in praise of this city, I think it of interest to introduce a few facts that are worth relating. It is truly the largest of all the cities in Europe, and there live in it Slavs and

---

[61] On the Dosse River, with their main settlement at Wittstock.

[62] Near Parchim on the Oder. Cf. Thietmar *Chronicon* I.xvi(9); VI.lix(39); VII.xx(VI.48).

[63] Probably near Fehrbellin.

[64] In the Havel country. Cf. Thietmar, *Chronicon* IV.xxix(20); *Helmold* I.xxxviii (Tschan, tr.).

[65] The temple was on an island in the Tollensee. The *burg* had three tower gates, and the town built about it had four; hence seven in all. Extensive excavations have long been conducted on the site. Cf. Thietmar, *Chronicon* VI.xxiii; *Helmold* I.xxi, xxiii, lii, lxxi (Tschan, tr.); Schmeidler, *Hamburg-Bremen*, pp. 341-58.

[66] Vergil *Aeneid* VI.439.

[67] Generally held to be the stronghold and city of the colony of Danes planted at the mouth of the Oder near Wollin by Harold Bluetooth (935-85) in order to break into the river trade between the Baltic and Byzantium. The coins found there and in the Baltic regions point to a prosperity at Jumne that absolves Adam of the charge that he had exaggerated the size and wealth of the place. Harold Bluetooth gave his colony the laws (reflected in Adam's account) that may be found in the garbled *Jómsvíkingasaga*. The Jómsborg was destroyed in 1043 by King Magnus of Norway. Cf. Kendrick, *History of the Vikings*, pp. 180-85; Petersens, ed., *Jómsvíkingasaga*.

many other peoples, Greeks and barbarians. For even alien Saxons also have the right to reside there on equal terms with others, provided only that while they sojourn there they do not openly profess Christianity. In fact, all its inhabitants still blunder about in pagan rites.[68] Otherwise, so far as morals and hospitality are concerned, a more honorable or kindlier folk cannot be found. Rich in the wares of all the northern nations, that city lacks nothing that is either pleasing or rare. There is *Olla Vulcani,*[69] which the inhabitants call Greek fire and of which Solinus[70] also makes mention. There Neptune may be observed in a threefold mood : that island is washed by the waters of three straits,[71] one of which they say is of a very green appearance; another, rather whitish; the third rages furiously in perpetual tempests. From that city it is a short passage in one direction to the city of Demmin, which is situated at the mouth of the Peene River,[72] where the Rugiani[73] also live. The other one reaches the province of Semland, which the Prussians occupy. The journey is such that it takes seven days to go from Hamburg or the Elbe River to the city of Jumne by land; for by the sea route one boards ship at Schleswig or Oldenburg to get to Jumne. From the latter city it is fourteen days' sail up to Ostrogard[74] of Russia. The largest city of Russia is Kiev, rival of the scepter of Constantinople, the brightest ornament of Greece.

[68] Cf. *Vita Bonifatii auct. Willebaldo* vi.

[69] This term occurs in classical, patristic, and medieval sources and often refers to a volcano on an island; thus Aetna and also Vesuvius, the craters of which would suggest a vulcan's jar. The term may also refer to a large receptacle holding an open fire to serve as a beacon for mariners threading the delta of the Oder, such as the ancient Pharos at Alexandria. Greek fire, therefore, readily comes to mind. It may have been a substance derived from volcanos, e.g., in Iceland, that was an article of commerce at Jómsborg. Cf. Beazley, *Dawn of Modern Geography,* II, 526-27; Kohlmann, *Adam von Bremen,* pp. 21-31.

[70] Solinus does not use the terms *Olla Vulcani* and *graecus ignis.*

[71] The Oder passes into the fresh-water Stettiner Haff, from which it enters the Baltic in three channels, the Peene, the Swine, and the Dievenow. Adam in this chapter calls the Baltic the Scythian marshes.

[72] Demmin is not at the mouth of the Peene River, but ships in Adam's time, drawing little water, could reach the city. Cf. Krabbo, "Nordeuropa in der Vorstellung Adams von Bremen," *Hansische Geschichtsblätter,* XV (1909), 37-51.

[73] The inhabitants of Rügen. Adam is inexact here. Cf. IV.xviii; Schol. 121(117).

[74] Identified either as Novgorod on the Volkhov River or as Ostrov.

Now, as was said before, the Oder River rises in the depths of the Moravian[a] forest, where our Elbe also has its source. At first not a great distance from each other, these rivers follow different courses. For the one, that is the Oder, tending toward the north, passes through the midst of the Winuli peoples until it passes by Jumne, where it divides the Pomeranians from the Wilzi. But the other, that is the Elbe, rushing toward the west, waters in its uppermost course the country of the Bohemians and the Sorbs;[b] midway in its course it divides the pagans from the Saxons; in its lower part it divides the diocese of Hamburg from that of Bremen and sweeps victoriously into the British Ocean.[c]

xxiii (20).   These remarks about the Slavs and their country may suffice, because through the valor of the great Otto they were all at that time converted to Christianity. Now we shall address our pen to what was done after the emperor's death and in the remaining years of our archbishop.

xxiv (21).   In the thirty-ninth year[75] of Archbishop Adaldag the great emperor Otto, the conqueror of all the nations of the north, departed happily to the Lord and received burial in his city of Magdeburg. His son, the second Otto, succeeded him and

a Schol. 17 (18). The Moravians are Slavic peoples who live to the east of the Bohemians and are encircled on one side by the Pomeranians and Poles, on the other by the Hungarians and the Petchenegs,* an extremely fierce folk that eats human flesh.

* An Asiatic people that pressed upon the Hungarians, forcing them into the plains of Hungary. Zeuss, *Die Deutschen und die Nachbarstämme,* pp. 752-53.

b Schol. 18 (19).† The Sorbs are Slavs who live on the plains lying between the Elbe and the Saale; and their bounds are coterminous with those of the Thuringians and Saxons. Beyond the Ohre River dwell other Sorb peoples.

† This and the following scholium occur in *A2* and are not by Adam.

c Schol. 19 (20). Bede,‡ Britain, an island in the Ocean, at one time bore the name Albion. It is situated between the north and west, facing, though at a great distance, Germany, Gaul, and Spain, the largest parts of Europe. To the south it has Belgic Gaul, from the nearest shore of which there appears to those who are crossing the city called Rutubi Portus.** Ireland is the largest of all the islands after Britain and is situated west of it. As Ireland tapers to the north, so it stretches far beyond the bounds of the latter into the farthest south, even to a point opposite the northern parts of Spain.

‡ *Hist. Eccl.* I.i.

** Probably Richborough on the Stour River, southwest of Ramsgate in Kent.

75 In 975, according to I.lxii(64) above. Otto died May 7, 973.

strenuously governed the Empire for ten years. When he had straightway overcome Lothair and Charles,[76] kings of the Franks, he transferred the war into Calabria and died at Rome after he had met the Saracens and Greeks in victory and defeat.[77] The third Otto, although still a boy, succeeded to the throne and for eighteen years distinguished the scepter by a strong and just rule. On account of the merits of his virtue and his mastery of learning the saintly Adaldag was held in such esteem and in such intimacy by these three equally mighty and most just emperors that he was scarcely, or rarely, ever separated from their sides. This is evident from the emperors' edicts which were drawn up on the archbishop's motion. In them it is also to be noted that the third Otto issued edicts while he stayed at Wildeshausen. At that same time Hermann, the duke of the Saxons, died and had as heir his son Benno,[78] who is also remembered for having been a good and valiant man, except that he departed from his father's ways by burdening the people with exactions. At Magdeburg, too, there followed in the see, on Archbishop Adalbert's death,[79] Gisiler. He too was a holy man who by his learning and virtues enlightened the lately converted Winuli peoples.

25 (22). Harold,[80] the king of the Danes, noted for his piety

---

[76] Sons of the Carolingian king of West Frankland, Louis IV or Louis d'Outremer (936-54). Charles, duke of Lower Lorraine, and his brother King Lothair (954-86) sought to detach Lorraine from Germany to increase the dwindling Carolingian patrimony and precipitated Otto II's invasion of Francia in 978. Charles was at best a weak contender for the crown in 987, when Hugh Capet was proclaimed king. Adam does not mention Otto II's expedition into Denmark for the reason that he had attributed it to Otto I. Cf. I.iii above.

[77] After freeing the pope from the Roman duke Crescentius in 980-81, Otto II marched against the Mohammedans who were expanding their holdings in southern Italy at the expense of Theophano's marriage portion. This portion Byzantium refused to cede to her husband's German empire. Otto was successful in 981-82, defeating the Mohammedans at Cotrone. A few days later he was ambushed with all his army and defeated. After an adventurous escape to Rome he died there December 7, 983.

[78] Hermann died March 27, 973. Cf. Widukind *Gesta Saxonum* III.lxxv; Thietmar *Chronicon* II.xxxi(20). Benno (Bernhard I) was duke, 973-1011.

[79] Adalbert died June 20, 982. Cf. *Annales Quedlinburgenses, an.* 981 (*MGH, SS*, III, 65); Thietmar *Chronicon* III.xi(8); Uhlirz, *Jahrbücher*, p. 156.

[80] Bluetooth.

and bravery, had long before benignantly admitted Christianity to his kingdom[a] and held it firm unto the end.[81] Hence, also, he strengthened his rule by holiness and justice[82] and extended his authority beyond the sea over the Norwegians and the Angles. Emund, Eric's son, then ruled in Sweden.[83] Since he was allied with Harold, he was favorably disposed toward the Christians who came there. In Norway Haakon[84] was the ruler. When the Norwegians drove him from the realm because he had acted haughtily, Harold valorously restored him and made him well-disposed to the worshipers of Christ. Exceedingly cruel, this Haakon, of the stock of Ivar and descended from a race of giants, was the first among the Norwegians to seize a kingship whereas chiefs had ruled before. Now Haakon, after completing thirty-five years on the throne, died and left as heir to his scepter Hartild,[85] who at the same time possessed Denmark and Norway. Anglia, as we have said above and as it appears in the *Gesta* of the Angles, remained after Gudröd's death[86] in the control of the Danes for nearly a

---

[a] Schol. 20 (21).* In the year of the Lord 996 the Danes were converted to the faith through a certain Poppo, who in the presence of the people carried without injury a white-hot iron fashioned in the form of a glove. When King Harold beheld this wonder, he renounced idolatry and with all his people turned to the worship of the true God. Poppo, moreover, was promoted to the episcopate.

* Found only in Codex *C* and not composed by Adam. Derived from Sigebert of Gembloux, *Chronographia*, an. 966 (*MGH, SS*, VI, 351).

---

[81] Heb. 3:14.

[82] Cf. Ephes. 4:24.

[83] Possibly Emund Ericsson, also known as Emund Slemme. His father probably was the Eric mentioned in I.lxi(63) above.

[84] Haakon the Bad (*c.* 971-995), who was a usurper. The Ivar from whose stock Adam states Haakon was descended probably was the Viking mentioned in I.xxxvii(39) above. Cf. *Theoderici Monachi Hist.* iv-x (*MGH, SS*, XXIX, 248-49). Haakon, however, was not the first king of all Norway, as Adam and Theodoric state, but rather Harold Fairhair (*c.* 862-932), who even put down the Vikings of the Hebrides, Orkneys, and Shetlands who were troubling his coastlands. Cf. Kendrick, *History of the Vikings*, pp. 108-16.

[85] Adam is full of errors here, perhaps pardonably, because the times were confused. Hartild's name is found nowhere else. Olaf Tryggvason, the great-grandson of Harold Fairhair, succeeded to the throne (c. 995-1000), but he did not also rule over Denmark.

[86] Cf. I.xxxix(41) above; Symeon of Durham, *Historia regum*, an. 920, 926, 937, 943, 950.

hundred years from the time of his sons, Aulaf, Sigeric, and Regi-
nold. But then Harold sent his son Hiring to England with an
army. When the latter had subjugated the island, he was in the
end betrayed and killed by the Northumbrians.

xxvi (23). Now Archbishop Adaldag consecrated for Denmark
several bishops whose names we have found indeed, but on what
see each was specifically enthroned we could not easily ascertain.
I think the reason is that, with Christianity in a rude state, none
of the bishops was as yet assigned to a fixed see, but that as each
of them pushed out into the farther regions in the effort to establish
Christianity, he would strive to preach the Word of God alike to
his own and to the others' people. This even now seems to be the
practice beyond Denmark, throughout Norway and Sweden. These,
then, were the bishops consecrated for Denmark: Hored, Liafdag,
Reginbrund;[87] and after them Harich, Sterkolf, Folgbracht, Adelbrecht, Marco,[88] and others. It is said that the elder Odinkar was
consecrated by Adaldag for Sweden and that he carried on his
mission among the heathen energetically. For he was, according
to report, a very holy man and learned in the things that belong to
God besides being, in that which pertains to the world, a noble and
a born Dane. Hence, also, he could easily convince the barbarians
of everything about our religion. Of the other bishops, however,
the past reveals hardly one as having been thus distinguished,
except Liafdag of Ribe who, they say, preached beyond the sea,
that is, in Sweden and Norway, and was also celebrated for his
miracles.

(24). For Oldenburg the archbishop first of all consecrated,
as we have said, Egward, or Evagrius, then Wago, thereafter Esico,
in whose times the Slavs remained Christian. And so Hamburg
also was at peace. Churches were erected everywhere in Slavia.
There were also very many monasteries built in which men and

---

[87] Cf. II.iv above.
[88] Cf. *Helmold* I.xiii, xiv (Tschan, tr.). Adelbrecht remains unidentified.

women served God.[a] Witness to this is the king of the Danes, Svein, who still lives. When he told how Slavia was divided into eighteen districts, he assured us that all but three had been converted to the Christian faith, adding also that their princes at that time were Mistislav, Naccon, and Sederich.[89] He said, "There was continuous peace under them, and the Slavs served paying tribute."

xxvii (25). In the last days of Archbishop Adaldag our cause among the barbarians was broken down, Christianity in Denmark was thrown into confusion, and, envying the fair beginnings of God's religion, a wicked man tried to oversow with cockle.[90] For then Svein Otto,[91] the son of the great Harold, king of the Danes, set on foot many plots against his father, taking counsel also with those whom his father had against their will compelled to embrace Christianity, to see how he might deprive him of the throne now that he was advanced in years and less strong. Of a sudden, therefore, the Danes entered into a conspiracy to renounce Christianity, to make Svein king, to declare war against Harold. As the latter had from the beginning of his reign placed all his trust in God, he then also most particularly commended to Christ the issue of the event and, although he abhorred war, decided to defend himself by arms. And like another David, mourning for his son Absalom,[92] grieving rather over his sin than over his own peril, he went forth to war. In that deplorable and worse than civil war[93] the party of Harold was vanquished. Wounded, Harold fled from the conflict, boarded ship, and escaped to the city of the Slavs which is called Jumne.

---

[a] Schol. 21 (22).* In the year of the Lord 973 Wenceslaus, the prince of Bohemia, was martyred by his brother Buggeslav, who seized the principate for himself. On Wenceslaus' account God made the city of Prague, where he rests, renowned for many miracles.

* This scholium is derived from Sigebert of Gembloux, *Chronographia, an.* 973 (*MGH, SS,* VI, 351). Wenceslaus was murdered in 929(?).

---

[89] Cf. Schmeidler, *Hamburg-Bremen,* pp. 318-30.

[90] Cf. Matt. 13:25.

[91] Svein Forkbeard, son of Harold Bluetooth, rebelled about 985-86. Cf. II.iii above.

[92] Cf. II Kings 18:33, 19:1.

[93] Cf. Lucan *Civil War* I.1.

xxviii (26). Kindly received by the Slavs, contrary to his expectations, because they were pagans, he failed from the wound after some days and passed away in the confession of Christ. His body was brought back to his fatherland by the army and entombed in the city of Roeskilde in the church which he himself had first constructed in honor of the Holy Trinity. When I would question his great-grandson, Svein, who now rules in Denmark, about his end, the king like another Tydeus[94] made no answer about his grandparent's crime. But when I preferred the charge that he was a parricide, the king said: "That is what we, his posterity, are expiating and what he himself, the parricide, made atonement for in exile." But he, the Harold of whom we speak, who first declared Christianity to the Danish people, who filled the whole north with preachers and churches, he, I say, wounded and driven out, though innocent, for the sake of Christ, will not fail, I hope, to gain a martyr's palm. He reigned fifty years. His death occurred on the feast of All Saints.[95] His memory and that of his wife, Gunnhild, will remain forever with us. These things took place, we learned, in the days of Archbishop Adaldag; still we could not find out all of the king's virtues. There[96] are, however, some who affirm that the grace of healing worked through him both then, while he still lived, and at his sepulcher after his death, and other things equally marvelous; for example, the blind were often given sight and many other wonders took place. Very certain is it, however, that in consideration of the man's repute our people as well as the Transalbingians and the Frisians still strive to observe the laws and customs he gave them. In the meantime, when the old and faithful Adaldag had accomplished his mission according to his desire and had prospered in his every work at home and abroad, he departed to the Lord at a fruitful old age in the fifty-fourth year of a priesthood laudably served. His death took place in the

---

[94] Adam probably meant his opponent, Polyneikes. Cf. Statius *Thebais* 1.465-66.
[95] In 985 or 986.
[96] Two readings occur here respectively, in *A*1, *B*, and *C*. The version in *B* has the same content, but the wording is slightly different.

year of the Lord nine hundred and eighty-eight, and he was buried in the church at Bremen at the head of Bishop Leuderic on the south side. He died in the first Indiction on the third day before the Kalends of May.

xxix (27).   Lievizo held the see for twenty-five years. He received the pallium from Pope John XV,[97] obtained the pastoral staff from the third Otto. He was the very first to be consecrated by suffragans. A very learned man and graced by every mark of moral probity, he had accompanied the lately deceased Archbishop Adaldag from Italy.[98] Imitating the latter's conduct in life and in office, he proved to be the only one at the disposition of the great father worthy of being entrusted with the care of the diocese of Hamburg. Some say that the episcopal vicar, Otto,[a] who prided himself on being Archbishop Adaldag's uncle, nevertheless yielded to the latter's choice of Lievizo, against whom not even an enemy could charge anything reprehensible.[99] They say that such was his chastity that he rarely permitted himself to be seen by women, such his abstinence that his face was pallid from fasting, such his humility and charity that he lived in the monastery like one of the brethren. Many were his virtues; content with what he had, he rarely went to court to acquire more. It is said that, staying quietly at home, he took most diligent care of his diocese and, turning every endeavor to the profit of souls, held all his communities most strictly to the rule. The archbishop in person attended to the care of the hospital, daily ministering dutifully to the brethren and the infirm; but the xenodochium he commended in his stead to his nephew, Lievizo. While there was still peace in Slavia, he

[a] Schol. 22 (23). This Otto, a man of very great eminence, was episcopal vicar and canon at Magdeburg.

---

[97] Correctly, John XVI. John XV died in 985 and Lievizo's episcopate extended from 988 to 1013. Cf. Schmeidler, *Hamburg-Bremen*, pp. 165-93.

[98] Cf. II.xiv(12), n.37 above.

[99] Adam moved this story from 1013 to 988. Lievizo had apparently recommended Otto as his successor, but Henry II declined to name him. Otto then went to Magdeburg. *Annales Quedlinburgenses an.* 1013, 1018 (*MGH, SS*, III, 81, 84); Thietmar *Chronicon* VII.xxviii *f* (VI.53-54).

frequently visited the Transalbingian peoples and cherished their mother at Hamburg with fatherly love. Like his predecessors, he prosecuted his mission to the heathen with great zeal even though he was hindered by evil days. At that time, while King Svein was preparing a fierce persecution of the Christians in Denmark, the archbishop is said through suppliant legates and by frequent gifts to have endeavored to mollify the king's ferocious spirit in regard to the Christians. But the king rejected these overtures and began to rage in his cruelty and perfidy. Divine vengeance pursued him in his rebellion against God for, when he undertook a war against the Slavs, he was twice captured[100] and led off into Slavia and as many times ransomed by the Danes for an immense amount of gold. Yet he still would not return to God, Whom he had first offended in the death of his father and then angered by the murder of the faithful. "And the Lord was exceedingly angry . . . and He delivered" him into the hands of his enemies that he might learn not to blaspheme.[101]

xxx (28). At that time Eric,[102] the most mighty king of the Swedes, collected an army as innumerable as the sands of the sea and invaded Denmark. Svein, abandoned by God and vainly trusting in his idols, went to meet him. The two forces joined in many naval battles—for thus that folk is wont to fight—and the whole Danish force was crushed. The victorious king Eric seized Denmark. Svein, driven from his realm, received from a jealous God[103] a reward befitting his deeds.[104] These things the younger Svein recounted to us as having by the just judgment of God happened to his grandfather because he had abandoned Him Whom his father had had as a good protector.

xxxi (29). At that time a fleet of the pirates whom our people

---

[100] Thietmar *Chronicon* VIII.xxxvi(VII.26) reports that Svein was once captured by the Norwegians.

[101] Cf. IV Kings. 21:14; Ps. 40:3; 105; 40-41; I Tim. 1:20.

[102] Segersäll, the Victorious. He was the son of Ring and his brother was Emund, according to *Annales Lundenses an.* 985, (*MGH, SS,* XIX, 200). Cf. I.*lxi*(63) above.

[103] Cf. Exod. 20:5; 34:14.

[104] Cf. Sallust *Catilina* lv.6.

call Ascomanni[105] landed in Saxony and devastated all the coastland of Frisia and Hadeln. And, as they went up the mouth of the Elbe River, they fell upon the province. Then the chief men of the Saxons met and, although their forces were small, engaged the barbarians, who had left their ships, at Stade, which is a convenient port and stronghold on the Elbe. Mighty and memorable, but exceedingly unhappy,[106] was that battle in which, though it was manfully contested on both sides, our men finally proved too few. The victorious Swedes and Danes completely destroyed the whole Saxon troop. Captured there were the margrave Siegfried,[107 a] Count Dietrich and other distinguished men whom the barbarians dragged to the ships with their hands tied behind their backs, and their feet shackled with chains. After that the barbarians ravaged the whole province with impunity. But since one of the captives, the margrave Siegfried, stealthily slipped away by night with the aid of a certain fisherman and escaped, the pirates forthwith fell into a rage and, mocking all the nobles whom they had in chains, severed their hands and feet and cut off their noses. Thus maimed and half dead, they cast them upon the land. Among them were some noble men who lived a long time after, a reproach to the Empire and a pitiful spectacle for all the people.

xxxii (30). Soon afterward Duke Benno and Margrave Siegfried came up with an army and took vengeance for that disaster. And those very pirates who, we said, had landed at Stade were destroyed by them.

The other party of Ascomanni, who had come by way of the Weser River, devastated the Hadeln country as far as Lesum. They

---

a Schol. 23 (24). A great miracle is related about this Siegfried. For when he fell upon the monastery of Ramelsloh to plunder it, he was immediately seized of a malignant spirit from which he did not earn freedom until he had restored to the church its property and had from his plunder presented the brethren with a rich villa for their service.

---

105 Literally, "ship men." This raid took place in 994. Cf. *Annales Hildesheimenses, an.* 994; *Annales Quedlinburgenses, an.* 994 (*MGH, SS,* III, 72); Thietmar *Chronicon* iv.xxiii-xxv (16).

106 Cf. I Kings 1:15; Vergil *Aeneid* iv.94.

107 Correctly, count.

came with a very great multitude of captives to the marsh called the Glinster Moor. There all the raiders were cut down to the very last man by our pursuing force. They numbered twenty thousand. A certain Saxon knight whom they had captured took them, when they made him guide their way, into the most untraversable parts of the swamp. There they were after a long time and much exertion fatigued and easily overcome by our men. The man's name was Heriward and his praise is sounded the year round by the Saxons.

xxxiii (31). Thereafter the pirates frequently made warlike sallies into that region. All the Saxon cities were terrified, and the people began to fortify Bremen itself with an exceedingly strong wall.[108] Then also, as the old men of the city recall, Archbishop Lievizo had the treasure of the Church and everything ecclesiastical removed to the canonry at Bücken, so great was the fear in all parts of this diocese. And, indeed, as report has it, Lievizo himself also smote the pirates who were ravaging his diocese with the sword of anathema. The body of one of them, who is said to have died in Norway, remained whole for seventy years until the time of Lord Archbishop Adalbert, in whose day Bishop Adalward went there and absolved the deceased. Soon after the corpse was resolved into dust.[109]

xxxiv (32). After receiving requital for the enormities he had perpetrated on the churches of God and the Christians, King Svein, vanquished and deserted by his own men, as one might expect of one whom God had abandoned, went, a wanderer and destitute of help, to the Norwegians over whom Tryggve,[110] the son of

[108] The pirates did not reach Bremen according to Thietmar *Chronicon* VII.xxviii (VI.53). The town itself would hardly have been walled—only the part about the cathedral.

[109] Cf. Schol. 67 (68) below.

[110] More probably the son of Olaf, whose father was Harold Fairhair. Tryggve, however, was king of only a part of Norway and lost his life at the hands of the sons of Eric Bloodaxe and Gunnhild, the sister of the Danish Harold Bluetooth, some years before the events narrated in this chapter. Harold Graafel (Greycloak), very unpopular in Norway, was king at this time. He was followed by a Jarl Haakon Sigurdson of Lade (971-95) and by Olaf Tryggvason (995-1000). Cf. Kendrick, *History of the Vikings,* pp. 121-23.

Haakon, then ruled. As Tryggve was a pagan, he was not moved with compassion for the exile. The latter, therefore, unhappy and rejected by all the world, shipped over to England, vainly seeking solace from his enemies. At that time Aethelred,[111] the son of Edgar, governed the Britons. Not unmindful of the outrages which the Danes had of old inflicted on the Angles, he drove the exile away. At length the king of the Scots,[112] taking pity on him for his misfortunes, received him kindly, and Svein stayed in exile there twice seven years until Eric[113] died. With these tribulations of his parricide grandparent King Svein to our astonishment acquainted us; then he turned his narrative to Eric, the victor.

xxxv (33). "Eric," he said, "held two kingdoms, that of the Danes and that of the Swedes, and, being a pagan, he was intensely hostile to the Christians."[a] The emperor and the bishop of Hamburg, it is said, sent a legate to him, a certain Poppo,[114] a holy and wise man and at the time consecrated for Schleswig, to insist on the emperor's interests in the kingdom of the Danes and on the peace of the Christians. They also say that to win them to Christianity, since it is the way of barbarians to seek after a sign, he straightway and without hesitation held a red-hot iron in his hand

[a] Schol. 24 (25). Eric, the king of the Swedes, entered into an alliance with Boleslav,* the most powerful king of the Poles. Boleslav gave his daughter or sister in marriage to Eric. Because of this league the Danes were jointly attacked by the Slavs and the Swedes.† In alliance with the third Otto the most Christian king Boleslav subjected all Slavia and Russia together with the Prussians, at whose hands Saint Adalbert had suffered martyrdom.‡ Boleslav at this time translated his remains into Poland.

* Boleslav Chrobry (992-1025), son of Miesko.

† According to Thietmar *Chronicon* VIII.xxxix (VII.28) Boleslav gave Eric the Victorious his sister in marriage. She remains nameless although referred to in later times as Sigrid Storråda. Boleslav's wars in Russia took place in 1013 and 1018; therefore, in the time of Henry II. Cf. Hirsch, *Jahrbücher,* III, 89-93.

‡ April 23, 997.

[111] Aethelred the Unready (978-1016). Svein, however, came as a plunderer according to the Anglo-Saxon Chronicle, *an.* 994.

[112] He is unknown.

[113] Eric the Victorious of Sweden, who died in 995. The phrase, "twice seven years," is biblical, referring to Jacob's service to Laban for Rachel. Cf. Gen. 19:27.

[114] Cf. II.xxv(22) above; Thietmar *Chronicon* II.xiv(8); Widukind *Gesta Saxonum* III.lxv. The miracles apparently took place about 965, but Poppo's see may not have been Schleswig.

and seemed to be unharmed. Although it would appear that every delusion of error should by this act easily have been removed from the minds of the pagans, the saint of God is said once again to have manifested another miracle—if you will, a greater one—in order to clear away that people's paganism. For he clad himself in a waxed tunic and, standing in the midst of the people, directed that it be set on fire in the name of the Lord. Then, with his eyes and hands lifted up to heaven, he so patiently bore the spreading flames that, after his garment was entirely consumed and reduced to ashes, his cheerful and pleasant countenance gave proof of his having not even felt or suffered from the smoke of the fire. Because of this unusual miracle many thousands then believed through him and to this very day Poppo's name is extolled by the peoples and in the churches of the Danes.

(34). Some affirm that these things were done at Ribe; others, that they were done at Haddeby, which is called Schleswig.

xxxvi (34). At this time the elder Odinkar, a man of happy memory, of whom we have spoken above, also was distinguished in Denmark.[115] By his preaching in Fyn, Zealand, Scania, and Sweden he converted many to the Christian faith. His disciple and nephew was another Odinkar, the younger,[a] himself a noble of the royal Danish stock,[116] rich in land, so much so that they say the bishopric of Ribe was founded from his patrimony. When not long ago he was admitted to the schools at Bremen, Archbishop Adaldag is said to have baptized him with his own hands and given him his own name, Adaldag. Now, consecrated by Archbishop Lievizo for the heathen, he received the see at Ribe. The conspicuous sanctity of his life made him acceptable both to God and to men, and he

---

[a] Schol. 25 (26). This Odinkar was taken to England by King Canute and there instructed in letters. After that, as he wandered through Gaul bent on learning, he acquired the reputation of being a wise man and a philosopher. Hence he also deserved the name he received, "dear to God."

---

[115] II.xxvi(23) above. Note the etymology of Odinkar, Odin-kar, Gottlieb, "dear to God," given in the scholium.

[116] Cf. Schol. 35(37) below. Odinkar was related by marriage to the Chnuba mentioned in I.xlviii(50) above.

most valiantly defended Christianity in Denmark. These men, we have learned, were at that time distinguished in this region. Others, who still survived from the days of Adaldag, were not idle. They also went on into Norway and Sweden[117] where they gathered many people unto Jesus Christ. Tradition has it that they baptized the son of Tryggve, Olaf, who then ruled the Norwegians, among which folk he was the first Christian. Olaf, the son of Tryggve, when expelled from Norway, went to England and there embraced Christianity, which he was the first to bring back into his fatherland.[118] He took a wife from Denmark, the haughty Thore,[119] at whose instigation he made war on the Danes.

xxxvii (35). Others say that of old and at this time certain bishops and priests of England left their home for the sake of doing mission work and that they baptized Olaf and others. Among these missionaries the principal one was a certain bishop John, and there were others who must be mentioned later.[120] If this is true, the mother church at Hamburg did not, I say, look askance even at strangers if they bestowed grace upon her children, saying with the Apostle: Some preach "out of envy and contention; but some also for good will"[121] and love. "But what then? So that by all means, whether by occasion, or by truth, Christ be preached; and," he says, "in this also I rejoice, yea, and will rejoice."[122]

xxxviii (36). Now Eric, the king of the Swedes, was converted to Christianity in Denmark and was there baptized. At this time missionaries went from Denmark into Sweden, "dealing confidently in the name of the Lord."[123] I myself have heard from the lips of the most judicious king of the Danes that after Eric had received

[117] But see II.xxxviii(36) below. Sweden is not mentioned in the B and C versions and may have been included later, possibly by Adam himself.

[118] Olaf Tryggvason became a Christian when he took refuge with the English in 994 and was by no means the first of his people to be baptized.

[119] Thore may have been the sister of Svein Forkbeard. Cf. II.xl(38) below.

[120] This John, later active in Sweden, is called Siegfried in I.lvii(55) above and IV.xxxiii below.

[121] Phil. 1:15.

[122] Phil. 1:18.

[123] Acts 9:28. Reference is to Eric the Victorious, previously mentioned in II.xxx(28), xxxiv(32) above.

Christianity he once more relapsed into paganism. As for his having had a war with the third Otto and having been vanquished, that I have learned from others; the king held his peace.[124]

xxxix (37). After the long-wished-for death of Eric,[125] Svein returned from exile and regained the kingdom of his fathers in the fourteenth year of his deposition and wanderings. And he married Eric's widow, the mother of Olaf, and she bore him Canute.[126] But this marital relationship was of no advantage to him, for God was angry with him. Olaf,[127] the king of the Swedes, was a very good Christian and took a wife from among the Abodrites, a Slavic maiden, named Estrith. Of her were born a son, James, and a daughter, Ingegerd, whom the saintly king Yaroslav of Russia married. For Olaf, who after the death of his father Eric acquired sovereignty over the Swedes, fell upon the unhappy Svein with an army, expelled him from the realm, and himself took possession of Denmark. Then Svein "knew that the Lord He is God,"[128] and, returning to himself,[129] considered his sins and in contrition prayed to the Lord. God heard him and gave him favor in the sight of his enemies.[130] And Olaf restored him to his kingdom[131] for the reason that he had married his mother.[132] Then they entered into a very binding pact with each other to the effect that they would hold to the Christian religion, which had

[124] I Macc. 11:5. This war is noted nowhere else. Adam doubtless had the incursion of the Ascomanni (994) in mind. Cf. I.xxxi(29) above.

[125] In 994 or 995.

[126] Canute the Great. His mother was the daughter or sister of Boleslav Chrobry of Poland, according to Scholium 24(25) above. Later writers refer to her as Sigrid Storråda, but this would appear to be legendary.

[127] The Lapp King. This and the next sentence occur in the *BC* versions with no attempt to work them smoothly into the context. Olaf's son was Anund James by Estrith-Edla. Some doubt has been cast on her being Olaf's legitimate wife. Anund's mother's name would, therefore, be unknown. Cf. II.lix(57) below. On his double name see Maurer, *Bekehrung des norwegischen Stammes,* I, 501 n. 129. Ingegerd was married to Yaroslav, the son of Saint Vladimir of Kiev.

[128] II Paral. 33:13 and elsewhere.

[129] Cf. IV Kings 4:33; Luke 15:17.

[130] Cf. Acts 7:10 and elsewhere.

[131] Cf. II Paral. 33:13. It appears rather that the kings of Denmark and Sweden attacked the king of Norway.

[132] Boleslav Chrobry's daughter or sister.

been planted in their kingdoms, and spread it among distant nations.

xl (38). Now when the king of the Norwegians, Olaf, the son of Tryggve,[133] heard of the engagement of the kings, he was enraged against Svein and reckoned that, as he was abandoned by God and had been driven out so many times, his own great numbers also could quickly expel him. Having brought together an innumerable fleet, he attacked the king of the Danes.[134] The encounter took place between Scania and Zealand, where kings usually go forth to war at sea.[135] Now, the short crossing of the Baltic Sea at Elsinore, where Zealand can be seen from Scania, is a covert well-known to pirates.[136] There, then, the Norwegians were attacked, defeated, and routed by the Danes. King Olaf, who was almost the only survivor, met with the end befitting his life by throwing himself into the sea. After the death of her husband, his wife[137] spent her life miserably, in hunger and want, as she deserved. Some relate that Olaf had been a Christian, some that he had forsaken Christianity;[138] all, however, affirm that he was skilled in divination, was an observer of the lots, and had placed all his hope in the prognostication of birds. Wherefore, also, did he receive a byname, so that he was called Craccaben.[139] In fact, as they say, he was also given to the practice of the magic art and supported as his household companions all the magicians, with whom that land was overrun, and, deceived by their error, perished.[a]

---

[a] Schol. 26 (27). On the suicide of Olaf, the son of Tryggve,* Craccaben possessed two kingdoms. He forthwith had idolatrous rites destroyed and by edict ordered Christianity to be received in Norway. At that time, also, he appointed a certain Bishop Gotebald, who came from England, to teach in Scania. It is related that at times he preached the gospel in Sweden and in Norway.
* Confused—but not by Adam.

---

[133] Olaf Tryggvason (995-1000).
[134] Rather, the kings of Denmark and Sweden attacked the Norwegian, who was betrayed by Sigvald of the Jomsvikings.
[135] Cf. II Kings 11:1; I Paral. 20:1.
[136] Cf. iv.vii below. Later accounts locate the battle at Svold near Rügen.
[137] Doubtless the sister of Svein Forkbeard. Cf. ii.xxxvi(34) above.
[138] All the Norwegian and Icelandic sources praise him for his zeal in propagating Christianity, and none mentions his having lapsed from the faith. Cf. Maurer, *Bekehrung des Norwegischen Stammes*, I, 282-452.
[139] A common name in Iceland: *Kräke* (bird of wisdom) + *Ben* (leg bone).

xli (39). On Craccaben's suicide Svein possessed two kingdoms. He then had idolatrous rites destroyed forthwith and by edict ordered Christianity to be received in Norway. At that time, also, he appointed a certain bishop Gotebald, who came from England, to teach in Scania. He is said to have preached the Gospel at times in Sweden, and often in Norway.

xlii (40). In the meantime the thousandth year since the incarnation of our Lord was happily completed and this was the archbishop's twelfth year. The following year[140] the most valiant emperor Otto, who had already conquered the Danes, the Slavs, likewise also the Franks and Italians, succumbed, overtaken by an untimely death, after he had thrice entered Rome as victor. After his death the kingdom remained in confusion. Then,[141] indeed, the Slavs, more than fairly oppressed by their Christian rulers,[a] at length threw off the yoke of servitude and had to take up arms in defense of their freedom. Mistivoi and Mizzidrag[142] were the chiefs of the Winuli under whose leadership the rebellion flared up.[b] Under these leaders the rebel Slavs wasted first the whole of Nordalbingia with fire and sword; then, going through the rest of Slavia, they set fire to all the churches and tore them down to the ground. They also murdered the priests and the other ministers of the churches with diverse tortures and left not a vestige of Christianity beyond the Elbe.

---

[a] Schol. 27 (30). The story* goes that a Slavic duke† sought for his son the hand of Duke Bernhard's niece and that he received the promise. Then the chief of the Winuli sent his son accompanied by a thousand horsemen with the duke into Italy, where nearly all were killed. And when the son of the Slavic duke asked for the woman that had been promised, the margrave Dietrich‡ broke up the plan, declaring that a kinswoman of the duke was not to be given to a dog.

* Scholia 27(30)-31(32) are by Adam and are more correct in their statements than his text.

† Mistivoi. The duke mentioned was Bernhard II, but the story fits only Bernhard I, who accompanied Otto II to Italy in 981-82.

‡ Of the Nordmark.

[b] Schol. 28 (31). Dietrich was the margrave of the Slavs whose villainy forced them to become rebels.

---

[140] January 24, 1002. Cf. II.xxxiff(29-31) above.
[141] Adam has referred events that occurred between 983 and 1018 to this time, 1011-13. Cf. Schmeidler, *Hamburg-Bremen,* pp. 317-30.
[142] Unknown under that name.

xliii (41).   At Hamburg, then and later, many clerics and citizens were led off into captivity, and even more were put to death out of hatred for Christianity. The long-to-be-remembered[143] king of the Danes who held in memory all the deeds of the barbarians as if they had been written down told us how Oldenburg[a] had been a city heavily populated with Christians. "There," he said, "sixty priests—the rest had been slaughtered like cattle—were kept for mockery.[144][b] The oldest of these, the provost of the place, and our kinsman,[145] was named Oddar. Now, he and others were martyred in this manner: after the skin of their heads had been cut with an iron in the form of a cross, the brain of each was laid bare;[c] with hands tied behind their backs, the confessors of God were then dragged through one Slavic town after another, harried either with blows or in some other manner, until they died. After having been thus made "a spectacle . . . to angels and to men,"[146] they breathed forth their victorious spirits in the middle of the course.[147] Many deeds of this kind, which for lack of written records are now

---

[a] Schol. 29 (29).* Oldenburg, a large city of the Slavs that are named Wagiri, is situated on the sea called the Baltic or Barbarian, a day's journey from Hamburg.
   * This is Scholium 15(16) of the *A2* codex. Oldenburg, of course, is not on the sea.
   [b] Schol. 30 (28). Since he would not give up Christianity, Mistivoi† was driven from his fatherland and fled to the Bardi, with whom he lived a believer to an old age.
   † Doubtless the Mistislav driven out in 1018. Cf. Thietmar *Chronicon* IX (VIII.4).
   Schol. 31 (32). The margrave Dietrich, deprived of his post of honor and of all his inheritance, ended his life as a prebendary at Magdeburg with the bad death he deserved.‡
   ‡ The margrave Dietrich mentioned in Schol. 28(31) died in 985. Two margraves of that name must, therefore, be posited.
   [c] Schol. 32 (33).** In the year of our Lord one thousand and ten the Hungarian nation was converted to the faith through the emperor's sister, Gisela who, married to the king of Hungary, induced him to have himself and his followers baptized, and he received the name Stephen in baptism. He later merited being declared a saint.
   ** This scholium was derived from Sigebert of Gembloux, *Chronographia, an.,* 1010 (*MGH, SS,* VI, 354).

---

[143] These words were evidently written after Svein had died, April 28, 1074. This date, established by Schmeidler, *Hamburg-Bremen,* pp. 288-303, corrects the one generally given, 1076.
   [144] This statement applies to the year 1018 rather than to the period of this chapter, 1011-13.
   [145] That is, Svein's, not Adam's.
   [146] I Cor. 4:9.
   [147] Codex *C* adds: the fourth day before the Nones of June.

regarded as fables, are remembered as having been done at this time in the several provinces of the Slavs. When I questioned the king further about them, he said: "Stop, son. We have so many martyrs in Denmark and Slavia that they can hardly be comprehended in a book."

xliv (42). And so all the Slavs who dwell between the Elbe and the Oder and who had practiced the Christian religion for seventy years[148] and more, during all the time of the Otto's, cut themselves off from the body of Christ and of the Church with which they had before been joined. Oh, truly the judgments of God over men are hidden: "Therefore He hath mercy on whom He will; and whom He will He hardeneth."[149] Marveling at His omnipotence, we see those who were the first to believe fall back into paganism; those, however, who seemed to be the very last, converted to Christ.[150] But He, the "just judge, strong and patient,"[151] who of old wiped out in the sight of Israel the seven tribes of Canaan, and kept only the strangers,[152] by whom the transgressors might be punished—He, I say, willed now to harden a small part of the heathen through whom He might confound our faithlessness.

xlv (43). These things were done in the last days of the elder Lievizo, under Duke Bernhard, the son of Benno, who grievously oppressed the Slavic peoples. At that time also the controversy of Bishop Bernar of Verden over Ramelsloh[a] was ended in the presence of Pope Sergius.[153]

[a] Schol. 33 (34). Ramelsloh is situated in the diocese of Verden not far from the village of the Bardi. When the bishop of Verden again made demand for its ordination and for the right of administration, he was estopped from what he had purposed by a decree of the Apostolic See. As the privilege has it, Oddo* was the legate.
* He represented Bremen, not Verden. Cf. II.xxix(27) above.

[148] The biblical phrase Adam used in I.xlvii(49) above to denote a long time.
[149] Rom. 9:18.
[150] The Norwegians and Swedes, who received Christianity long after the Slavs, now are faithful, while the Slavs have lapsed. Cf. Matt. 19:30, 20:16, and elsewhere.
[151] Cf. Ps. 7:12.
[152] Cf. Deut. 7:1; Judges 3:1; Acts 13:19.
[153] Pope Sergius IV (1009-12). Codex C adds: "At that same time the venerable count Henry established a canonry at Harsefeld. Archbishop Lievizo approved the foundation and consecrated its church."

xlvi (44).   In the archbishop's twenty-second year Benno,[154] the duke of the Saxons, died; also his brother, Liudger, who with his wife, the venerable Emma, did very much good to the Church at Bremen. At Magdeburg Tagino[155] succeeded Archbishop Gisiler; next Walthard merited the see. Our archbishop in the meantime was sedulous about his mission to the heathens and consecrated several bishops whose names and sees are uncertain because persecution weighed upon the times. But as we have learned from what the fathers related, Esico[156] succeeded Poppo at Schleswig; Odinkar,[157] of whom we have spoken above, was outstanding at Ribe. And report has it that from the death of Archbishop Adaldag to our own age all the region of Jutland was divided into two dioceses; the third, at Aarhus, passed out of existence. For Slavia the archbishop consecrated Folcward,[158] after that Reginbert;[159] the former of whom, when driven from Slavia, was sent by the archbishop to Sweden and Norway, and when he had won many to the Lord he returned full of joy. After that, with everything set in good order, the blessed archimandrite Lievizo died, at the same time as the bishop of Verden,[160] in the year of our Lord one thousand and thirteen. And he was interred in the middle of the choir before the sanctuary steps. That was the day before the Nones of January,[161] the eleventh Indiction.

xlvii (45).   Archbishop Unwan held the see for sixteen years.[162] He received the staff from Henry and the pallium from the elder

---

[154] Bernhard I, who died February 9, 1011, in Lievizo's twenty-third year. Liudger died February 26. For Emma, see II.lxvii(65), lxxx(76) below.

[155] In 1004; and Walthard in 1012, but he died the same year.

[156] Otherwise known as Ekkehard (1000-1026). Poppo either had resigned the see or accepted another in Denmark. Cf. II.xlix(47) below.

[157] The Younger. Cf. II.xxxvi(34) above.

[158] Cf. II.lxiv(62) below. Adam's statement about his having been expelled from the Slav country and then having gone into Norway and Sweden is refuted by Bresslau, Zur Chronologie und Geschichte der ältesten Bischöfe von Brandenburg, Havelberg und Aldenburg, *Forschungen zur brandenburgischen und preussischen Geschichte,* I (1880), 78-83. The dates of the consecration of the Slavic bishops are not known.

[159] Cf. Thietmar *Chronicon* VI.xliii(30).

[160] Bernar II died July 25, 1014. Cf. Thietmar *Chronicon* VIII.xxxi(VII.22).

[161] Correctly, January 24, 1013.

[162] 1013-29.

Pope Benedict.[163a] Selected from the choir at Paderborn and sprung from the very illustrious Immedinger family,[164] he was, besides being rich and generous, acceptable to all men; but he was especially benevolent to the clergy. Indeed, at the request of Lievizo, who was then provost, he presented them with the estate of Botegun, the rent of which was to be rendered on the feasts of the Apostles.[165]

xlviii (46). Unwan was the first of all to impose the rule of canons on his communities, which, indeed, had lived before according to a mixed rule of life, partly that of monks and partly that of canons. He ordered all pagan rites, of which superstition still flourished in this region, to be entirely uprooted in such a manner that he had new churches built throughout the diocese in place of the sacred groves which our lowlanders frequented with foolish reverence. Among these groves he also commanded the Basilica of Saint Vitus to be built outside the town and the Chapel of Saint Willehad restored because it had burned.

At that time, they say, he strengthened the wall of the town of Bremen against the plots and attacks of the king's enemies, chiefly because Duke Bernhard, who had dared to rebel against Emperor Henry, was terrorizing and throwing into confusion all the churches of Saxony. For, from the time that the duke was established in this region, discord never ceased between the two houses: namely,

---

a Schol. 34 (35). Report has it that he was enthroned through the curse of simony because he was possessed of a great inheritance.* Of this heritage he unwillingly relinquished one part to the emperor; another part, however, he presented to his Church, which he ruled devoutly; a third part he left to his relatives. He was a venerable old man and a lover of the poor, especially of those who were children. On this occasion† the brethren, leaving the cloister too freely, sought rendezvous with women which for a time they kept secret.

* Oddo had been elected but had not been approved by Henry II. Cf. Hirsch, *Jahrbücher*, I, 404-6.

† The occasion is not clear.

---

163 Benedict VIII, in 1022. Cf. Lappenberg, *Hamburgisches Urkundenbuch*, Vol. I, No. 64.

164 Said to be that of the Saxon hero of the wars with Charles the Great. Cf. Widukind *Gesta Saxonum*, I.xxxi; Uslar-Gleichen, *Das Geschlecht Wittekinds des Grossen und die Immedinger*.

165 Peter and Paul, June 29-30.

that of the archbishop and that of the duke, the one fighting against the king and the Church, the other struggling for the welfare of the Church and for fidelity to the kings. This partisan rivalry, hitherto concealed, from this time gathered strength and grew to immense proportions. For Duke Bernhard, forgetful both of his grandfather's humility and of his father's piety, in the first place cruelly oppressed by his avarice the Winuli nation and drove it, as a last resort, to paganism.[166] Then, in his pride unmindful of favors, he moved all Saxony to rebel with him against Caesar. Rising, finally, against Christ, he did not hesitate to attack the churches of his fatherland, and especially ours, which at the time was obviously richer than the others and farther from the emperor's reach. Our Archbishop Unwan is said by his magnanimity to have so broken the man's impetuosity[167] that, for shame of the bishop's wisdom and liberality he was in the end obliged to be well-disposed and friendly in all respects to [the Church] which he previously had attacked. By taking counsel with our bishop, too, the rebellious prince was at length prevailed upon to make submission as a suppliant to the Caesar Henry at Hausberge.

(47). Soon, also through the favor of Unwan, he subjected the Slavs to tribute[168] and returned peace to the Nordalbingians and to their mother at Hamburg.

xlix (47). To restore the latter, the venerable metropolitan is said to have built a new city and church after the destruction wrought by the Slavs. At the same time he selected three brethren from each of his communities[169] of men so that twelve might live at Hamburg in canonical association and convert the people from the error of idolatry. On Reginbert's death he consecrated for

---

[166] Cf. ii.xlv(43), where Adam dates the uprising 1011-13, while the Annals of Quedlinburg (*MGH, SS,* III, 84-86) record it as of the year 1020, and the Annals of Hildesheim, incorrectly, a year earlier. Cf. Thietmar *Chronicon* ix.v(viii.4); Hirsch, *Jahrbücher,* III, 93-96, 117-18.

[167] Through the mediation of Empress Cunigunde. *Annales Quedlinburgenses* (*MGH, SS,* III, 84-86).

[168] Canute the Great warred on the Slavs in 1019, but the Saxon duke did not join him. Hirsch, *Jahrbücher,* III, 185-86.

[169] Bremen, Bücken, Harsefeld, and Ramelsloh.

Slavia Bernhard,[170] a prudent man, whom he selected from the brethren of the Church of Hamburg, and who brought forth much fruit in preaching among the Slavic people. In Denmark, however, there still lived the theologian Poppo[171] and the noble bishop Odinkar,[a] who because of the fidelity and sanctity of his life was on most intimate terms with the archbishop. We have learned of only these two bishops in Jutland previous to Canute's entry into the realm. Odinkar was the only one of our bishops who ever visited the churches beyond the sea. Esico stayed at home;[172] the persecution deterred the rest. The archbishop also consecrated other very learned men for Norway and Sweden. But because of his friendship with the kings he also sent out others, who had been consecrated in England, to build up the Church, if they were satisfactory. Many of them he kept with him, but all he loaded with gifts when they left, making them willing to acknowledge subjection to the Church at Hamburg.

1 (48). Although, indeed, Unwan was a very noble man, he received a bishopric which was equally noble and sufficient for his liberality,[b] one in which he could display his greatness of soul and at the same time adequately meet the needs of the Church. Therefore, the treasure of the Church, which had been carefully accumu-

---

[a] Schol. 35 (37). Odinkar was the son of Toki, the duke of Vendsyssel, and had his see at Ribe. A third part of the land of Vendsyssel is said to have been his patrimony. Although he was a man of such great wealth he possessed remarkable moderation. One example of his virtue I learned about was that he had himself scourged by one of his priests, invariably every other day, throughout the whole season of Lent.

[b] Schol. 36 (36). Unwan had with him at most of the Easter festivals seven bishops, also abbots, and no less, the duke and some of the counts of this province, every one of whom he treated with great respect.

---

[170] Bernhard was bishop of Oldenburg in 1014. Thietmar *Chronicon* VIII.iii(VII.4). A Bernhard, who died in 1023, is also listed as bishop of Mecklenburg. *Annales Quedlinburgenses, an.* 1023 (*MGH, SS,* III, 88-89). He was taken from the chapter at Magdeburg and not from that of Hamburg, which was suspended from 983 until after 1020. Cf. Thietmar *Chronicon* VII.xiv(VI.4), IX.vi(VIII.4); Hirsch, *Jahrbücher,* II, 406 n.l.

[171] Doubtless the Poppo mentioned in II.xxxv(33) above.

[172] Unable to function in his see because of the troubled times, he spent most of his years in Hildesheim assisting Bernward. Cf. Tschan, *Saint Bernward,* I, *passim.*

lated over a long period of time and which it seemed hardly necessary to keep guarded behind walls—that treasure he took care so to expend to the advantage of his mission that by the cheerfulness of his giving he made the most ferocious kings of the north friendly and attentive to his every wish. In doing so he did not, in my opinion, sin much, for he sowed things carnal to reap things spiritual.[173] Indeed, his largess appeared to be most conducive to the conversion of the heathens in recent years; and it did not thus far harm the Church, which through the diligence of the fathers who preceded him was most opulent. I believe also that he followed the example of Saint Ansgar[174] and a certain Scythian bishop, Theotimus, mentioned in the Ecclesiastical History.[175] The first of these, one reads, had placated unbelieving kings with gifts; the other is praised for having tamed barbarians of ferocious nature with sumptuous repasts and presents. These remarks will suffice in apology for the prelate. Now we shall return in the order of our history to the mission of the Church which, it is acknowledged, was very successfully carried on in Unwan's time.

li (49).   To avenge the outrages he had suffered long before, both the killing of his brother[176] and his own expulsion, Svein, king of the Danes and Norwegians, sailed over to England with a large fleet, taking along with him his son, Canute,[177] and Olaf, the son of Craccaben[178] of whom we have spoken above. And so, after he had spent much time and won many battles from the English, Svein expelled the aged king Aethelred and held the island in his power—but only for a short while. For he succumbed there, overtaken by death, the third month after he had achieved victory.[179]

---

[173] Cf. I Cor. 9:11.

[174] Cf. *Vita Anskarii* xxiv, xxvi, xxxii.

[175] Cf. Cassiodorus *Hist. Eccl. Triparta* IX.xlvii (Migne, *PL*, LXIX, 1162).

[176] Hiring, son of Harold Bluetooth. Cf. II.xxv(22) above. Adam here resumes the story of Svein Forkbeard.

[177] Canute the Great, then said to have been but fourteen years old.

[178] Correctly, Olaf the Saint, the son of a Harold Grenske of the line of Harold Fairhair. Craccaben was the Olaf Tryggvason noted in II.xxxvi(34), xl(38) above.

[179] At Gainsborough on the Trent, February 2, 1014.

lii (50). The king's son, Canute,[a] who had returned with the army to his fatherland, in his turn plotted war against the English. When Olaf[180] was chosen leader by the Norwegians, he seceded from the kingdom of the Danes. Disturbed by this twofold blow, Canute then entered into a pact with his brother Olaf,[181] the son of Eric, who reigned in Sweden, and, assured of his aid, decided first of all to subjugate England and after that Norway. Equipped with a thousand large ships,[182] Canute therefore crossed the British Ocean. Over this sea sailors say it is a three-day sail from Denmark to England with a southeast wind blowing. This sea, very large and exceedingly dangerous, has the Orkneys on the left and touches Frisia on the right.[183]

liii (51). Canute made war on Britain for three years. Aethelred, the king of the English, died while he was being besieged in London,[184] losing his life at the same time as his kingdom.[b] And this by a just judgment of God; for he had befouled the scepter with blood for thirty-eight years after his brother died a martyr.[185] Thus he expiated the murder of his brother; he left a child, a son named Edward[186] whom his wife Imma had borne him.

[a] Schol. 37 (38). Having put away his pagan name, Canute, the son of King Svein, received the name Lambert in baptism. Hence, it is written in the book of our brotherhood: "Lambert, the king of the Danes, and Queen Imma and their son Canute* devoutly commended themselves to the prayers of the brethren at Bremen."
  * Harthacanute.
[b] Schol. 38 (39). Edgar, the most mighty king of the English, had by his legitimate wife a son, Edward,† a very holy man. His stepmother was Aelfthryth, who murdered her stepson, the king, and set her own son, Anund, on the throne.‡
  † The Confessor's mother was Aegelfled, also known as Aened.
  ‡ Aethelred, not Anund, was the son of Aelfthryth.

---

[180] The Saint.
[181] The Lapp king was Canute's half-brother. Canute's father, Svein Forkbeard, had married Olaf's mother, Sigrid Storråda, Canute's mother, the widow of Eric the Victorious.
[182] Greatly exaggerated. Thietmar *Chronicon* VIII.xl(VII.28) gives the number as 340, each armed by eighty men, but other sources of the time give a much lower figure.
[183] Cf. IV.x below.
[184] Aethelred died April 23, 1016. The war extended over the years 1014-17.
[185] Edward was murdered March 8, 978, but Aethelred was then only ten years old and innocent of the deed. Adam corrects himself in Scholium 38 (39).
[186] The Confessor (1042-66).

Aethelred's brother, Edmund, a warlike man, was put out of the way by poisoning to favor the victor; his sons were condemned to exile in Russia.[187]

liv (52).   Canute received Aethelred's kingdom and married his wife named Imma,[a] who was a sister of Count Richard of Normandy.[188] The king of the Danes gave the latter his own sister, Margaret,[189] in marriage by way of alliance, and when the count repudiated her, Canute gave her to Duke Ulf of England and married this Ulf's sister[190] to another duke, Godwin, because he shrewdly reckoned that the English and Normans would prove more faithful to the Danes through intermarriage. In this reasoning he was not mistaken. To turn away Canute's wrath this Count Richard,[191][b] indeed, set out for Jerusalem, where he died, leaving a son, Robert, in Normandy. Robert's son is the William whom the Franks call the Bastard. By King Canute's sister, Ulf had as sons Duke Björn and King Svein.[192] By Duke Ulf's sister, Godwin had Svein, Tostig, and Harold.[193] This line of descent appeared worth inserting here because we considered that it would be useful in reading what will follow.

lv (53).   Canute returned victorious from England and for many years held in his power the kingdoms of Denmark and England.

[a] Schol. 39 (40). Canute gave his sister Estrid in marriage to the son of the king of Russia.

[b] Schol. 40 (41). When he had put away King Canute's sister, Richard exiled himself from his fatherland out of fear of the Danes and went to Jerusalem, where he died. His forty associates are related to have stayed in Apulia on their way back and from that time the Normans possessed Apulia.

---

[187] Edmund Ironside was Aethelred's son and died November 30, 1016. His sons are reported to have been in Hungary, not Russia.

[188] Imma was a sister of Richard I, the Fearless, of Normandy.

[189] Her pagan name was Estrith. She became the wife, not of Richard II of Normandy, but of his son, Robert I. Her marriage to the Russian prince must have been a third, following the murder of Ulf in 1025, as Adam noted in Scholium 39(40).

[190] Named Gythe.

[191] Correctly, Robert I, who died at Nicaea, July 22, 1035, leaving a son, William, by Arlette, the daughter of a tanner of Falaise. William, called the Bastard by the French, conquered England in 1066.

[192] Duke Björn died in 1049. Svein was Adam's friend, Svein Estrithson of Denmark.

[193] Svein died on a pilgrimage in 1052; Tostig was killed at Stamford Bridge, September 25, 1066; and Harold, king of England, at Senlac, October 14, 1066.

At that time he introduced many bishops from England into Denmark. Of these he placed Bernhard over Scania, Gerbrand over Zealand, Reginbert over Fyn. Our archbishop Unwan took offense at this and is said to have seized Gerbrand as he was returning from England. Unwan had learned that he had been consecrated by Aethelnoth, the archbishop[194] of the English. Persuaded by necessity, Gerbrand made satisfaction and promised the fidelity and subjection due the see of Hamburg, thereafter becoming very intimate with the archbishop. By his agency the latter also sent his legates to King Canute, congratulating him with gifts upon his successes in England but reproving him for the presumption of the bishops whom he had brought over from England.[195] This admonition the king received graciously and thereafter entered into such close union with the archbishop that thenceforth he gladly would do everything to Unwan's satisfaction. The king of the Danes made known to us these facts about his uncle and he did not pass over in silence the arrest of Gerbrand.

lvi (54). In the twelfth year of Archbishop Unwan Emperor Henry, eminent for his justice and sanctity, departed to the heavenly realm after having subjected to his sway the Saxons, Italians, and Burgundians. The most valiant Caesar, Conrad, succeeded to his scepter and by his great might soon subdued the Poles and their king, Mising,[196] and he made their allies, the Bohemians and other Slavic peoples, tributary. On the mediation of the archbishop he made peace with the king of the Danes and English. The emperor even asked that Canute give his daughter in marriage to his son[197] and ceded Schleswig and the march which lies across the Eider,[198]

---

[194] Of Canterbury (1020-38).

[195] The bishops mentioned probably were Germans. Gerbrand must have been in England, June 23, 1022, as Unwan's emissary, because he signed a document by Canute there on that date. *Regesta Hist. Dan.*, Vol. I, No. 60.

[196] In 1033.

[197] Gunnhild was betrothed to Henry (later Emperor Henry III) in 1035 and was married to him in 1036. The betrothal was not connected with the treaty of friendship, which was probably concluded in 1025.

[198] Liliencron, *Beziehungen des deutschen Reichs zu Dänemark*, pp. 39-47, concludes that the existence at this time of a march across the Eider at Schleswig cannot be fully proved.

in token of their treaty of friendship. From that time it belonged to the kings of Denmark.

lvii(55). Between Canute and Olaf,[199] the king of the Norwegians, there was continual war, and it did not cease all the days of their lives,[200] the Danes struggling for dominion, the Norwegians in truth fighting for freedom.[201] In this case it seems to me that Olaf had the juster cause. The war was for him necessary rather than voluntary. And whenever there was a lull in hostilities, the same Olaf governed his realm with judgment and justice. They say that among other virtuous characteristics of his was a great zeal for God, so that he routed out the magicians from the land.[202] Although all barbarism overflows with their number, the Norwegian land in particular was full of these monsters. For soothsayers and augurs and sorcerers and enchanters and other satellites of Antichrist live where by their deceptions and wonders they may hold unhappy souls up for mockery by the demons. All these and others of their kind the most blessed king Olaf decreed must be pursued in order that, with their scandals removed, the Christian religion might take firmer root in his kingdom. And he had with him many bishops and priests from England by whose admonitions and teaching he prepared his heart to seek[203] God, and he committed his subjects to their direction. Of their number Siegfried,[204] Grimkil,[205] Rudolf,[206] and Bernhard[207] were noted for their learning and virtues. At the king's command they also went to Sweden, Gothia, and all the islands beyond Norway, preaching the Word of God and the Kingdom of Jesus Christ to the barbarians. He also sent

---

[199] Saint Olaf. The war was by no means so continuous as Adam states.
[200] Cf. III Kings 14:30; 15:6, 16.
[201] Cf. Sallust *Jugurtha* xciv.5.
[202] Cf. Zach. 13:2.
[203] II Paral. 12:14.
[204] The Bishop John of II.xxxvii(35) above.
[205] Reappears in England, 1042-46. Cf. IV.xxxiv(33) below.
[206] Returned to England, became abbot of Abingdon, and died 1052. Cf. *Hist. Coenobii Abendoniensis, an.* 1050.
[207] Perhaps the Bernhard of II.lv(53) above and III.lxxviii, IV.xxxiv(33) below.

messengers with gifts to our archbishop, entreating him graciously to receive these bishops and to send his bishops to him, that they might strengthen the rude Norwegian people in Christianity.

lviii (56). The other Olaf in Sweden[208] is said to have been filled with like devotion to religion. In his desire to convert the people subject to him to Christianity he made great endeavor to destroy the temple of idols situated at Uppsala in central Sweden. Apprehensive of his intentions, the pagans are said to have entered into an agreement with the king to the effect that if he himself wished to be a Christian he might take under his jurisdiction the part of Sweden he liked best. In that part he might establish the Church and Christianity, but not force any of the people to give up the worship of their gods unless anyone of his own accord wished to be converted to Christ. Delighted with an agreement of this kind, the king soon established for God a church and an episcopal see in western Gothia, which is the region nearest the Danes and the Norwegians. The largest city is Skara, in which, on the petition of the most Christian king Olaf, Archbishop Unwan consecrated Thorgaut[209] as the first bishop. This man energetically conducted his mission to the heathen and by his efforts gained for Christ the two noble Gothic peoples.[210] And through this bishop King Olaf sent very many gifts to the metropolitan Unwan.

lix (57). This king is said also to have had two sons, each of whom he ordered to be baptized, together with his wife and people. One of them, born of a concubine,[211] was named Emund. The other, whom the king begot of his legitimate wife, was Anund, who received a second name of faith and grace, James. He was, to be sure, a youth in respect of age, but in wisdom and piety he excelled

---

[208] The Lapp king.

[209] Mentioned by Thietmar *Chronicon* VII.xxix(VI.54) as a bishop in attendance when Unwan was consecrated in 1013. At that time he may have been a mission bishop without a fixed see.

[210] The East and West Goths of Scandinavia.

[211] Estrith-Edla. The name of the legitimate wife is unknown. Cf. II.xxxix(37) above.

all who were before him; nor was any of the kings as acceptable in the eyes of the Swedish people[212] as Anund.

lx (58). Since at that time there was a firm peace between the Slavs and the Transalbingians, Archbishop Unwan rebuilt the metropolis of Hamburg and, bringing together the clerics who had been dispersed, assembled there a great number both of citizens and canons. For this reason he frequently visited there with Duke Bernhard, often living in Hamburg half the year, and he invited the most glorious King Canute to a conference with the Slavic leaders Udo and Sederich.[213] In such wise Archbishop Unwan, distinguished at home and abroad, is said to have carried out his mission among the heathen. Now there remains to be told what we have ascertained from fleeting reports[214] about the martyrdom of King Olaf.

lxi (59). Now Olaf,[a] the most illustrious king of the Norwegians, fought on in perpetual warfare against Canute, the king of the Danes, who had attacked his kingdom. At length, they say, the most blessed King Olaf was driven from the throne of Norway by a rebellion of the nobles whose wives he had apprehended for sorcery. Then Canute reigned in Norway as well as in Denmark and—which it had not been possible for any king to attain before— in England. Now Olaf, placing all his trust in God, a second time resumed his war for the suppression of idolatry. So he gathered an innumerable multitude of armed men from the king of the Swedes,

---

[a] Schol. 41 (42). Olaf, a most fervent observer of the feasts, since he had for the sake of God's religion been driven from his kingdom and had again recovered his kingdom by means of war, is said to have had a vision as he lay sleeping in his tent on that very battlefield. And as his enemies came up while he was still resting, a leader of his army, one named Finn, went to the king and awakened him. Then Olaf sighed and said: "O! what have you done? I saw myself going up a stair the top of which touched the stars. Alas, I had reached the top of this stair and heaven was open for me to enter, if you had not called me back by awakening me." After the king had had this vision he was surrounded by his own people and, since he did not resist, was put to death and crowned with martyrdom.

---

[212] I Kings 18:5.
[213] Udo was the son of Mistivoi, the Mistislav of Thietmar *Chronicon* ix.v(viii.4). Cf. ii.lxvi(64) below. Sederich was probably the Sederich mentioned in ii.xxvi(24) above.
[214] Cf. Vergil *Aeneid* xi.139 and elsewhere.

whose daughter he had married,[215] and from the peoples of Iceland,[216] and by force of arms recovered his paternal realm.[217] The most Christian king, noted for firmness toward his enemies and justice toward his own people, believed that God had restored him to his kingdom in order that henceforth no one should be spared who either would persist in sorcery or would not become a Christian. He had for the most part made good his resolution when a small number of the sorcerers, who had survived, struck him down in revenge for those of their number whom the king had condemned. Some say he was slain in battle, but certain others that he was publicly exposed in the midst of the people for derision by the sorcerers. There are others who assert he was secretly murdered for the favor of King Canute, and we readily accept this assertion as being more likely to be true because the latter had invaded his kingdom. Thus Olaf, king and, as we believe, martyr, came to such an end. His body was entombed with becoming honor in the great city of his realm, Trondhjem. There even today the Lord by the numerous miracles and cures done through him deigns to declare what merit is his in heaven who is thus glorified on earth. The feast of his passion, observed on the fourth Kalends of August, is worthily recalled with eternal veneration on the part of all the peoples of the Northern Ocean, the Norwegians, Swedes, Goths, Sembi, Danes, and Slavs.

lxii (60). Report has it that at this same time a certain Englishman named Wolfred, inspired by divine love, entered Sweden and with great courage preached the Word of God to the pagans. And as by his preaching he converted many to the Christian faith, he proceeded to anathematize a popular idol named Thor which

[215] Astrid, the illegitimate daughter of Olaf the Lapp king of Sweden. The latter, however, had died in 1021 or 1022. His successor, Anund James, befriended Olaf the Saint.

[216] According to customary law Icelanders living in Norway at a time when the country was attacked had to render certain military service and might not leave before the danger was over. Maurer, *Bekehrung des norwegischen Stammes,* I, 572-73.

[217] Olaf fell in the first armed effort to recover his kingdom, the battle of Stiklestad, July 29, 1030. Scholium 41(42) is more in accord with the facts.

stood in the Thing[218] of the pagans, and at the same time he seized a battle ax and broke the image to pieces. And forthwith he was pierced with a thousand wounds for such daring, and his soul passed into heaven, earning a martyr's laurels. His body was mangled by the barbarians and, after being subjected to much mockery, was plunged into a swamp. These facts, truthfully ascertained, I deliver to the memory of men, even though there also are others to this day worthy of record. But enough has been said—and, in my estimation, truthfully—about Unwan and what happened in his years. At the same time Gero succeeded Walthard at Magdeburg, then Hunfrid, both holy men and worthy of the episcopal title.[219] Then died our glorious archbishop. He is said to have passed away on the sixth day before the Kalends of February, in the year of our Lord one thousand and twenty-nine, the twelfth Indiction,[220] and was buried by the side of his predecessor, on the left.

lxiii (61). Lievizo occupied the see almost four years.[221] Since he was a nephew of the other Lievizo and at that time the major provost of the cathedral, he received the staff from Caesar Conrad, through the favor of Empress Gisela, and the pallium from Pope John XIX. "And that man was simple and upright, and fearing God."[222a] Although he was gracious to all, he cared for the clergy with singular affection and was intensely compassionate with the needs of the poor. For this reason he bought a village[223] across the river from the inhabitants of the land and, presenting it to the

---

a Schol. 42 (43). And as for the women who had already cohabited with the canons in open sin, the pastor commanded that not one of them should remain in the city. They were, then, dispersed under custody through the nearby villages; and this vice ceased until the church burned and the monastery was ruined.*

* In 1041. Cf. iii.lxxxi(77) below.

[218] Doubtless at Uppsala, about 1030. Cf. iv.xxvi below.
[219] Gero, 1012-23, Hunfrid 1023-51.
[220] The date and year are uncertain, but most probably January 29, 1029.
[221] Correctly, three years and seven months, 1029-32.
[222] Job 1:1, 8; 2:3.
[223] Probably Liudwinestein (Ledenze), near Bremen. Cf. Lappenberg, *Hamburgisches Urkundenbuch*, Vol. I, No. 66.

brethren, stipulated that thirty meals be provided every year from its revenues. Most of all, he exercised such solicitude in every way for the xenodochium that he seemed in this respect alone to make up for the negligence of all his predecessors. To such an extent did the bishopric and the provostship and the xenodochium prosper that a needy person could hardly be found. This perhaps seems incredible to those who see the poverty of this time,[224] and perhaps no one would then have believed that the conditions now seen would occur in the future.

lxiv (61). And so Lievizo, good in the provostship and even much better in the see, entered upon his mission to the heathen with a fervent spirit.

(62). After winning to his side first of all Canute, the king of the Danes, he put Avoco in Gerbrand's place in Zealand, consecrated Meinher for Oldenburg, and appointed Gottschalk of Ramelsloh bishop in succession to Thorgaut.[a] In those days the most blessed bishop Thorgaut stayed a long time with the archbishop to preach at Bremen and, as he had been stricken with the dreaded disease of leprosy, he is said to have awaited the day of his summons with great patience. When at length his life was happily ended, he was interred in Saint Peter's Basilica, where Folcward and Harich, the great Odinkar, and Poppo also rest in peace.[bc] With the archbishop at that time were the renowned

[a] Schol. 43 (45). They say that Thorgaut, and also Bishop Odinkar, predicted long in advance that the Church at Hamburg and Bremen would sometime be destroyed for its sins. And now we see this prophecy fulfilled.

[b] Schol. 44 (44). At this same time died Poppo, the very celebrated bishop of the Danes. When Esico,* who was soon after selected to succeed him, reached the Eider River, he was there taken sick and died.

* Schol. 51 (52) below refers Esico's consecration to Archbishop Hermann's time, 1032-35, although the scholium above would seem to refer it to 1029. As a matter of fact, Esico, identified as Ekkehard, was bishop of Schleswig about 1000-1026. Cf. II.xlvi(44) above. Cf. Hauck, *Kirchengeschichte Deutschlands,* III, 998.

[c] Schol. 45 (46). Bishop Odinkar had a sister, Asa, a very holy woman, who also held a prebend at Bremen. She always went about barefoot and is said to have spent twenty years in fasting, prayer, and almsgiving. She seldom left the church and, when she later died a good death, left her books to the church because she had no other possessions.

[224] After Adalbert's fall, about which Adam wrote in IV *passim* below.

preachers, the younger Odinkar from Denmark, Siegfried from Sweden, Rudolf[225] from Norway. They told him what the Lord had wrought[226] for the salvation of the heathen who daily were being converted. And the archbishop dismissed them honorably, as was right, and sent them back to their preaching.

lxv (63). The Emperor Conrad at that time[227] received the daughter of King Canute for marriage to his son Henry. In royal state he at once proceeded to Italy with them to do justice to that kingdom. Accompanying him on the expedition was King Canute, very dreadful in his power over the barbarian peoples of three realms. Since, indeed, he had three sons, he placed one over each of his kingdoms. At one time he himself visited the Danes, at another the Norwegians; most of the time, however, he stayed in England.

lxvi (64). The archbishop frequently visited the metropolis of Hamburg. Because of the valor of Canute, the king, and of Bernhard, the duke, there was at that time a firm peace beyond the Elbe, since Caesar also had reduced the Winuli by war.[a] Their chiefs, Gneus and Anadrag, were pagans; the third, Udo, the son of Mistivoi,[228] was a bad Christian. On this account and also because of his cruelty, he was murdered by a certain Saxon deserter. He had a son, Gottschalk, who at this very time was being instructed in the learned disciplines in the duke's monastery at Lüneburg. Of this abbey Gottschalk, the bishop of the Goths, then had charge. But when he learned of his father's death, the prince Gottschalk, in his wrath and indignation, rejected the faith along with his

---

[a] Schol. 46 (47). The Emperor Conrad led his army against the Slavs for several years,* and for this reason there was great peace beyond the Elbe.
* In 1033, 1035, and 1036.

---

[225] Siegfried and Rudolf were mentioned in ii.lvii(55) above. When Olaf the Saint died, Rudolf came to Lievizo, who then sent him to Iceland.

[226] Cf. Acts 15:22.

[227] Adam confused events and their dates in this chapter, dated from the royal marriage (1036). Canute had visited Rome ten years before, in 1026, and one of his sons, Svein of Norway, died the year of the nuptials.

[228] Cf. ii.xlii(40); Schol. 30(28) above; Thietmar *Chronicon* ix.v(viii.4).

letters, seized his arms, and, passing over the river,[229] joined the enemies of God, the Winuli. With their help he attacked the Christians and, it is said, struck down many thousands of Saxons out of revenge for his father. At last Duke Bernhard captured him and held him in custody as if he were a robber captain. But because he respected him as a man of great bravery, the duke made an alliance with him and let him go. He went to King Canute and, proceeding with him to England,[230] stayed there a long time.

lxvii (65). In the meanwhile our archbishop, by pious works ever intent upon heaven, as a prelate graced his Church and as a pastor reared the sons of the Church, acceptable to all, even to the princes—which is difficult. In his days Duke Bernhard and his brother Thietmar did our Church much good through the exhortation of the most devout Emma,[a] who loved the Church at Bremen exceedingly and offered nearly all her fortune to God, to His mother, and to the holy confessor Willehad. Out of love for the bishop she likewise cherished all the sons of the Church as if they were her own. The fates envied us that we should not long delight in a pastor such as Lievizo, acceptable, I say, both to God and to men. Although he was ailing, it is said that he celebrated two Masses on the feast of the apostle Bartholomew and, when he had finished the psalter as usual, that same day departed to Christ. But his people mourned forever. His death took place the ninth day before the Kalends of September, that is in the year of our Lord a thousand and thirty, the thirteenth Indiction.[231]

lxviii (66). Hermann held the see barely three years.[232] He

---

[a] Schol. 47 (48). Heeding the admonition of Archbishop Lievizo, the illustrious and senatorial Emma gave the holy Church at Bremen two crosses, an altar table, and a chalice—all made of gold and set with gems worth twenty marks of gold; likewise, she gave sacred vestments and many ornaments and golden stoles and dorsals and books.

---

[229] The Elbe.
[230] In 1029?
[231] August 24th, but 25th below. Lievizo died in 1032.
[232] 1032-35.

obtained the pastoral staff from Caesar Conrad[a] and the pallium from the younger Pope Benedict.[233]   He was elected from the chapter of Halberstadt, of which church he was the provost.[234] They say he was a man harmless as a dove but possessed too little of the wisdom of the serpent;[235] therefore he was easily misled by those subordinate to him. He rarely visited his diocese. He came once to Hamburg and then with an army, despoiling the bishopric as if it were not his own, and he left, deriding the land as if it were a briny waste.[236]   The instigator of his rapacity and the promoter of his counsels was one Macco, the archbishop's episcopal vicar. As chaplains, however, he had the noble men, Thiaderic and Suidger,[237] whom the Roman see afterwards named Clement.[b] His subdeacon was Adalbert, later archbishop of Bremen, then already menacing of countenance and bearing and, because of his lofty talk, mistrusted by those who heard him. Making little of everything he found in the diocese, the archbishop[c] first of all brought to Bremen the music master Guido,[238] at whose instance he reformed the chant and cloistral discipline. Of the archbishop's

---

[a] Schol. 48 (49). Hermann acquired from the inhabitants of the land the marsh Eterinbroch,* which by an edict of Emperor Conrad was confirmed to the Church. The manuscript of this deed can be seen in the archives where it is preserved.

* Marshland on the Eider River, confluent of the Weser, south of Bremen.

[b] Schol. 49 (50). This Suidgar was transferred from the bishopric of Bamberg to the Apostolic See after three schismatics† had been ejected from that post.

† Popes Benedict IX, Silvester III, and Gregory VI were deposed by Henry III at Sutri, 1046.

[c] Schol. 50 (51).‡ They say that if he had lived longer, he would have renewed everything. Hence, also, he began to gird the city with a wall and tore down the oratory and did many other things, in all of which one can see that his intentions were not bad.

‡ This scholium is by Adam.

---

[233] Benedict IX (1033-45). The document is no longer extant.

[234] *Annales Hildesheimenses, an.* 1032, 1035.

[235] Cf. Matt. 10:16.

[236] Cf. Job 39:6; Jer. 17:6. Hermann may have seen the fields about Bremen covered with water because at that time dikes had not been built.

[237] Bishop of Bamberg, 1040-46; named pope at Sutri by Henry III, he reigned as Clement II, 1046-47.

[238] Not the famous Guido of Arezzo. Cf. Schumacher, "Die älteste Geschichte des bremischen Domkapitels," *Bremisches Jahrbuch,* I (1864), 109-73, in refutation of Manitius, *Geschichte der lateinischen Literatur,* II, 748-56.

efforts this was the only one that was successful. Next he tore down the venerable old Oratory of Saint Michael and moved the remains of three predecessors—namely, Adalgar, Hoger, and Reginward—from that place, recommitting them in the major basilica directly under the choir. Then he planned to build a wall about the city,[239] a great and useful undertaking, but scarcely had the foundations been laid when his life came to an end with his work. Thus also did the great high priest Heli,[240] because he did not restrain his own from rapine, displease, even in many good deeds, God, to whom belongs revenge.[241] Hermann died within the bishopric of Halberstadt while he was on his estate Hüttenrode. His remains were brought back to Bremen and buried in the middle of the choir. His death occurred on the fourteenth day before the Kalends of October.[242] d

lxix (67). Bezelin, called Alebrand, held the see for ten years.[243] He was a man graced with every kind of perfection, worthy of the episcopal office, acceptable both to God and to men. He was presented to us by the Church of Cologne. The Emperor Conrad gave him the staff, and Pope Benedict sent him the pallium.[244] He was consecrated with great splendor here in the metropolitan city of Hamburg by his suffragans and seven other bishops of Saxony. Everything we say in praise of the blessed man is inadequate, and never have I heard anyone dissent from this praise of him. To picture his virtues by briefly listing them: he was the father of his country, the splendor of the clergy, the salvation of the people, the dread of powerful evildoers, an exemplar for the

---

d Schol. 51 (52). He consecrated Esico** for Haddeby, but the latter soon died, before he entered upon his bishopric.
** This scholium is not by Adam. Cf. Schol. 44 above.

[239] That is, the cathedral quarter. Cf. II.xxxiii (31) above.
[240] Cf. I Kings 2:22-5.
[241] Cf. I Kings 3:13; Ps. 93:1.
[242] September 18, 1035.
[243] Adam would have it 1034-43; correctly, 1035-43. Cf. *Annales Hildesheimenses an.* 1035; *Chronicon breve Bremense, an.* 1035, 1045 (*MGH*, SS, VII, 391).
[244] Benedict IX. The papal document is not extant.

benevolent, surpassing in piety and in wishing to bring everything
to perfection. All his sayings and deeds are stored up pleasantly
in the memory of posterity. And though he was to everyone such
as each one wished, his concern and affection for the clergy[a] were
so exceptional that he could hardly bear to have anyone say an ill
word of them.[245][b] He also rebuilt the monastery and himself first
instituted a noonday meal for the canons. As it was altogether
evident that the prebend had previously been too meager, he seems
to have so appointed the thirty meals, which Bishop Lievizo had
ordered to be given every year,[246] that by the addition on his part
of certain tithes the brethren daily received white bread over and
above the usual portion and on Sundays each of them was allowed
a double measure of mead.[247] He arranged, too, that the brethren
be given wine, even though it is foreign to Saxony,[248] and this
provision was nearly always carried out in his days. When he had
adjusted the noonday meal, he turned his attention to the monastery.
This building, which previously had been of wood, he constructed
in stone, rectangular of form, as was customary, with lattices
alternately ordered, embellished and pleasing to behold.[249] Next,
he built the wall encircling the city, which his predecessor Hermann
had begun, raising it in some places up to the battlements, leaving
it in others half finished, from five to seven cubits high. In this
wall, opposite the market on the west side, there was a great portal
and over the portal an exceedingly strong tower, fortified in the

a Schol. 52 (53). To clerics of his Church who he saw were in need of help
he secretly gave, to some from four to ten *solidi* of silver, to many also a prebend,
to others his own clothes. In his compassion, too, for a good many who had received shameful treatment at the hands of laymen he had the ones who had struck
them both buffeted with fists and beaten with stripes in his presence.

b Schol. 53 (54). When, however, he beheld the pestiferous vice of clerical
marriage daily gaining in strength, he determined to proceed in the way thought
out by his predecessor Lievizo,* if only he had previously brought the church and
the monastery to their proper state.

* Cf. Sallust *Catiline* 1.4; Schol. 42(43) above; iii.xxx(29) and Schol. 76(77) below.

---

245 Cf. Judges 8:8.
246 Cf. ii.lxiii(61) above.
247 A honied drink.
248 Cf. Sallust, *Catiline* ii.18.
249 Cf. Ducange, "*Claustrum.*"

Italian way and provided with seven chambers to meet the various needs of the town.

lxx (68). While he left these monuments of his activity at Bremen, he forthwith addressed himself with all the love of his heart to the building up of the church at Hamburg. There, indeed, after the Slavic cataclysm of which we have given an account above,[250] Archbishop Unwan and along with him Duke Bernhard had built a stately fortress from the ruins of the old city and erected a church and dwelling places, all of wood.[251] Archbishop Alebrand, however, thought a somewhat stronger defense against the frequent incursions of enemies was necessary for an unprotected place, and first of all rebuilt of squared stone the church that had been erected in honor of the Mother of God. Then he constructed for himself another stone house, strongly fortified with towers and battlements. In emulation of this work the duke was roused to provide lodging for his men within the same fortified area. In a word, when the city had thus been rebuilt, the basilica was flanked on one side by the bishop's residence, on the other by the duke's palace. The noble archbishop also planned to have the metropolis of Hamburg girded with a wall and fortified with towers,[a] had his swift death not interfered with his desires.

lxxi (69). Across the Elbe and throughout the realm there was a firm peace at that time. The princes of the Slavs, Anadrag and Gneus and Ratibor, came peacefully to Hamburg and rendered military service to the duke and prelate. But then as now the duke and bishop worked at cross purposes among the Winuli people; the duke, indeed, striving to increase the tribute; the archbishop, to spread Christianity. It is clear to me that because of the efforts

[a] Schol. 54 (55). When the city* had been surrounded by the wall, he intended to fortify it with three portals and twelve towers in such wise that the bishop would be assigned to provide guards for the first tower, the advocate for the second, the provost for the third, the dean for the fourth, the master of the schools for the fifth, the brethren and canons for the sixth, and the citizens for the other six.
* Cf. ii.lxix(67) above.

[250] Cf. ii.xlii-xlv(40-43) above.
[251] Cf. ii.lx(58) above.

of the priests the Christian religion would long ago have become strong there if the avarice of the princes had not hindered the conversion of the folk.[252]

lxxii (70). The archbishop was also, in the manner of his predecessors, solicitous about the mission among the heathen with which he had been entrusted,[a] and he consecrated as coadjutors in the preaching bishops Rudolf,[253] one of his chaplains, for Schleswig; Abhelin[254] for Slavia; Wal,[255] of the chapter at Bremen, for Ribe; while the others, who were mentioned above,[256] still lived and were not idle in the vineyard of God.[257]

lxxiii (71). The mighty emperor Conrad died[258] in the archbishop's sixth year and his son Henry, he who subdued the Hungarians, succeeded him. At the same time died those memorable northern kings, the blood brothers Canute and Olaf.[259] The one, namely Olaf, king of the Swedes, had a son, James, of whom we have spoken above,[260] to succeed him in the realm. Under him the younger Svein, the son of Ulf,[261] served twelve years in Sweden, and he told us that while James reigned Christianity was widely diffused in Sweden. The other brother, that is, Canute, died in England; he held the kingdoms of the Danes, the English, and the Norwegians under his sway for twenty-two years.[262]

[a] Schol. 55 (56). They say that the right noble archbishop of Cologne, Herimann,[*] renewed the old plaint about Bremen.[†] Repulsed, however, by Bezelin's reputation as well as by a silence of three years, he gave satisfaction to our archbishop and for a whole month entertained him as a guest at Cologne.

[*] 1036-55.
[†] Cf. ii.vi(5) above.

[252] Cf. iii.xxiii below for a like opinion of Svein Estrithson.
[253] Consecrated bishop of Schleswig in 1026, before Bezelin's time.
[254] Seated at Oldenburg.
[255] Succeeded Odinkar the Younger. Cf. Schol. 59(60) below.
[256] Cf. ii.lxiv(62) above.
[257] Cf. Matt. 20:1-16.
[258] January 4, 1039, in Bezelin's sixth year, for Adam had reckoned his consecration to have taken place in 1034. Cf. ii.lxix(67) above.
[259] Canute and Olaf the Lapp King of Sweden were half-brothers. Canute had died November 11, 1035, and Olaf in 1021 or 1022. Cf. Schol. 24(25), ii.xxxix(37) above.
[260] Anund James, the son of Ulf who had married Canute's sister, Astrith.
[261] Svein Estrithson.
[262] 1014-35.

lxxiv (72). After his death his sons succeeded him in the realm, as he had determined—Harold in England, Svein in Norway, Harthacanute in Denmark. Since the last-named was the son of Queen Imma, it was his sister[263] whom Caesar Henry later received in marriage. As for the others, Svein and Harold had been born of a concubine;[264] but they, as is the custom with the barbarians, were then allotted an equal share of the patrimony with Canute's legitimate children. Harold ruled in England for a period of three years. His brother, issuing forth against him from Denmark, assembled a fleet in Flanders. But since the English king was overtaken by death,[265] the war was broken off. Harthacanute possessed England as well as Denmark.

lxxv (73). At that time the younger Svein, while on his way to England, put ashore[266] with his ships on the coast of Hadeln. When, after the manner of pirates, he had ravaged whatever places were nearest to hand, some of the archbishop's knights captured him and dragged him into the prelate's presence. But the latter received the captive with honor, took him to Bremen, and on concluding friendship with him permitted him to depart some days later with royal gifts. This the king in person told us about himself, heaping the utmost praise upon the archbishop, who was highly regarded by all for his physical appearance and liberality of soul. He also told the bystanders about the kingly magnificence of the archbishop and about the inestimable church treasure he said he had seen in Bremen, and many other things.

lxxvi (74). Accepted by all, Archbishop Alebrand was highly esteemed for his liberality of soul by Duke Bernhard and his blood brother Thietmar. Only malefactors, like the margrave Udo,[267] whose pride he confounded by his magnanimity, hated the prelate.

lxxvii (74). In the meanwhile the second of Canute's sons,

---

[263] Gunnhild. Cf. ii.lvi(54) above.
[264] Aelgifu.
[265] Harold Harefoot died March 17, 1039.
[266] Because of a storm, according to *BC2*.
[267] Count of Stade, later margrave of the Nordmark.

Svein, who ruled in Norway, died.[268] The Norwegians then chose Magnus, who was the son of Olaf, the martyr, by a concubine. Straightway invading Denmark, while Harthacanute, the king of the Danes, was lingering in England with his army, Magnus got possession of two kingdoms. Intending at once to fight against Magnus, Harthacanute put his kinsman Svein in command of a fleet. Magnus defeated Svein, who, on returning to England, found Harthacanute dead.[269] At the same time the piratical Ascomanni are said to have entered the mouth of the Weser and gone as far as Lesum, unexpectedly ravaging everything. As they were returning to their ships, then, they were attacked at Aumund, and there most of them are said to have been cut down.

lxxviii (74). In Harthacanute's place the English had previously chosen his brother Edward,[270] whom Imma had conceived by her former husband. Edward was a holy man and one fearing God. Since he suspected that Svein would claim the English scepter for himself, Edward made peace with the despot, designating him to be, on his death, the next heir to the English throne, even if Edward had sons. Appeased by this arrangement, Svein returned to Denmark. Svein is said to have fought many battles with Magnus. As often as Svein was defeated, he came fleeing to the king of the Swedes, Anund.

lxxix (75). The victorious Magnus possessed Denmark and Norway. To hold a conference with him our archbishop went as far as Schleswig,[271] having in his company Duke Bernhard, Bishop Thietmar of Hildesheim, and Rudolf, the bishop of the city. This Thietmar, born a Dane, came with Queen Gunnhild, through whose patronage he obtained the bishopric of Hildesheim.[272] In the barbarous tongue he was called Tymmo. In that conference King Magnus' sister[273] was betrothed to the duke's son, Ordulf. The

---

[268] About 1036.
[269] June 8, 1042.
[270] The Confessor, son of Aethelred the Unready, was crowned April 3, 1043.
[271] In 1042.
[272] He was bishop of Hildesheim, 1038-44.
[273] Wulfhild, daughter of Olaf the Saint.

nuptials had hardly been celebrated when, for the sake of his brother-in-law, Ordulf murdered a certain innocent Danish prince, Harold,[274] across the Elbe, as the latter was returning from the city of the Apostles. The reason for this murder was that, since he was of the royal Danish stock, Harold appeared to stand nearer the scepter than did Magnus. This deed bore the beginning of calamity in the duke's household.[275]

Now King Magnus was beloved by the Danes for his justice and valor but dreaded by the Slavs who attacked Denmark after Canute's death. Ratibor, the Slavic chief, was slain by the Danes. This Ratibor was a Christian and a man of great influence among the barbarians. He had eight sons, Slavic princes, every one of whom the Danes killed when they sought vengeance for their father. To avenge Ratibor's death the Winuli at that time also came with all their forces as far as Ribe, ravaging as they pressed forward. But King Magnus, returning from Norway, happened just then to land at Haddeby.[a] He at once collected the armed strength of the Danes from all sides and came upon the pagans in the heath near Haddeby as they were leaving Denmark. Fifteen thousand[276] are said to have been slain there, and the Christians enjoyed peace and happiness all the time Magnus lived. At that same time, after the death of King Canute and of his sons, Gottschalk also returned from England and made raids into Slavia, fighting all and striking great terror into the hearts of the barbarians. Of his valor and the influence he had over the barbarians we shall speak presently.[277]

lxxx (76). While, indeed, these things were with varying fortunes taking place abroad, the state of affairs in Bremen became

---

[a] Schol. 56 (57) Attended by a large Danish fleet, King Magnus laid siege to Jumne, the richest city of the Slavs. The losses were the same. Magnus terrified all the Slavs and, being a young man holy and blameless of life, God for that reason granted him victory in every enterprise.

---

[274] The son of Ulf who had married Astrith, Canute's sister. Harold's wife was a Gunnhild and, therefore, Canute's niece. Cf. Steindorff, *Jahrbücher,* I, 277.
[275] Cf. Sallust *Catiline* li.33.
[276] September 28, 1043.
[277] Cf. iii.xix(18) below.

unstable.[278] "The speedy fall no eminence can escape"[279] also grudged our good fortune. In those days died the most noble, senatorial lady, Emma. Once the wife of Count Liudger and sister of Bishop Meinwerk of Paderborn, she had been a widow then for forty years[280] and she dispersed almost all her immense fortune to the poor and the churches. Her body rests in the church at Bremen; may her soul rejoice in the repose of heaven. While she still lived, she gave the Church at Bremen the estate called Stiepel on the Rhine[281] but, through what fault of her daughter I do not know, she ceded Lesum to the portion of the Emperor Conrad. On this account Queen Gisela came to Bremen, did the brethren, the Church, and all the residents many favors, and then visited Lesum with the archbishop.

lxxxi (77). In the archbishop's last year but one the Cathedral of Saint Peter at Bremen burned down, and the flames of this conflagration consumed the monastery with its workshops, the whole city with its buildings, and of the old habitation not a vestige remained.[282] There the treasure of the consecrated church, there the books and the vestments, there all the furnishings were destroyed.[a] The loss of these possessions, indeed, could easily have been made up, if we had not suffered greater harm in respect of morals. As someone has said,[283] "There is vast difference between the loss of morals and the loss of temporal goods, because the former are within us, the latter without us." Indeed, from that time on the brethren, who formerly had lived canonically, roved

---

a Schol. 57 (58).* The archbishop gave Edo the provostship. Jealous at this appointment, the younger Edo, his nephew, set fire to the monastery in his anger. To make atonement for this sacrilege Edo's father gave his patrimony to the Church. The provost, however, went as a pilgrim to Jerusalem, leaving about the time of the feast of Saint James, and he returned the following Easter.
* This scholium is probably not by Adam.

---

[278] Cf. Cicero *In Catilinam* I.i.3.
[279] Lucan *Civil Wars* I.70-71.
[280] Really twenty-eight years, 1011-38. *Chron. breve Bremense* (*MGH, SS*, VII, 391).
[281] On the Ruhr, in Westphalia.
[282] The fire took place September 11, 1041, i.e., in the archbishop's seventh year, his next "to the last but one." Adam's account of it is probably exaggerated.
[283] Pseudo-Isidore, *Decretales Pseudo-Isidorianae*, Hinschius, *ed.*, pp. 81-87.

outside the cloister and began at first to observe the rule of the holy fathers, which for many ages previously had been scrupulously kept, more negligently and then, as it became antiquated, they threw it aside altogether. And from the consecration of Saint Willehad, when the church at Bremen was founded, to the death of Alebrand, when that church was burned, it is almost two hundred and seventy years.[284]

The conflagration took place early in the autumn, that is, the third day before the Ides of September.

lxxxii (78). The archbishop was on his way into Frisia at that time.[a] As soon as he heard of the burning of the temple, he retraced his steps. Having laid the foundations during the following summer, he provided that the dimensions of this our new church should correspond in beauty with that at Cologne. And we really believe that, if the fates had granted him a longer life, he would in a few years have completed all the work on the church—so great were the prelate's ardor and perseverance in every work, but particularly in the building of the temple. Indeed, that summer alone, in which he began this work, saw the foundations of the church laid, the columns and the arches and the side walls erected. When the winter had passed and the feast of Easter[285] was at hand, the most blessed archbishop Alebrand came barefooted the day before Holy Thursday, not unaware of his summons in my belief, from the church at Scharmbeck to Bremen. There after a long prayer, poured forth amid tears, he commended the church to God and to His saints. And as he was taken with a fever, they

---

[a] Schol. 58 (59).* Indeed, some who envied him said that the bishop had only the fault of pride. On this account there was strife unbecoming to bishops between him and Bishop Brun of Verden,† and this very especially because of the pride of a certain Wolfrid, an advocate. And this man died a sudden and miserable death like the archbishop.

* This scholium is not by Adam; certainly not the last sentence.

† Brun II, 1034-49.

---

[284] Correctly 254 years, according to Adam's own reckoning.

[285] April 3, 1043. The archbishop must have come to Bremen on March 30 and died about April 15.

carried him by ship to the canonry at Bücken, where he lived seven days longer. Exchanging thus its earthly phase for a heavenly Easter,[286] his soul passed rejoicing to the Lord. Great was the grief[287] of those who accompanied or met the prelate's remains as they were taken to Bremen by way of the Weser River. He was entombed in the middle of the new basilica which he had started, to wit, in the place in which the main altar had formerly been located, hard by the sepulcher of the holy father Willehad. In the course of the same time Archbishop Hunfrid,[288] of happy memory, died at Magdeburg, and Engelhard succeeded him after the one, Winither, who disdained the bishopric, had been rejected. The burial of our beloved father Alebrand took place in the year of our Lord one thousand and forty-three,[a] about the seventeenth Kalends of May. That is the eleventh Indiction. Farewell in Christ, beloved pastor, never to be forgotten by your flock. Pass to the heavenly Easter, where you may eat with the Lamb of "the unleavened bread of sincerity and truth."[289] May you be happily received into the everlasting dwellings,[290] there to delight with the angels in never-failing bliss. For as long as you enjoyed the earthly life with us,[291] you fulfilled nobly the duties of your pastoral office; your life and teachings, everything was sweet to us. Yea, speedily were you now taken away, lest wickedness alter your understanding;[292] and so the pious Lord hastened to take you out of the midst of iniquities, that you might receive in full measure the reward

a Schol. 59 (60). Bishop Odinkar of Ribe also passed away the year in which the archbishop died. Certain of his end, he set his affairs in order after celebrating Mass on Easter day.*
    * April 3, 1043.

[286] Cf. Lev. 23:5.
[287] Cf. Vergil *Aeneid* VI.868; XI.62-63, 231.
[288] Hunfrid died February 28, 1051. Engelhard succeeded the same year. Winither was Henry III's chancellor for Germany.
[289] I Cor. 5:8.
[290] Cf. Luke 16:9.
[291] Cf. Sallust *Catiline* i.3.
[292] Wisd. 4:11, 14.

of your labors,[293] even though you had not done all the good you wished. Therefore, shall your righteousness endure and your memorial shall not be forsaken for ever and ever.[294]

[293] Cf. Wisd. 3:15.
[294] Cf. Ps. 101:13; 110:3; 111:3, 9; 134:13.

Book Three

Adalbert's fame is weighed in this third part.

i (1). Archbishop Adalbert held the see for twenty-nine years. He received the pastoral staff from the Emperor Henry, the son of Conrad, who was, counting from Caesar Augustus, the ninetieth Roman emperor to sit upon the throne, those excepted who ruled at the same time with others. The archiepiscopal pallium was brought to him, as it had been to his predecessors, by legates from the Pope Benedict mentioned above, who, we have learned, was the one hundred and forty-seventh after the Apostles in the succession of the Roman pontiffs.[1] His consecration took place at Aachen in the presence of Caesar and of the princes of the realm. Twelve bishops assisted and laid their hands on him. He himself referred to this copious consecration in opposition to those who many times execrated him, smiling as he said that no one can speak ill of one who from the start and at one time had been so solemnly blessed by so many patriarchs of the Church. Although it is difficult to write worthily of this man's deeds and character, necessity compels us to record them, because we promised to extend the content of this book, O venerable prelate Liemar, up to the day of your pontificate. Hence, even if I have foolhardily and boldly embarked upon this sea, I shall by no means appear to be acting imprudently now if I hastily put to shore. On coming to this shore I hardly discern a haven for my inexperience. So beset is everything with the crags

---

[1] Benedict IX was the 149th pope. The extant document transmitting the pallium is a forgery.

of envy and the reefs of detraction that what one says in praise may
be carped at as if it had been spoken in flattery, while what one
says in criticism of shortcomings may be put down as having been
inspired by ill will.

This remarkable man may for all that be extolled with praise of
every kind in that he was noble, handsome, wise, eloquent, chaste,
temperate. All these qualities he comprised in himself and others
besides, such as one is wont to attach to the outer man: that he
was rich, that he was successful, that he was glorious, that he
was influential. All these things were his in abundance. Moreover,
in respect of the mission to the heathen, which is the first duty of
the Church at Hamburg, no one so vigorous could ever be found.
Likewise, in the solemn conduct of the divine ministry, in reverence
for the Apostolic See, in fidelity to the commonwealth, and also in
solicitude for his diocese, he could hardly have an equal nor would
anyone have in every respect been as vigilant in the pastoral cure,
if he had so continued. Although he was such in the beginning,
he seemed to fail toward the end. Not being well on his guard
against any defect in his virtue, the man met with ruin as much
through his own negligence as through the driving malice of others.
About these matters we shall speak more extensively in the proper
place. Since I can with difficulty portray all the man's acts either
well or fully or in order, I shall pick out summarily whatever deeds
of his were important. My desire is to give a sympathetic account
of the misfortunes by which the noble and wealthy cities of the
diocese of Hamburg and Bremen were devastated, the one by pagans,
the other by pseudo-Christians. Therefore I shall so begin my
narrative that everything can at once be perceived from his character.

ii (2). He was truly a man of the noblest stock.[2] His first
position was that of provost at Halberstadt. Keen and well trained
of mind, he was skillful in many arts. In things divine and human
he was possessed of great prudence and was well known for

---

[2] He was the son of Count Frederick of Goseck and of Agnes, probably of Weimar.
Steindorff, *Jahrbücher,* I, 282 n. 3.

retaining in memory and setting forth with matchless eloquence what he had acquired by hearing or by study. Then, besides, although handsome of physical form, he was a lover of chastity. His generosity was of a kind that made him regard asking favors as unworthy, that made him slow and humble in accepting them but prompt and cheerful in giving, often generously, to those who had not asked.[3] His humility appears doubtful in that he exhibited it only in respect of the servants of God, the poor, and pilgrims, and it went to such lengths that before retiring he often would on bended knees personally wash the feet of thirty or more beggars. To the princes of the world, however, and to his peers he would in no way stoop. Toward them he even broke out at times with a vehemence that at last spared no one he thought outstanding. Some he upbraided for luxury, others for greed, still others for infidelity. If, therefore, his many merits could have been put together into one vessel, the man was one who could be blessed and called such, except for one contravening fault, the ugliness of which beclouded all the prelate's grace. That fault was vainglory, the handmaid of the wealthy. This vice brought the shrewd man so much ill will that many said[4] even the good, of which he did very much, was done for the sake of earthly glory. But let men of this kind take care that they do not judge him rashly, knowing that there ought not to be an absolute judgment in doubtful cases and that wherein thou judgest another, thou condemnest thyself.[5]

To us, however, who lived with him and observed his everyday way of life it is known that as a man he did some things for the sake of earthly glory, but that as a good man he did many things in the fear of God. And although his liberality toward all was boundless, still I have found reason in his largess; that to enrich his Church he sought by his favors to win over certain men, such as kings and those very high in their counsels. Others, however, who appeared in any way harmful to his Church, he attacked with

---

[3] Cf. Sallust *Jugurtha* lcvi.2.
[4] Cf. Lambert of Hersfeld, *Annales, an.* 1072; Bruno *De bello Saxonico* ii-iv.
[5] Rom. 2:1.

consuming hatred, such as our dukes and some bishops. Very often have we heard him say that he had sacrificed himself and his relatives to the advantage of the Church. "So much so," said he, "will I spare no one, neither myself, nor the brethren, nor money, nor the Church itself, but that my bishopric shall some time or other be freed from bondage and made the equal of others." [6] All these matters will be better disclosed in the text of this history, so that the wise may realize how under compulsion and not rashly, but indeed with commendable reason, he did some things that appear silly or senseless to those who do not understand.

iii (3). In the first year following his consecration the archbishop celebrated his nuptials with the Church of Bremen by solemn enthronement. On seeing that the basilica which had lately been started was an immense structure requiring very great resources, he with too precipitate judgment immediately had the city wall, begun by his predecessors, pulled down, as if it were not at all necessary, and ordered its stones built into the temple. Even the beautiful tower, which we said [7] had been fitted out with seven chambers, was then razed to its foundations. What shall I say about the monastery which, constructed of polished stone, by its beauty gave cheer to those who looked upon it? This building, too, the archbishop ordered to be pulled down without ado, as though he would speedily build another more beautiful. For, as he himself made known to us, when we questioned him about the matter, he intended to construct a refectory, dormitory, storehouse, and the rest of the workshops for the brethren, all of stone, if time and leisure sufficed. Although he boasted that he would have at hand plenty for all these works—I say it with the good leave of the brethren [8]—he often complained only about the lack of clerics and of stone. In the meantime all aglow was the work, [9] the wall of the church rose up. Alebrand before him had begun it in the

---

[6] Sallust *Catiline* xiv.4.

[7] II.lxix(67) above.

[8] Cf. Sulpicius Severus, Ep. 2 (Migne, *PL,* XX, 179).

[9] Vergil *Aeneid* 1.436-37; *Georgics* IV.169.

style of the church at Cologne, but he planned to carry it out in the manner of the cathedral at Benevento.[10]

iv (4). At length, in the seventh year after the building began the fore part of the structure was erected and the main altar of the sanctuary dedicated to the honor of Saint Mary.[11] The second altar, in the western apse, he intended to have consecrated in affection for Saint Peter, under whose invocation, one reads, the old basilica had been erected. As many difficulties then arose for the archbishop, the work stayed unfinished until the archbishop's twenty-fourth year[12] when also I, most unworthy servant of the Church of God, came to Bremen. Not till then were the walls of the temple whitewashed and the western crypt dedicated to Saint Andrew.

v (5). And because the great prelate saw that his Church and bishopric, which his predecessor Adaldag's prudence had freed,[13] was troubled again by the iniquitous might of the dukes, he made a supreme effort to restore to that Church its former freedom, that thus neither the duke nor the count nor any person of judicial position would have any right or power in his diocese.[14] But this objective could not be attained without incurring hatred, since the wrath of the princes, rebuked for their wickedness, would be further inflamed. And they say that Duke Bernhard, who held the archbishop under suspicion because of his nobility and wisdom, often said that Adalbert had been stationed in this country like a spy, to betray the weaknesses of the land to the aliens and to Caesar.[15] Consequently the duke declared that as long as he or any of his sons lived, the bishop should not have a happy day in the bishopric

[10] Adalbert's cathedral was pulled down by his successor, Liemar. Albert of Stade, *Chronicon, an.* 1089 (*MGH, SS,* XVI, 316). The cathedral at Benevento was later altered so extensively that, like that of Cologne, it no longer affords any clue as to what Adalbert's structure was like.

[11] In 1051. Cf. iii.xxx(29) below.

[12] 1066.

[13] Cf. ii.ii, ix-xi, xxiii(21) above.

[14] Adam's text runs close to that of charters, issued by Otto II in 967 and 974, defining the freedom of the diocese of Hamburg-Bremen. Lappenberg, *Hamburgisches Urkundenbuch,* Vol. I, Nos. 44-45.

[15] Cf. Gen. 42:9.

This remark sank more deeply into the bishop's heart than anyone supposed.[16] And so from that moment he was a prey to resentment and fear, planned and schemed, and considered only what would be a disadvantage to the duke and his followers. After he had dissembled the anguish of his soul for a time, he relied altogether on the help of the imperial court, for he did not find counsel any other way. And he did not spare himself or his followers, or even his bishopric,[17] to please Caesar and his courtiers if that only would accomplish his purpose—that the Church should be free. Accordingly, he was seen to undertake so many services at court, of his own accord to exert himself and his followers to the utmost[18] in so many expeditions to every part of the world, that Caesar, marveling at this man's indefatigable perseverance, was pleased to retain him even as his chief adviser in all concerns of the realm.

vi (6). The expeditions which the archbishop made with Caesar into Hungary, Slavia, Italy, and Flanders were indeed many.[19] Although they were all carried out at great expense to the bishopric and at the cost of many exactions from his vassals, we need to mention only two of them—that is, the one into Italy, which was the first, and the one into Hungary, which was the last—for the reason that they were more important than the others and that both turned out unhappily for us. The Hungarian campaign will be discussed toward the end. We shall now consider the Italian.

vii (7). When he had put down or settled the rebellions of the Pannonians,[20] King Henry was drawn to Rome by ecclesiastical exigencies, as it is said, and in his company, along with other great nobles of the Empire, was also our archbishop. After the king had

---

[16] Cf. Sallust *Jugurtha* xi.7-8.

[17] Adalbert evidently is quoted here. Cf. iii.ii above.

[18] Cf. Lucan *Civil War* ix.881.

[19] Adam returns to the Hungarian expedition in iii.xliii(42) below. The Slavic campaign was carried on against the Liutici in the vicinity of Rügen in 1045. Cf. *Annales Augustani, an.* 1045 (*MGH, SS*, III, 125); Steindorff, *Jahrbücher*, I, 285-86. The Flemish expedition was directed against Baldwin V in 1049 or 1050. Cf. Schol. 5(6); Steindorff, *Jahrbücher*, II, 83-84.

[20] The Hungarians, so called from the former Roman province they occupied at this time.

deposed the schismatics Benedict, Gratian, and Silvester, who were contending for the Apostolic See, Archbishop Adalbert would have been elected pope but for the fact that he proposed in his stead a colleague, Clement.[21a] By him King Henry was crowned emperor on Christmas day and hailed as Augustus.

viii (8). When, after this, the emperor returned from Italy,[22] our archbishop is said to have invited him to Bremen on the pretext that the emperor might visit Lesum or summon the Danish king to a conference, but in reality to test the dukes' loyalty. On having been received at Bremen with royal pomp, as was proper, the emperor presented the brethren with the estate called Balge,[23] and the Church with the county in Frisia[24] which Godfrey[25] had previously held. Thence Caesar went soon after to Lesum, protected by our archbishop's vigilance from Count Thietmar,[26] who, they say, beset the emperor with snares. When Caesar for this reason summoned that count to justice, he elected to clear himself by combat. In this ordeal he was killed by a vassal of his named Arnold. And this Arnold was himself caught not many days after by Thietmar's son and hanged by the legs between two dogs until he died.[27] The emperor also arrested Thietmar's son for this deed and condemned him to perpetual exile. In their fierce rage against the archbishop over Thietmar's death, his brother, the duke, and his sons from that time on pursued the prelate, his Church, and

---

[a] Schol. 60 (61). Pope Clement renewed for our Church at Hamburg all the privileges that had of old been conceded by the Roman See.*

* April 24, 1047. Cf. ii.lxviii(66), Schol. 49(50); Lappenberg, *Hamburgisches Urkundenbuch,* Vol. I, No. 72.

---

[21] The contest of the Italian factions for control of the papacy in which the Tusculan Benedict IX, the Crescentian Silvester III, and the worthy though simoniacal archpriest John Gratian (Gregory VI) were involved. Henry put them all aside at the Synod of Sutri (December 20, 1046) in favor of Adalbert's nominee, Bishop Suidger of Bamberg, who as pope assumed the name Clement II.

[22] Very probably in 1048.

[23] Cf. Lappenberg, *Hamburgisches Urkundenbuch,* Vol. I, No. 73.

[24] Fivilgau and Hunesgau; but the actual transfer was not effected until 1057. Cf. iii.xlv(46) below.

[25] Duke of Upper Lorraine, related both to Duke Bernhard of Saxony and to Baldwin of Flanders.

[26] Brother of Duke Bernhard of Saxony. His son probably bore the same name.

[27] Cf. *Lambert of Hersfeld,* an. 1048; *Annalista Saxo, an.* 1048.

the tenantry of the Church with deadly hatred. Although a patched-up peace now and then made the two parties appear to have been reconciled, nevertheless those who followed the duke kept in mind the old hatred which their fathers had borne toward the Church and did not stop attacking our people, afflicting them in every way. "Arise, O Lord, judge thy own cause: be mindful of the reproaches of thy servants."[28]

ix (9). The metropolitan, striving in opposition with good endeavors and redeeming the time by good deeds,[29] because the days were evil, made peace with the dukes. In his solicitude thereafter for his diocese he considered it something great and worthy of himself to leave a memorial of his nobility everywhere. With little regard for the golden mean[30] of his predecessors, in his endeavor to make everything new he indeed at first despised the old. With great efforts of soul and with lavish outlay of wealth, he labored to make Bremen like other cities. Forthwith he established two provostships from the riches he himself had acquired: one for Saint Willehad, where his body either rests or was translated; the other for Saint Stephen, whose servant the archbishop many times prided himself on being. These two he founded at the start, but he later also established others, to wit, a third house in Bremen for Saint Paul, from property that belonged to the hospital; and a fourth at Lesum, from the land of that estate. He planned to found a fifth at Stade and a sixth across the Elbe on the Süllberg.[31] He began a seventh at Esbeck,[32] a wooded and mountainous place in the diocese of Minden. At Goseck[33] on the Saale River there is an eighth abbey, which was founded by the archbishop's relatives.

---

[28] Ps. 74:22.
[29] Cf. Gal. 2:7; Eph. 5:16. Adalbert gave the duke a number of benefices. Steindorff, *Jahrbücher,* II, 41.
[30] Cf. Horace *Odes* ii.x.5.
[31] Cf. iii.xxv(26) below; Lappenberg, *Hamburgisches Urkundenbuch,* Vol. I, No. 80.
[32] Completed by Liemar in 1091. Lappenberg, *ibid.,* Vol. I, Nos. 118, 119.
[33] Not transferred to the diocese of Bremen until 1053. *Ibid.,* Vol. I, No. 76.

x(10). He also began at different places numerous other works, most of which failed while he still lived and was intent upon affairs of state;[34] for example, the stone house at Esbeck, which of a sudden slipped and fell to pieces in his presence. Other enterprises are proved to have come to nothing because of the rapacity or negligence of the provosts. When their dishonesty was uncovered, the archbishop at times punished them severely. In this connection one can see how, through the wickedness of those in whom he had unduly trusted, the prelate's intentions often were diverted from the good he purposed.

xi(10). In the beginning, indeed, this man provided well and praiseworthily for affairs at home. What he did abroad in behalf of the mission to the heathen will be briefly set forth in the following account.

(11). As soon as the metropolitan had entered upon his episcopate, he sent legates to the kings of the north in the interest of friendship. There were also dispersed throughout all Denmark and Norway and Sweden and to the ends of the earth admonitory letters in which he exhorted the bishops and priests living in those parts faithfully to keep the churches of our Lord Jesus Christ and fearlessly to forward the conversion of the pagans.

xii(11). Magnus[35a] at that time held two kingdoms; namely, that of the Danes and that of the Norwegians. James[36] still held the scepter in Sweden. With his support and that of Duke Tove,

---

a Schol. 61 (62). On being overcome by Magnus,* Svein bowed to fate and, taking an oath of fidelity to the victor, became his vassal. But when on the advice of the Danes he undertook to rebel a second time, he was none the less defeated by Magnus.† Taking to flight, then, Svein came to James. grieving in particular about the pledged faith he had violated.

* In the war of 1042. Cf. ii.lxxvii(74) above.

† In 1046-47 or 1047-48.

---

34 Cf. Sallust *Catiline* ii.9; liv.4; *Jugurtha* lxxxix.3.

35 Magnus, son of Saint Olaf of Sweden, was elected king of Norway when Canute's son Svein and his mother Aelfgifu were driven out on Canute's death in 1035. Magnus was chosen king of Denmark in 1042, succeeding Canute's son Harthacanute.

36 Anund James succeeded his father, Olaf the Lapp King, in 1021.

Svein[37] drove Magnus from Denmark. When the latter again resumed the war, he died on shipboard. Svein[38] possessed two kingdoms and is said to have got ready a fleet to subject England to his jurisdiction. But as the most saintly king Edward governed his realm with justice, he then also preferred peace to victory and, proffering tribute, ordained, as has been stated above,[39] that Svein should inherit the kingdom after him. Since the young king Svein had three kingdoms at his disposition, he by and by forgot the heavenly King as things prospered with him[40] and married a blood relative from Sweden.[41] This mightily displeased the lord archbishop, who sent legates to the rash king, rebuking him severely for his sin, and who stated finally that if he did not come to his senses, he would have to be cut off with the sword of excommunication. Beside himself with rage,[42] the king then threatened to ravage and destroy the whole diocese of Hamburg. Unperturbed by these threats, our archbishop, reproving and entreating, remained firm, until at length the Danish tyrant was prevailed upon by letters from the pope[43] to give his cousin a bill of divorce.[44] Still the king would not give ear to the admonitions of the priests. Soon after he had put aside his cousin he took to himself other wives and concubines, and again still others. And the Lord raised up against

[37] Jarl of Västergötland.

[38] Svein Estrithson, Canute's nephew, was made regent in Denmark by Magnus and became king in his own right in 1047, when Magnus died. Svein must have given Adam a very one-sided account of the doings recorded in this chapter. Svein, for example, did not hold Norway. On Magnus' death Harold Hardrada ruled Norway, and Svein fought him with little success. In 1064 the two kings at length made peace.

[39] Cf. II.lxxviii(74). Although Edward the Confessor agreed to have Svein succeed him, there was no mention of tribute. Cf. Schmeidler, *Hamburg-Bremen*, p. 97. Warfare between Magnus and Svein prevented Magnus' invasion of England, according to the *Anglo-Saxon Chronicle, an.* 1046.

[40] Cf. Gen. 40:23.

[41] Schmeidler, *Hamburg-Bremen*, pp. 303-12, holds that Svein was married but once, according to III.xv(14) below. Scholia 66(67) and 72(73), however, refer to another legitimate queen, Gythe, the widow of Anund James. Hofmeister opposes Schmeidler's contention that Svein had but one legitimate queen, Gunnhild, in his review of his book, *Historische Zeitschrift*, CXXI (1920), 476-77.

[42] Cf. Mark 3:21.

[43] Probably Leo IX. No such letter is known.

[44] Cf. Matt. 5:31 and elsewhere.

him many adversaries on all sides as He had against Solomon through his own servants.[45]

xiii (12). A certain Harold,[46][a] the brother of Olaf, king and martyr, left his fatherland while his brother still lived and went an exile to Constantinople. Becoming there the emperor's knight, he fought many battles with the Saracens by sea and with the Scythians by land, and he was distinguished for his bravery and much exalted for his riches. Now, when he was recalled to his fatherland on his brother's death, he found his kinsman Svein ruler.[b] To his hands, it is said, Harold commended himself, swearing an oath of fidelity to the victor, and received his father's kingdom in fief as a duchy.[47] But when soon after he came to his own people and clearly perceived that the Norwegians were true to him, he was easily persuaded to rebel, and he devastated all the coastlands of Denmark with fire and sword. The church at Aarhus was burned at that time and that at Schleswig despoiled. King Svein retreated. Between Harold and Svein there was war all the days of their lives.[48]

xiv (13). At that same time the English also seceded from the Danish kingdom. The rebellion was started by the sons of Godwin, who, we said, were the sons of the aunt[49] of the Danish king whose sister King Edward had taken in marriage.[c] Entering into a con-

---

a Schol. 62 (63). When Harold returned from Greece, he married the daughter of the king of Russia, Yaroslav. Andrew, the king of Hungary, married another daughter, of whom Solomon was born. Henry, the king of the Franks, married a third daughter, who bore him Philip.*

* Harold Hardrada married Elizabeth. Andrew (1046-58) married Anastasia, and their son Solomon (1064-74), succeeded Béla I (1060-63). The third daughter, Anna, married Henry I of France (1031-60), whom Philip I (1060-1108) succeeded.

b Schol. 63 (64). Harold fought with Magnus against Svein, after whose death he became the former's vassal.

c Schol. 64 (65). For, as we said before,† Canute, the king of the Danes, gave

---

45 Cf. III Kings 11:14, 23.

46 Hardrada.

47 This account also is colored in favor of Svein, against whom, as Schol. 63(64) states more correctly, Harold fought in alliance with Magnus.

48 Cf. Ps. 22:6, 26:4.

49 Gythe, the sister of Ulf. Cf. Schol. 64(65).

spiracy, they forthwith slew Björn,[50] one of King Svein's brothers who were dukes in England, and drove the other, Osbern, with all his followers out of the fatherland. And Godwin's sons held England in their power, for Edward[51] was contented with life alone and the empty title of king.

xv (14). While these events were taking place there, the most Christian king of the Swedes, James, departed this world, and his brother, Emund the Bad,[52] succeeded him. He was born of a concubine by Olaf and, although he had been baptized, took little heed of our religion. He had with him a certain bishop named Osmund,[53] of irregular status, whom the bishop of the Norwegians, Sigefrid, had once commended to the school at Bremen for instruction. But later he forgot these kindnesses and went to Rome for consecration. When he was rejected there, he wandered about through many parts and so finally secured consecration from a Polish archbishop. Going to Sweden then, he boasted that he had been consecrated archbishop for those parts. But when our archbishop sent his legates to King Gamular, they found this same vagabond Osmund there, having the cross borne before him after the manner of an archbishop. They also heard that he had by his

---

his sister, who had been repudiated by Count Richard, to his duke, Ulf, and of her were born Duke Björn and King Svein. Duke Ulf married his sister to Godwin, the duke of the English, and of her were born Svein, Tostig, Harold, and that Eadgyth whom King Edward‡ had in wedlock. Svein, Godwin's son, afterwards slew Björn, his uncle's son. But as Harold was a very valiant man, he beheaded Griffith,** the king of Hibernia; drove Svein, the king of the Danes, from England; and had no regard for his kinsman and lord, Edward. There followed the vengeance of God and the Norman disaster and the overthrow of England.

† Cf. ii.liv(52) above.
‡ Edward the Confessor.
** Griffith was king of Wales. He was slain in an uprising of his subjects, who sent his head to Harold.

---

[50] Cf. *Anglo-Saxon Chronicle, an.* 1049.
[51] The Confessor. Cf. Lucan *Civil War* v.389.
[52] Called Emund Gamular, the Old, and the Bad, the son of Olaf the Lapp King.
[53] Commended, as stated, to the school at Bremen by the younger Sigefrid; consecrated by Stephen I, who was archbishop of Gnesen about 1038-58. He presently went to England and died in the monastery of Ely about 1070.

unsound teaching of our faith corrupted the barbarians, who were still neophytes. Frightened by their presence, he with his accustomed cunning induced the people and the king to drive the legates away, on the ground that they had not been apostolically accredited. And they went from the presence of the council, rejoicing that they were accounted worthy to suffer reproach for the name of Jesus.[54] The legates were brethren of the Church at Bremen, and the most prominent of them was the elder Adalward,[55a] at one time dean of our monastery, but then consecrated bishop for the Swedish people. Of this man's merits much might be said if we were not hurrying on to other matters. When the legates had thus been turned away from Sweden, a certain one, whether a grandson or a stepson of the king I do not know, is said to have followed them with tears, beseechingly commending himself to their prayers. His name was Stenkil.[56] He alone was moved with compassion for the brethren, offering them gifts and conveying them safely over the Swedish mountains to the most saintly queen Gunnhild.[57b] After her separation from the king of the Danes on the ground of consanguinity, she lived on her estates across from Denmark, devoting her time to hospitality and almsgiving and busying herself with other works of charity. She received the legates with great respect, as having been sent by God, and as their host sent valuable gifts to the archbishop by them.

xvi (15). The Swedes, who had expelled their bishop, were in the meantime pursued by divine vengeance. First, indeed, when

---

a Schol. 65 (66). On his departure the monastery at Bremen declined in respect of the rule, the discipline, and concord of the brethren, as heretical persons threw everything into confusion.

b Schol. 66 (67). There was another Gunnhild, the widow of Anund, another Gythe whom Thore* murdered.

* Cf. iii.lxxii below.

---

[54] Acts 5:41.

[55] Later bishop of Öster- and Västergötland and probably the Albert mentioned in Schol. 148(142) below.

[56] Of Västergötland, king of Sweden, 1051-56.

[57] Cf. iii.xii(11) above.

one of the king's sons, named Anund,[58] was sent by his father to extend his dominions, he came into the land of the women, who we think were Amazons, and he as well as his army perished there of poison which the women mingled in the springs. After that, the Swedes were visited, among other misfortunes, by so great a drought and failure of crops[59] that they sent legates to the archbishop asking again for their bishop and pledging the good faith of the people along with amends. Joyfully the archbishop gave the petitioning flock a willing pastor. When he then came into Sweden,[60] he was afforded so eager a reception on the part of everyone that he won all the people of Värmland to Christ and is said also to have worked many miracles among the folk.[61a] At that same time Emund, the king of the Swedes, died. After him his nephew Stenkil, of whom we have spoken above, was raised to the throne. He was faithful to our Lord Jesus Christ, and all our brethren who had gone to those parts bore witness to his devotion. Everything that happened in Sweden in his time the lord Archbishop Adalbert described in grandiose language, as was his way, and he also took care to add the vision Bishop Adalward had, in which he was admonished not to hesitate pressing the cause of conversion.

xvii (16). In Norway great events also took place at that time; King Harold[62] surpassed all the madness of tyrants in his savage

---

[a] Schol. 67 (68). On the invitation of King Harold, Adalward came into Norway, and there the body of a certain man who died sixty years before could not at all decompose, but soon after the bishop pronounced the absolution effecting reconciliation it was resolved into dust. For, as was in a vision revealed to Adalward himself, that man had at one time been excommunicated for piracy by Archbishop Lievizo.[*]

[*] This story also occurs in II.xxxiii(31) above, where, however, the time is given as seventy years, which figure checks with other chronological data.

---

[58] Son of Emund. The text of this passage is also that of Schol. 123(119), except that Adam there cites Adalward as his informant. For other remarks about the Amazons, see IV.xix below.

[59] The drought in 1056-57 was not confined to Sweden. Cf. Norlind, "Einige Bemerkungen über das Klima der historischen Zeit," *Lunds Universitets Aarskrift,* Vol. X (1914), No. 1, p. 24.

[60] Before 1060.

[61] Cf. IV.xxiii below.

[62] Harold Hardrada.

wildness. Many churches were destroyed by that man; many Christians were tortured to death by him. But he was a mighty man and renowned for the victories he had previously won in many wars with barbarians in Greece and in the Scythian regions.[63] After he came into his fatherland, however, he never ceased from warfare; he was the thunderbolt of the north, a pestilence to all[64] the Danish islands. That man plundered all the coastlands of the Slavs; he subjected the Orkney Islands to his rule; he extended his blood-stained sway as far as Iceland.[65] And so, as he ruled over many nations, he was odious to all on account of his greed and cruelty. He also gave himself up to magic arts and, wretched man that he was,[66] did not heed the fact that his most saintly brother[67] had eradicated such illusions from the realm and striven even unto death for the adoption of the precepts of Christianity. The miracles that take place every day at that king's tomb in the city of Trondhjem testify to his extraordinary merits. Although this man whom God had forsaken beheld these wonders, he was nothing moved. With clawed hands[68] this Harold grasped at and dispersed to his henchmen the offerings, and in particular the treasure, which the supreme devotion of the faithful had collected at his brother's tomb. For these reasons the archbishop, inflamed with zeal for God, sent his legates to the king, rebuking him by letter for his tyrannical presumption. In particular, however, did the prelate reprimand him about the offerings, which it was not lawful to appropriate to the use of laymen, and about the bishops[a] whom

[a] Schol. 68 (69). From that day forth King Harold sent his bishops to Gaul; he also received many who came from England. One of these was Asgot, whom the archbishop ordered to be apprehended as he was returning from the city of the Apostles. When he had tendered the oath of fealty, the archbishop dismissed him, laden with presents and free to go his way.

---

[63] Cf. III.xiii(12) above.
[64] Cf. Lucan *Civil War* x. 34-35.
[65] Harold did not conquer Iceland. Cf. Orosius *Hist. adv. Paganos* v. 4, 16 (Migne, *PL,* XXXI, 927).
[66] Cf. II Paral. 33:6; II Macc. 7:16.
[67] Olaf the Saint. Cf. II.lvii(55) above.
[68] Cf. Vergil *Aeneid* III.217; vi.360; *Georgics* II.365-66.

he had had unlawfully consecrated in Gaul or in England, in contempt of the archbishop himself, who by authority of the Apostolic See should rightly have consecrated them. Thrown into a rage by these mandates, the tyrant scornfully ordered the bishop's legates to depart, vociferating that he did not know of any archbishop or authority in Norway save only Harold himself. Many other things he later did and said that threatened his pride with speedy fall.[69] Pope Alexander without delay also sent that king a letter[a] commanding that both he and his bishops tender the respectful submission due the vicar of the Apostolic See.

xviii (17). After these occurrences in Norway the archbishop earnestly endeavored to conciliate the Danish king, to whom he had previously given offense, by repudiating his cousin. For he realized that if he could attach a man of this kind to himself, approach to other matters he had in mind would be easier. Relying, therefore, on the good will won by the generosity he showed to everyone, he presently went to Schleswig.[70] There he easily became acquainted and reconciled with the proud king and by gifts and

---

[a] Schol. 69 (70). "Alexander,[*] bishop, servant of the servants of God, to Harold, king of the Norwegians, greeting and apostolic benediction. Because you are still immature in the faith and after a fashion halting in respect of ecclesiastical discipline,[†] it behooves us, to whom has been committed the governance of the whole Church, to visit you more frequently with admonitions of a divine nature. But as it is not at all possible for us to do this because the way is long and difficult, know that we have immovably intrusted all these matters to Adalbert, the archbishop of Hamburg, our vicar. And so the aforesaid venerable archbishop, our legate, has complained to us by letter that the bishops of your country either have not been consecrated or, contrary to the Roman privileges that have been granted to his Church and to him, have for a pecuniary consideration been very unacceptably consecrated in England or in Gaul. Wherefore we admonish you by the authority of the Apostles Peter and Paul that, as you are obligated to show reverend subjection to the Apostolic See, so you and your bishops render the same to the aforesaid venerable archbishop, our vicar and functioning in our stead. And so forth."

[*] Alexander II. The letter here condensed is dated variously, 1061 or 1065.

[†] Cf. III Kings 18:21.

---

[69] Harold was killed at Stamford Bridge, September 25, 1066. Cf. Prov. 16:18; iii.lii(51) below.

[70] In 1052 or 1053—therefore not after the events narrated in the preceding chapter; so also the emperor's conference with Svein, which took place at Merseburg, Easter 1053.

banquets endeavored to put the archiepiscopal power above royal wealth. Finally, as is the custom among the barbarians, they feasted each other sumptuously on eight successive days to confirm the treaty of alliance. Disposition was made there of many ecclesiastical questions; decisions were reached about peace for the Christians and about the conversion of the pagans. And so the prelate returned home full of joy and persuaded Caesar to summon the Danish king to Saxony that each might swear the other a perpetual friendship. By virtue of this alliance our Church gained great advantages and, with the cooperation of King Svein, the mission to the northern nations steadily received prosperous increase.

xix (18).   Across the Elbe and in Slavia our affairs were still meeting with great success. For Gottschalk, who was mentioned above, a man to be praised for his prudence and valor, married a daughter[71] of the Danish king and so thoroughly subdued the Slavs that they feared him like a king, offered to pay tribute, and asked for a peace with subjection. Under these circumstances our Church at Hamburg enjoyed peace, and Slavia abounded in priests and churches. For Gottschalk, "a religious man and one who feared God,"[72] also an intimate friend of the archbishop, cherished the Church at Hamburg like a mother. He was in the habit of going to her frequently to fulfill his vows. No mightier and more fervent propagator of the Christian religion has ever arisen in hither Slavia. For he had in mind, if a longer life had been granted him, to make all the pagans embrace Christianity, since he converted nearly a third part of those who previously under his grandfather Mistivoi had fallen back into paganism.

xx (19).   Now all the Slavic peoples who belonged to the diocese of Hamburg practiced the Christian religion devoutly under that prince; that is, the Wagiri and Abodrites and Reregi and Polabingi; likewise, the Linguones, Warnavi, Kicini, and Circipani, as far as the Pane River which in the privileges of our Church is called the

---

[71] Sigrid or Siritha. Cf. ii.lxvi(64), lxxix(75) above.
[72] Acts 10:2.

Peene.[73a] The provinces now were full of churches, and the churches full of priests. And the priests attended freely to "those things that pertain to God."[74] Their common servant, the prince Gottschalk, is said to have been inflamed with such ardent zeal for the faith that, forgetting his station, he frequently made discourse in church in exhortation of the people[b]—in church because he wished to make clearer in the Slavic speech what was abstrusely preached by the bishops or priests.[75] Countless was the number of those who were converted every day; so much so that he sent into every province for priests. In the several cities were then also founded monasteries for holy men who lived according to canonical rule, likewise for monks and nuns, as those testify who saw the several communities in Lübeck, Oldenburg, Lenzen, Ratzeburg, and other cities. In Mecklenburg, which is a noted city of the Abodrites, there are said to have been three communities of those who served God.

xxi (20). The archbishop rejoiced over the new plantation of churches and he sent the prince, of his bishops and priests, wise men who were to strengthen the untutored folk in the Christian religion. For Oldenburg he consecrated the monk Ezzo when Abhelin died.[76] John the Scot he appointed to Mecklenburg. He assigned a certain Aristo, who had come from Jerusalem, to be in Ratzeburg,[77] and others elsewhere. When he came to Hamburg

---

[a] Schol. 70 (72). At the mouth of the Peene River is the very large city that is called Demmin; there is the end of the diocese of Hamburg.

[b] Schol. 71 (71). The story goes that two monks at that time came from the wooded highlands of Bohemia into the city of Rethra. Because they publicly proclaimed the Word of God there, they were tried in a council of the pagans first by diverse tortures, as they had desired, and finally beheaded for the sake of Christ. Their names indeed, although unknown to men, are, as we truly believe, recorded in heaven.

---

[73] Cf. II.xxii(19) above.

[74] Exod. 4:16, 18-19.

[75] That is to say, allegorically, not that the clergy did not preach in Slavic. Cf. *Helmold* I.xcii, n. 3 (Tschan, tr.).

[76] Between 1055 and 1060 according to Dehio, *Hamburg-Bremen,* Vol. I, App., pp. 68-69. For John the Scot see III.li(50) below.

[77] Ratzeburg did not become an episcopal city until 1154. Aristo doubtless was stationed there as a bishop without a fixed see.

himself, furthermore, he invited the same Prince Gottschalk to a conference, earnestly exhorting him resolutely to carry through to the finish the work he had begun for Christ, assuring him that victory would attend him in everything; finally, that he would be blessed if he suffered adversity for the name of Christ. And he assured him that there were laid up for him in heaven many rewards for his conversion of the pagans, many crowns for the saving of individual souls. With the same words and to the same endeavor the metropolitan exhorted the king of the Danes, who many times came to him as he tarried by the Eider River. He noted attentively and remembered everything the archbishop drew from the Scriptures, with the exception that he could not be convinced about gluttony and women,[a] which vices are inborn with that people. As to everything else, the king was obedient and yielding to the prelate.

xxii (21).   In the course of that same time, events of great importance took place in Slavia that for the glory of God may not be withheld from posterity, for "the God of revenge hath acted freely," rendering "a reward to the proud."[78] Although many tribes of the Winuli are renowned for their valor, there are only four, called by us Leutici, by themselves Wilzi, among whom existed contention for leadership and power. These are, namely, the Kicini and Circipani who live this side of the Peene River, the Tholenzi and Redarii who live beyond the Peene. When the quarrel reached the stage of war, the Tholenzi and Redarii, although helped by the Kicini, were nevertheless overcome by the Circipani. When the war was once more renewed, the Redarii were crushed. There was a third attempt, and the Circipani came off victorious. Then they who had been vanquished called to their aid the prince Gott-

---

a Schol. 72 (73). The most illustrious king of the Danes was afflicted with incontinence only in respect to women, yet not of his own will, in my opinion, but from racial vice. Nevertheless, he did not escape vengeance for his evil doing, for one of his concubines, Thore, put his legitimate queen, Gythe, to death with poison. And when King Svein sent Thore's son, named Magnus, to Rome to be consecrated there for the kingship, the unhappy youth died on the way. After him the wicked mother did not have another son.

78 Ps. 93:1-2.

schalk and the duke Bernhard and the king of the Danes. And they proceeded against their enemies. For seven weeks they maintained the immense host of the three rulers from their own resources, and the Circipani fought back valiantly. Many thousands of pagans were laid low on both sides, many more were led off into captivity. At last the Circipani bought peace, offering the rulers fifteen thousand talents.[79] Our forces came home in triumph, but of Christianity there was no mention. The victors were intent only upon booty. Such was the valor of the Circipani, who belong to the bishopric of Hamburg. A certain man prominent among the Nordalbingians told me that these and other things really so happened.

xxiii (22). I have also heard the most veracious king of the Danes say, when in conversation he commented on these matters, that the Slavic peoples without doubt could easily have been converted to Christianity long ago but for the avarice of the Saxons. "They are," he said, "more intent on the payment of tribute than on the conversion of the heathen."[80] Nor do these wretched people realize with what great danger they will have to atone for their cupidity, they who through their avarice in the first place threw Christianity in Slavia into disorder, in the second place have by their cruelty forced their subjects to rebel,[81] and who now by their desire only for money hold in contempt the salvation of a people who wish to believe. By the just judgment of God,[a] therefore, we

---

[a] Schol. 73 (74). For the Scripture saith unto Pharaoh, "And therefore have I raised thee, that I may shew my power in thee, and that my name may be spoken of throughout all the earth. Therefore he hath mercy on whom he will; and whom he will, he hardeneth." *
* Exod. 9:16; Rom. 9:17-18.

---

[79] Helmold corrects Adam's account of this war of 1057. He has the Kicini and Circipani live east of the Peene and the Tholenzi and Redarii west. He also has the Circipani allied with the Kicini and the defeated tribes support the armies of the Danish kings, the Saxon duke, and the Abodrite chief for six weeks. Cf. *Helmold* I.xxi (Tschan, tr.).
[80] Cf. II.lxxi(69) above; Lucan *Civil War* I.461.
[81] The reference here evidently is to the Slav rebellion of 1011-13. Cf. II.xlii(40) and Schol. 28(31) above.

see prevailing over us[82] those who by God's leave have been hardened to the end that by them our iniquity may be scourged. For in truth as we, sinning, see ourselves overcome by our enemies, so, when we are converted, shall we be victorious over our enemies. If only we earnestly sought their conversion, they would ere now have been saved and we should surely be at peace."

xxiv (23).   While by its ministry our Church was carrying on this work abroad in its mission to the heathen, the lord metropolitan Adalbert, still intent upon good endeavors, vigilantly and zealously provided that the pastoral office should not through any negligence on his part appear to have fallen off in the matter in which the Apostle gloried,[83] namely, the care of all the churches. And so the prelate, illustrious at home and abroad, conducted himself in such wise that, though he was the equal of the rich and greater than the great, he tried none the less to be "the father of orphans and the judge of widows."[84] Of all he took such care that, a most accomplished provider, he attended to the needs even of the least. And though, burdened with earthly business, he had presently to relax his care for the spiritual, he remained in respect of the heathen mission alone vigorous in service and without reproof, and such as both the circumstances of the times and the ways of men would have him. So affable, so generous, so hospitable, so desirous of divine and at the same time of human glory was he that because of his ability little Bremen was, like Rome, known far and wide and was devoutly sought from all parts of the world, especially by all the peoples of the north. Among those who came the longest distances[85] were the Icelanders, the Greenlanders, and legates of the Orkney Islanders. They begged that he send preachers thither, which he also did.

xxv (25).   In those days the bishop of the Danes, Wal, departed

---

[82] Cf. Ps. 64:4.

[83] Cf. II Cor. 11:26.

[84] Ps. 67:6.

[85] The rest of this chapter is repeated nearly verbatim at the end of III.lxxiii below.

this world.[86] With the sanction of the metropolitan, King Svein divided his diocese into four bishoprics, in each of which he enthroned one of his bishops. Then our prelate also sent laborers to Sweden and Norway and the islands of the sea into the Lord's harvest.[87] About the consecration of each of these bishops fuller mention will be made at the end.

xxvi (25). And though he made very careful provision for his diocese as a whole, the archbishop regarded the metropolis Hamburg as the prime source of his joy.[88] Calling her the fruitful mother of peoples, one to be revered with all manner of devoted service, he declared that she ought to be accorded so much the more consolation because she had been tried by so much greater misfortunes and plotting close to her and by such prolonged molestation on the part of barbarians. The while he often thought of fortifying Hamburg, and at the same time of embellishing the diocesan seat, whenever peaceful times should be at hand. He undertook to build a work, therefore, that would be serviceable against the attacks of the barbarians, one in which both the Nordalbingian people and the Church would find protection the year round. Now, the entire province of the Sturmarians, in which Hamburg is situated, levels off into a flat plain. In the part which borders on the Slavs there is neither a hill nor a stream at hand to afford the inhabitants protection. Woods are to be met with only here and there, but from the protection of their coverts the enemy at times suddenly breaks in unexpected raids upon our people who, thinking themselves secure and suspecting nothing, are either killed or, what is worse than death, led away captive.[89] The only hill in that country rises near the Elbe with its ridge sloping gently

---

[86] Wal, bishop of Ribe, died after 1057. The reorganization of the Danish Church must have been effected between 1057 and 1060. Cf. Schmeidler, *Hamburg-Bremen*, pp. 284-87.

[87] Cf. Matt. 9:38.

[88] Cf. Ps. 136:6.

[89] Cf. Sallust *Jugurtha* xiv.15.

westward, and the inhabitants call it the Süllberg.ᵃ Regarding this eminence, a fit one on which to erect a stronghold for the protection of the people, the archbishop immediately ordered the woods which covered its top to be cut down and the place to be cleared. Thus, at great expense and with much effort on the part of men his wish was accomplished and the rugged mountain made habitable.[90] There he established a canonry, planning to form a community of men who served God, but they soon turned into a gang of robbers. For from that stronghold certain of our men began to plunder and harry the countrymen of the vicinity, whom they had been posted to protect. For this reason the place was later destroyed in an uprising of the co-provincials. The Nordalbingian people, however, were excommunicated. This, we have learned, was done to favor the duke who, as usual, envied the successful enterprises of the Church.

xxvii (26). Now the duke at that time also abandoned the old stronghold at Hamburg and established for himself and his followers a new fortress[91] between the Elbe and the stream called the Alster. Thus the two were separated from each other in their dwelling places as they certainly were in their hearts; and the duke lived in the new town, the archbishop in the old. Like all his predecessors, the archbishop truly loved this place because it was the metropolitan seat for all the northern nations and the chief town of his diocese. For this reason, while there still was peace across the Elbe, he wished to celebrate there nearly all the feasts of Easter and Pentecost, as also those of the Mother of God. On these occasions he assembled from the several communities a very great number of clerics, those especially who could please the

---

ᵃ Schol. 74 (75). And there he deposited the head of Saint Secundi, who we read was one of the leaders of the Theban legion. This relic the metropolitan had received in Italy through the generosity of a certain bishop of Turin.*
* Cunibert was bishop of Turin when Adalbert was in Italy.

---

[90] Still in Bernhard II's time; therefore, before 1059.
[91] Still called the Neueburg.

people with their resonant voices. Since at that time he rejoiced in a full complement of clerics, he ordained that all the offices of divine service be carried out with great reverence as well as external splendor. Certainly he was so much given to pomp that he would no longer conduct the ecclesiastical mysteries in accordance with the Latin rite[a] but, warranted by what usage of the Romans or of the Greeks I do not know, he ordained twelve offices to be sung during the three masses at which he assisted. He sought for everything that was grand, everything that was resplendent, everything that was glorious whether in things divine or human. And on this account he is said to have delighted in the smoke of spices and the glittering of lights and the resounding of deep sonorous voices. All this he drew from the reading of the Old Testament, in which the Majesty of the Lord appeared on Mount Sinai.[92] Many other things he also used to do that were uncommon in the eyes of moderns and those who did not know the Scriptures. Nevertheless he did nothing without the sanction of the Scriptures. Even then, he obviously thought of making his church excel others in riches and prestige if he could bend the pope and the king to his will. Accordingly, he hastened to make them amenable to him in every way.

xxviii (27). Making use of the vast wealth of his realm, the Caesar Henry at that time founded in Saxony Goslar,[93] which he, as they say, transformed from a small millstead or hunting lodge, building it up with good luck and speed into as great a city as can now be seen. In this city he also built a palace for himself and founded two congregations for Almighty God. One of these he granted to our archbishop to direct and to hold because Adalbert was his inseparable associate and cooperated with him in everything. Then he also held out hope to the archbishop of acquiring

[a] Schol. 75 (76). "Hard is it that the praise of men does not seduce one who lives praiseworthily." Pope Leo.

---

[92] Cf. Exod. 24:16-17.

[93] Goslar came into prominence as a result of the mines of the Rammelsberg in the tenth century. Cf. Tschan, *Saint Bernward*, II, 151.

or receiving the counties and abbacies and estates which we later purchased at the cost of great peril to the Church;[94] for example, the monasteries of Lorsch and Corvey; the counties of Bernhard[95] and Egbert,[96] the estates of Sinzig, Plisna, Groningen, Duisburg, and Lesum. Having under dubious circumstances already got possession of these properties, the metropolitan thought, as it is well said of Xerxes, that he could walk on the sea and sail over the land;[97] in short, that he could easily accomplish everything he had in mind.

xxix (28). He was especially encouraged because the most powerful pope Leo[98] came to Germany for the purpose of bettering the needs of the Church, for the archbishop knew that on account of their old friendship the pope would refuse him nothing which might rightfully be assured anyone.

xxx (29). At that time then there was held the general synod at Mainz, presided over by the apostolic lord and by the Emperor Henry and attended by bishops Bardo of Mainz, Eberhard of Trier, Herimann of Cologne, Adalbert of Hamburg, Engelhard of Magdeburg,[99] and other priests of provincial jurisdiction. In that council a certain bishop of Speyer, Sigebod, who stood accused of the crime of adultery, was cleared by sacrificial ordeal. Many other measures besides were there adopted for the welfare of the Church, in the fore of which simoniacal heresy and the abomination of clerical marriage were forever condemned, over the signatures of the synod. That our lord archbishop, when he came home, did not keep silence about these evils is proved. As to women he ordained the same

---

[94] Most of the cessions may have been contemplated by Henry III, but actually they were not made until the next reign. Cf. ii.xlv(44), xlvi(45); Lappenberg, *Hamburgisches Urkundenbuch,* Vol. I, Nos. 87-89, 91, 94-95, 97.

[95] Count of Werl.

[96] Count of Brunswick and margrave of Meissen.

[97] Cicero *De finibus bonorum et malorum* ii.34.

[98] Leo IX spent some time at the court of his cousin, Conrad II, where Adalbert may have made his acquaintance.

[99] Correctly, his predecessor, Hunfrid. Adam may have used an official account of this synod, October, 1049.

policy[a] that his predecessor, the memorable Alebrand, and before him Lievizo[100] had inaugurated: namely, that they "be put out of the synagogue" and city,[101] that by their seductive presence the strumpets might not affront the chaste of vision. This synod was held in the year of our Lord one thousand and fifty-one.[102] That was the seventh year of the archbishop; then also was dedicated the main altar of the choir to the honor of the Mother of God.

xxxi (30). I purposely made mention of this synod because at a time when the Church counted men of such great distinction the lord Adalbert excelled nearly all, thanks to his wisdom and virtues. So much did he avail with the pope, so much with Caesar, that nothing was done in public matters without his counsel. On this account, while the emperor was making ready for wars, a business in which a cleric had hardly any proper part, he would not do without the man whose invincible counsel he knew from experience had often overcome his enemies. The shrewdest of the Italians, Duke Boniface,[103] was aware of this fact, likewise Godfrey,[104] Otto,[105] Baldwin,[106] and others who, filling the realm with tumult, apparently wore out Caesar by their troublesome rivalry. When at length they were humbled, they gloried in having been subdued by Adalbert's prudence alone.

xxxii (31). What shall I say about the barbarian peoples, the Hungarians and the Danes, also the Slavs, and certainly the North-

---

[a] Schol. 76 (77). Many times have we heard our most pious archbishop Adalbert say, when he exhorted his clerics in respect of the continence to be observed: "I warn you and, in requesting, command you to free yourselves from the pestiferous bonds of women, or if you cannot bring yourselves to what belongs to perfection, at all events preserve the marriage tie with modesty in accord with the saying, "If you are not chaste, at least be cautious." *

* The origin of this saying defies discovery.

[100] Cf. ii.lxxxi(77); Schol. 42(43) and 53(54) above.
[101] John 9:22.
[102] The seventh year of Adalbert is 1049. Adam miscalculated the date of the synod.
[103] Margrave of Tuscany.
[104] Duke of Upper Lorraine.
[105] Doubtless Otto of Nordheim, duke of Bavaria.
[106] Baldwin V, count of Flanders.

men,[107] whom the emperor reduced by counsel oftener than by war? By the advice and the management of our archbishop he learned a noble lesson, how

to spare

The humbled and to tame in war the proud.[108]

To this our store of good fortune there was added the fact that when the most valiant emperor of the Greeks, Monomachus,[109] and Henry[110] of the French sent gifts to our Caesar, they congratulated the archbishop for his wisdom and fidelity and for the happy conduct of affairs through his counsel. The latter, in replying then to the Constantinopolitan, took pride among other things in being descended from Greek stock, since Theophano and the most valorous Otto were the founders of his line.[111] And for this reason it was not surprising that he loved the Greeks, whom he wished to imitate also in dress and deportment; and this he also did. He dispatched letters of similar purport to the king of France and to others.

xxxiii (32). Elated by his success in these affairs and because he beheld the pope and Caesar disposed to do his will, the metropolitan worked with great zeal to establish a patriarchate in Hamburg.[112] To this purpose he was first of all directed of necessity, because the king of the Danes, now that Christianity had been spread to the ends of the earth, desired to have an archbishopric erected in his own kingdom. For carrying this design into effect—

---

[107] Henry III is not known to have had any dealings of the kind implied by Adam with the Norwegians. Our author may have had the Normans of southern Italy in mind. On the whole Adalbert's rôle in the emperor's foreign affairs seems much exaggerated. For the other peoples, cf. iii.vi, xviii(17) above, xliii(42) below.

[108] Vergil *Aeneid* vi.854.

[109] Constantine IX (1042-54).

[110] Henry I (1031-60).

[111] "The latter" refers to Emperor Henry III, who was the grand-grand-grand nephew of Otto II and Empress Theophano.

[112] The pseudo-Isidorian decretals required at least eleven or twelve suffragan sees to warrant the establishment of an archiepiscopate. The plan presented here belongs to a later stage of Adalbert's thinking. Cf. iii.lix(58); Dehio, *Hamburg-Bremen,* I, 207-10; Hauck, *Kirchengeschichte Deutschlands,* III, 658-64; "Decreta Annitici de ordinatione archiepiscoporum," in Hinschius, ed., *Decretales Pseudo-Isidorianae,* pp. 120-21; "Decreta secunda Pelagii," *ibid.,* p. 724.

it was near the point of being sanctioned by authority of the Apostolic See, since canonical decretals were in concurrence—only the word of our prelate was still awaited. He promised, albeit unwillingly, that he would give his consent to this proposal provided that patriarchal rank were conceded to him and his Church by Roman privileges. To this patriarchate he proposed to subject twelve bishoprics, which he would carve out of his own diocese, besides the suffragan bishops that our Church had in Denmark and over other peoples, in such wise that the first would be in Pahlen on the Eider River, the second in Heiligenstedten, the third in Ratzeburg, the fourth in Oldenburg, the fifth in Mecklenburg, the sixth in Stade, the seventh in Lesum, the eighth in Wildeshausen, the ninth in Bremen, the tenth in Verden, the eleventh in Ramelsloh, the twelfth in Frisia. For he boasted more than once that he could easily acquire the bishopric of Verden.[113]

xxxiv (33). In the meantime, during protracted negotiations on both sides, the most holy pope Leo departed this life and in the same year the most valiant emperor Henry died.[114] Their passing occurred in the twelfth year of the archbishop. Not only was the Church thrown into confusion by their deaths, but the state also appeared to have come to an end. And so with our pastor intent only on the affairs of the court, all kinds of disasters befell our Church from that time on.[115] A woman and a boy[116] succeeded in the conduct of the realm to the great detriment of the Empire. For the princes, indignant both at being constrained by the authority of a woman and over the rule of a child king, at first as a group arrogated to themselves their former freedom not to lend obedience. Then they proceeded to quarrel among themselves over "which of them should seem to be the greater."[117] Finally, they boldly took

[113] Cf. Schmeidler, *Hamburg-Bremen*, pp. 183-84.
[114] Leo IX died April 19, 1054, and Henry III two years later, October 5, 1056, respectively in the eleventh and fourteenth years of Adalbert's episcopate.
[115] Cf. Sallust *Catiline*, xxxix.4.
[116] Agnes, daughter of Count William of Poitou, was regent for the young King Henry IV until her removal from the regency in 1062.
[117] Luke 22:24; Mark 9:33.

up arms and attempted to depose their lord and king. But all this can better be seen with the eyes than written with the pen.

When rebellion at length gave way to peace, archbishops Adalbert and Anno were declared consuls, and the general welfare thereupon depended on their judgment.[118] Although both were prudent men and vigorous in the administration of public affairs, the one nevertheless apparently far surpassed the other in his good fortune and industry.

[Consequently, the feigned fellowship of the bishops lasted but a short time; however much the words of each seemed to sound peace, their hearts nevertheless battled with each other in mortal hatred. The bishop of Bremen, indeed, assumed the more righteous cause, in that he was more inclined to mercy[119] and declared that fidelity to the king and lord must be observed even unto death. But the bishop of Cologne, a man of atrocious disposition, was even charged with having betrayed his trust with respect to the king; furthermore, he was always the central figure in all the conspiracies that were hatched in his time.][120]

xxxv (34). For the archbishop of Cologne, who was noted for his avarice, devoted everything he could lay hands on either at home or at court to the embellishment of his Church. Although this Church had been great before, he made it so far the greatest that now it passed out of comparison with all the other churches of the realm. He exalted also his relatives and friends and chaplains, bestowing on them all the principal posts of honor that they might help others who were less powerful. Of these the foremost were his brother, Archbishop Werinhar of Magdeburg, and their nephew Burchard, bishop of Halberstadt; similarly, Kuno, who was elected

---

[118] Not until June 27, 1063, at Allstedt. Oddly enough, Adam does not mention the abduction of the boy king from his abode at St. Suitberts below Düsseldorf to Cologne in May, 1062, by Anno. Archbishop Anno had conspired with Otto of Nordheim and Egbert of Brunswick. Their strategy apparently was that the prelate in whose jurisdiction the king happened to reside should be the regent. Adalbert must, then, have been very active to become consul a year after the abduction.

[119] Cf. Prov. 22:9.

[120] The text in brackets occurs in codices of the *B* and *C* families. It will be noted that the next chapter begins as if there had been no interpolation.

archbishop of Trier, but who was crowned with martyrdom by the ill will of the clergy before he was enthroned; likewise, Egilbert of Minden and William of Utrecht. In Italy, furthermore, the bishops of Aquileia and of Parma,[121] and others whom it would take too long to enumerate, were exalted by Anno's efforts and favor, and they too strove to further their patron's undertakings with aid and whatever was appropriate. We have learned, however, that this man did many splendid things in the divine and human order.

xxxvi (35).   But our metropolitan, striving only for earthly fame and glory,[122] thought it improper to elevate anyone associated with him. Although he drew many needy persons into his following, he regarded it as something of a reflection on himself for either the king or any of the great to favor them. As he put it, "I myself can reward these people as well or better." Therefore only a few among his following attained to the heights of the episcopate through his favor. Many, however, if only they were apt of speech or adroit at service,[a] were showered with enormous riches. Hence it was that, to catch at worldly glory, he took into his confidence men of various kinds and of many arts, but chiefly flatterers. He drew their burdensome throng along with him to court and through the diocese or wherever else he journeyed, protesting that he was not only not put to inconvenience by the great multitude of traveling companions but even found it diverting. The money he received from his people or from friends or also from those who frequented

[a] Schol. 77 (78). Among them was the foreigner Paul, a convert from Judaism to the Christian faith, who had, I do not know whether out of avarice or out of a desire for knowledge, wandered into Greece. When he returned thence, he attached himself to our prelate. He boasted that he was so adept at many arts that he could in the course of three years make learned men of persons ignorant of letters and render fine gold from copper. He easily persuaded the archbishop to believe everything he said, topping all his lies with the statement that he would soon have the public money at Hamburg coined of gold and bezants paid out instead of denarii.

[121] Probably Ravenger and Eberhard, bishops respectively of Aquileia and Parma.
[122] Cf. Sallust *Jugurtha* cxiv.2. This chapter opens the second part of this book, in which Adam stresses the flaws in Adalbert's character that led to his fall and consequent misfortunes.

the palace or who were answerable to his royal majesty, that money, I say, even though it amounted to a very large sum, he promptly dispersed to disreputable persons and hypocrites, healers and actors and others of that sort. Unwisely, to be sure, he thought that the favor of such persons would either make him the only one accepted at court or give him preferment before all as the first lord of the palace, and that in this way he might accomplish what he had in mind about the advancement of his Church. When, moreover, he adopted as his vassals all the honorable and distinguished men in Saxony and in other parts by giving many of them what he had and by promising the rest what he did not have, he bought an empty title to vainglory at great loss to his body and soul. Indeed, the archbishop's manners, corrupted thus from the beginning, in the course of time and toward the end became ever meaner.

xxxvii (36). Puffed up, therefore, by the great honors then accorded him at court and now hardly tolerant of his destitute diocese, he came to Bremen with a great number of armed men, as was usual, and loaded new taxes on the people and country.[123] At this time were erected the strongholds which most of all fired our dukes to wrath.[124] He ceased to take the interest he previously had in establishing holy congregations. Marvelous, to be sure, were the man's strength of purpose and his impatience with idleness, which would never let him tire, though he was occupied at home and abroad with so many tasks. Although this wretched bishopric had often before been in distress because of the enormous costs of his expeditions and his extraordinary activities at a ravenous court, it was now unmercifully impoverished for the building of canonries and strongholds. He even planted gardens and vineyards on arid land. Although he put ineffectual effort into many things he tried, it was nevertheless his desire to reward magnificently the labor of all who gratified his wishes. Thus the man's lofty mind contended

---

[123] Probably in the fall of 1063, on his return from the Hungarian expedition. The following January Adalbert was at the court again.

[124] Probably in the course of 1063. They were leveled again within the next two years. Cf. iii.xliv(43) above.

against the nature of the land. There was nothing splendid anywhere which, if he got knowledge of it, he did not also wish to
possess himself. From a long and careful probing into the causes
of his distemper, I have concluded that this knowing man was
brought to this weakness of spirit[125] by the worldly glory which he
esteemed too highly. It was that which, when his worldly enterprises prospered, lifted him up to a pride whose quest for glory
knew no bounds but which in times of adversity depressed him more
than it should and gave free rein to his anger or worry.[126] And so,
in what is good, when he was compassionate, as well as in what is
bad, when he was in a passion—in both he exceeded measure.

xxxviii (37). In proof of this statement I present the fact that
in his fierce anger[127] he struck some persons with his hand so that
blood came, as he did in the case of the provost[128] and others. But
in his compassion, which in this case is better called prodigality,
he was so profuse that—in his estimation a pound of silver was like
a penny—at times he ordered a hundred pounds lavished upon
ordinary persons, and more upon those of greater importance.
Hence it happened that whenever he was angry, everyone fled him
as if he were a lion, but when he was calm he could be caressed like a
lamb. Very quickly, also, could either his friends or strangers by
praising flatter him out of a rage into cheerfulness and then, as if
changed from the man he had been, he started smiling upon his
panegyrist. We often saw the opportunity to do this seized by the
sycophants who flowed from different parts of the earth into his
quarters as into a cesspool.[129] In his judgment princes needed such
men in order to obtain the esteem of the world. The moment
anyone was better known at court or to the king, he was honored
by being received into the circle of his intimates; the rest he let go
away with presents. The ambition to be on intimate terms with him

---

[125] Sallust *Catiline* lii.28.
[126] Lucan *Civil War* vii.124.
[127] Cf. Sallust *Catiline* ix.4; Lam. 2:3.
[128] Probably the Suidger mentioned in iii.lvii(56) below.
[129] Sallust *Catiline* xxxvii.5.

lured even respectable persons and men conspicuous in the priestly order to this most disgraceful business of flattery. Finally, we have seen one who did not know how to flatter, or perhaps would not, shut out of doors as if he were witless or stupid. It was one might say:

> Let him who would be just from court depart[130]

and

> Informer will he be who speaks the truth.[131]

Liars at last prevailed so much among us that they who spoke the truth would not be believed even under oath.[132] With persons of this sort, then, was the bishop's house filled.

xxxix (38). In addition to these persons there came daily other mountebanks, parasites, interpreters of dreams, and newsmongers who gave out that the stories they had made up and trumpeted to us for the sake of winning favors had been revealed to them through angels. Already they publicly prophesied that the patriarch of Hamburg—for such he preferred to be called—would soon become pope, that his rivals would be driven from court, even that he would for a long time govern the state by himself, and that he would live to so ripe an age that he would exceed fifty years in the episcopate; finally, that through this man a golden age would come upon the earth.[133] Although, indeed, these predictions had been fabricated by the sycophants and were put forth for the sake of gain, the bishop for all that thought everything was true, as if it had been cried down from heaven, and he drew from the Scriptures that certain signs about things that were to happen were given to men either in dreams or omens or everyday conversational expressions or unusual manifestations of the elements. Therefore, he is said to have formed the habit of being entertained with fables when he went to bed, with the interpretation of dreams when he awakened, even of taking the auspices whenever he undertook a journey. At

---

[130] Lucan *Civil War* VIII.493-94.
[131] Juvenal *Satires* I.161.
[132] Cf. Jerome *Epist.* vi (Migne, *PL*, XXII, 337).
[133] Cf. Vergil *Aeneid* VI.793-94; VIII.324-25.

times, also, he gave up a whole day to sleep and kept vigil during the night, either playing at dice or sitting at table. When, however, he reclined at table, he commanded everything to be set before his guests in cheerful abundance. Now and then he himself got up from the repast without having eaten, but he always had some persons at hand whose duty it was to receive the guests as they arrived, taking particular care that they did not lack anything. Hospitality he furthermore extolled as a virtue of the highest order, which, though it is not without its divine reward,[134] often also wins the greatest possible applause among men. As he reclined, however, he took pleasure not so much in food or drink as in witticisms or the histories of kings or the rare sayings of philosophers. But if he was by himself, which rarely happened, that he might be alone and without guests or royal legates, then he would waste his leisure[135] with fables and in reveries, always, however, with continent speech. Rarely did he admit minstrels whom, however, he considered needful at times in order to lighten his anxious cares. As for pantomimes, who made a practice of entertaining the common folk by obscene movements of their bodies, he drove them absolutely from his presence.[136] Physicians alone ruled with him. For others access was difficult. Only if a matter of grave importance required it were some laymen admitted. Hence it also came to pass that we saw the door of his chamber, which at first had been open to every stranger and pilgrim, later so closely guarded that legates on important business and persons of consequence in the world at times had to wait unwillingly a week before the doors.

xl (39). At dinner, furthermore, he had a way of criticizing eminent men, noting foolishness in some, avarice in certain others, reproaching many, too, for the meanness of their origin. But all he charged with infidelity, for the reason that they were ungrateful to him, who had lifted them out of the dunghill,[137] and to the king,

---

[134] Cf. Heb. 13:2.
[135] Lucan *Civil War* I.488; Sallust *Catiline* IV.1; Vergil *Aeneid* IV.271.
[136] Cf. Exod. 10:11; 23:31.
[137] Cf. Ps. 112:7; I Kings 2:8.

whom he himself alone loved, whose rule he alone evidently protected for the sake of what is right, not for the sake of his own
advantage. His proof of this was that whereas they, baseborn that
they were, were ravishing the goods of others, he, noble that he
was, was lavishing his own; this was the clearest indication of his
nobility. With defamatory invective of this sort he abused each
in turn, finally sparing no one if only he might exalt himself above
all. Briefly, therefore, one must say that for the mere sake of the
worldly glory in which he delighted this man forswore all the
virtues of which he was in the beginning possessed. Such traits of
his and many others of like nature were evinced at the time when
his superstition or his boasting or, I might better say, his thought-
lessness bore him much bad repute and the hatred of all mortals,
but especially that of the great nobles.

xli (40). Of these the most hostile both to him and to our
Church were Duke Bernhard and his sons. Their envy, enmity, and
hatred,[138] likewise also their plottings, reproaches, and calumnies
drew the archbishop headlong to make all those offensive remarks
of which we have spoken above and made him as it were insane,
as long as he appeared to be less than they and yielded to them.
Still he gave way at times of his own accord because of his priestly
office, wishing to overcome ill will with kindness and to render
good for evil.[139] But he labored in vain,[140] as all his efforts to mend
his ill-tied friendship with the dukes came to naught in every respect.
Baffled, finally, by the harassments of his persecutors and embit-
tered by sorrow over his afflictions,[141] he more than once cried out
with Elijah: "Lord God, [they have] thrown down thy altars, they
have slain thy prophets . . . and I alone am left, and they seek my
life, to take it away."[142] As for how unjustly our bishop suffered

---

[138] Cf. Einhard *Vita Karoli* xviii. Adam here recapitulates briefly events of the
years before 1059, narrated in III.xxxiv(33) above.
[139] Cf. Gen. 44:4 and elsewhere.
[140] Cf. Job. 9:29; 39:16.
[141] Cf. Ps. 106:39.
[142] I Kings 19:10.

such things,[143] it is enough to give here one example from which it can be seen that the friendship he maintained with the envious was of no use.

xlii (41). Spurred on by avarice, the duke moved against the Frisians because they did not pay the tribute they owed.[144] He came into Frisia accompanied by the archbishop, who went only for the sake of reconciling the mutinous folk with the duke. And since the duke was fond of Mammon, he demanded the total sum of the duty, and when he could in no wise be placated with seven hundred marks of silver, the people forthwith became barbarous and furiously enraged and " . . . rushed on the sword for freedom's sake."[145] Many of our men were then wounded, the rest saved themselves by flight. The camps of the duke and the archbishop were sacked. The Church lost much treasure there. Still the loyalty of friendship tested in danger gained us nothing with the duke and his followers, nor did it restrain them from their determination to persecute the Church. They say that the duke, apprehensive of the future, often declared with a sigh that his sons were by the fates destined to destroy the Church of Bremen. For in a dream[146] he saw bears and boars, then stags, and last of all hares going out of his chambers into the church. "The bears and boars," he said, "were our fathers, armed in their fortitude as with teeth. My brother and I are the stags, fitted out only with horns.[147] But our sons are the hares, of moderate strength and timid. For them I fear that in attacking the Church they will incur divine vengeance." With the solemn charge of the fear of God, therefore, he forewarned them not to plan anything impious against the Church and its pastor; to injure either her or him is perilous, because an assault on

---

[143] Cf. Luke 13:2.

[144] We have no record of tribute due the Saxon dukes from the Frisians before the time of Henry the Lion. Meyer von Knonau, *Jahrbücher,* I, 158, n.77.

[145] Vergil *Aeneid* VIII.648.

[146] For a like vision, see Gregory of Tours *Hist. Franc. epitomata per Fredigarium scholasticum* I.xii (Migne, *PL,* LXXI, 581-82).

[147] Cf. Matt. 8:26.

them falls ultimately upon Christ. These injunctions fell on deaf ears. Now let us see how vengeance immediately pursues the sinners.

xliii (42). Bernhard, the duke of the Saxons, died in the seventeenth year of our archbishop. Ever since the days of the elder Lievizo, for forty years,[148] indeed, he had vigorously administered the affairs of the Slavs and the Nordalbingians and our own. After his death his sons Ordulf and Hermann received their father's inheritance, which boded ill for the Church at Bremen. For they were mindful of the ancient though concealed hatred which their fathers had borne against that Church and made up their minds that vengeance was now openly to be wrought on the bishop and the whole vassalage of the Church. Indeed, while his father still lived, Duke Ordulf, attended by a hostile multitude, devastated, first, the bishopric of Bremen in Frisia and blinded the vassals of the Church;[149] then he ordered others, even legates sent to him to sue for peace, to be publicly whipped and shorn; lastly, he in every way assailed, plundered, struck, and insulted the Church and its ministers. Although the bishop was, as he ought to be, fired with ecclesiastical zeal at this treatment and visited the sword of anathema upon those who contemned him, and even referred the dispute to the royal court, he met with nothing but derision. For, as they say, the king, a mere boy, was at first also treated with derision by our counts. Accommodating himself to circumstances, therefore, the archbishop is said to have adopted Count Hermann[150] as a vassal in order to part the oath-bound brothers from each other. The archbishop made use of his knightly service at the time when he, as the king's tutor and chief counselor, set out on an expedition into Hungary, leaving the archbishop of Cologne to oversee the affairs of the kingdom. On having restored to his throne Solomon,

---

[148] Bernhard died June 26, 1059. He had ruled, as Adam reckons, from 1010; therefore, nearly fifty years. Cf. ii.xlvi(44) above.

[149] In 1058 or 1059. Cf. Meyer von Knonau, *Jahrbücher*, I, 158-60.

[150] Ordulf's younger brother.

whom Béla had expelled, our archbishop returned victorious from Hungary with the boy king.[151]

xliv (43). Then Count Hermann hoped for and solicited a large fief, which the bishop would not grant him. Immediately beside himself with rage,[152] he moved against Bremen with a large army. There he seized everything that came to hand, sparing only the church. All the herds of oxen and horses were taken as spoil. Going in like manner through the entire diocese, he left the men of the Church naked and in want. At that time, too, all the strongholds which the bishop, foreseeing the future, had built in different places were laid level with the ground.[153]

xlv (44). At that time the archbishop held the first place at court. When his charge against the count was heard, the latter was banished in accord with a decision of the palace, but after a year was pardoned through the king's clemency. Then the same Count Hermann and his brother, Duke Ordulf, made satisfaction to the Church for their offense by presenting it with fifty hides of land, and the land rested for a few days.[154]

Distressed at the desolation of the Church at Bremen, the king at that time sent it for consolation nearly a hundred vestments besides silver vessels, likewise books, candlesticks, and censers adorned with gold. These[155] are the gifts that the king sent for refurnishing Hamburg: three golden chalices in which there were ten pounds of gold, one chrismal vessel of silver, a silver shield gilded with gold, a psalter written in golden letters,[156] silver censers and candlesticks, nine royal dorsals, thirty-five chasubles, thirty copes, fourteen dalmatics and tunics, and many other things; also a reliquary-chest, whose cover was supposed to contain nine pounds

---

[151] In 1063. Cf. Meyer von Knonau, *Jahrbücher*, I, 344-48.

[152] Cf. Mark 3:21.

[153] Cf. III.xxxvii(36) above; Bernold, *Chronicon, an.* 1064 (*MGH, SS*, V, 428); *Chronicon breve Bremense, an.* 1064 (*MGH, SS*, VII, 392).

[154] In 1066. Cf. Judges 3:30 and elsewhere.

[155] This interpolation is not by Adam. Cf. Schmeidler, *Hamburg-Bremen*, p. 99.

[156] Before the Second World War in the Viennese Kgl. Hofbibliothek, No. 1861. Cf. Schmeidler, *Adam*, p. 187 n.6.

of gold. The monasteries of Lorsch and Corvey, for which the archbishop had long striven hard, also are said to have been at that time conveyed to the Church at Hamburg by privileges.[157] Then, too, Lesum, which had long been desired,[158] came under the jurisdiction of the Church. That estate, they say, appears to have comprised seven hundred hides of land and held possession of the coastal territory of Hadeln. To make this cession surer by freeing it of every obligation, the archbishop is said to have given Queen Agnes nine pounds of gold, because she averred that its revenues had been assigned as a portion of her widow's estate. The archbishop held fifty royal estates, of which the largest, Altenwalde, rendered one month of service; whereas the smallest, Ambergen, rendered fourteen days. So great was the wealth of this bishop.

xlvi. (45). Our Church could be rich, our archbishop could not envy Cologne or Mainz in all the glory of their goods. There was only the bishop of Würzburg who is said to have had no rival in his bishopric: since he himself held all the counties of his diocese,[159] the bishop also possessed ducal authority over the province. Jealous of him, our prelate determined to bring under the authority of the Church every count who had any semblance of jurisdiction in his diocese. For this reason, indeed, he began by getting from Caesar the most important county of Frisia, that of Fivilgau, which Duke Godfrey had first held and now Egbert.[160] They say that the income amounts to a thousand pounds of silver, of which the count pays two hundred and is the vassal of the Church. Now this same county the archbishop had possessed for ten years, to the day of his expulsion. Another county was that of Udo, which was scattered here and there throughout the whole diocese of Bremen, mostly along the Elbe. For this the archbishop gave Udo precarial title to so

---

[157] Cf. III.xxviii(27) above; *Chronicon Laureshamense, an.* 1056 (*MGH, SS,* XXI, 413-14); *Lambert of Hersfeld, Annales, an.* 1063.

[158] As early as Alebrand's time. Cf. II.lxxx(76) above; Meyer von Knonau, *Jahrbücher,* I, 335.

[159] Only partly true.

[160] Cf. III.viii, xxviii(27) above; Lappenberg, *Hamburgisches Urkundenbuch,* Vol. I, No. 79, dated 1057.

much of the property of the Church as was estimated to yield annually a thousand pounds of silver.[161] Although in any case greater benefit to the Church than merely gaining worldly glory might have been secured each year from so large a sum of money, the gift did give us the occasion to be paupers in order to have many rich persons in our service. In the neighborhood of our diocese there was in Frisia a third county, called the Emsgau.[162] Gottschalk[163] was slain by Count Bernhard in maintaining the rights of our Church to this county. For this territory our archbishop agreed to pay the king a thousand pounds of silver. Since he could not easily raise this sum of money, he ordered—alas!—the crosses, the altars, the coronary candelabra, and other ornaments of the church to be taken down. By the sale of these objects he hastened the execution of this unhappy agreement. He protested, however, that he would soon make the church over in gold instead of in silver and that he would restore tenfold everything he had taken away, even as it appears he had previously done in the case of the monastery he had pulled down. Oh, the sacrilege! Two crosses of gold adorned with gems, a main altar and chalice, both radiant with gold and set with costly stones, were broken up. The wieght of the gold in them amounted to twenty marks. The lady Emma had given it to the church at Bremen along with numerous other gifts.[164] The goldsmith who melted them down said that he had to his great sorrow been forced to this sacrilege, the breaking up of those crosses. Privately he told some people that in the clanging of his hammer he had heard what sounded like the voice of the craftsman moaning. Then and in such a manner were the treasures of the church at Bremen, collected by the men of old and with the utmost effort for their time and with the great devotion of the faithful, in one miserable hour reduced for nothing. Still

[161] *Ibid.,* Vol. I, No. 89, dated 1063.
[162] By the same document cited in Note 160 above.
[163] Gottschalk, not otherwise identifiable, doubtless was killed after Adalbert's fall in 1066.
[164] Cf. II.lxvii(65), Schol. 47(48) above.

hardly half of what was owing was paid with this money. We have heard that the gems that had been taken from the holy crosses were presented by certain persons to courtesans.

xlvii (46). I confess that I shudder to reveal everything as it happened, for the reason that these were only the first stages of our sorrows,[165] and grave vengeance followed. From that day, therefore, our good fortune changed to ruin, everything turned out adversely for us and the Church, so that every one hissed our bishop and his followers as they would heretics. But he paid little attention to what all were saying. At the same time, also, he gave up looking after his domestic concerns. He passionately devoted his whole being to the court and rushed headlong[166] after glory for the reason he himself gave: that he was striving for primacy in the control of the affairs of state[167] because he could not bear to see his lord and king fall captive into the hands of those by whom he was being plundered. He had already attained the consulship. With his rivals removed, he alone now held the citadel of state, yet not without the envy that always follows hard upon glory.[168] At this time our metropolitan is also said to have contemplated the renewal of a kind of golden age in his consulate, by extirpating from the city of God all who work iniquity,[169] evidently those especially who had laid hands on the king or had plundered the churches. Since nearly all the bishops and princes of the realm were afflicted with guilty consciences, they were unanimous in their hatred and conspired to destroy him so that the rest should not be imperiled.[170] They all met together therefore, at Tribur and, since they had the support of the king's presence, drove our archbishop from court as if he were a magician and seducer.[171] So much was his hand

---

[165] Cf. Mark 13:8; Matt. 24:8.
[166] In 1065. Cf. Juvenal *Satires* vi.648-49; Lucan *Civil War* ix.122; Lambert of Hersfeld, *Annales, an.* 1062.
[167] Sallust *Catiline* lii.6, *Jugurtha* lxxxv.47.
[168] Sallust *Jugurtha* lv.3.
[169] Cf. Ps. 5:7, 13:4, and elsewhere.
[170] Cf. John 11:50.
[171] January 13, 1066. Cf. *Annales Weissemburgenses, an.* 1066 (*MGH, SS,* VI, 71); Meyer von Knonau, *Jahrbücher,* I, 487-91.

"against all men, and all men's hands against him"[172] that the end
of the controversy[173] reached the point of bloodshed.

xlviii (47).   Now, when our dukes heard that the archbishop
had been expelled from the senatorial order, they were filled with
great joy and thought that the time to take vengeance on him was
also at hand, to deprive him of his bishopric altogether, declaring,
"Raze it, even to the foundation thereof," and cut him "off out
of the land of the living."[174] Thus, many were their plots, many
their taunts against the archbishop, who, because he had no safer
place, stayed then in Bremen as if he were besieged and hemmed
in by a watchful enemy. Although all the duke's vassals derided
the pastor and the Church and the people and the sanctuary, still
Magnus[175] raged more than all the others and boasted that the
taming of the rebel Church had been at length reserved for him.

xlix (48).   And so the duke's son, Magnus, collected a multitude
of brigands and undertook to attack the Church, not in the manner
in which his forebears had operated but by attacking the person of
the pastor of the Church. Evidently to put an end to the long-
drawn-out contest he sought either to maim the bishop in his
members or utterly to destroy him. The latter, nevertheless, did
not lack craft[176] in protecting himself, but he got absolutely no aid
from his vassals. As he was at that time hard pressed by Duke
Magnus, the archbishop secretly fled by night to Goslar and stayed
there half a year in the security of his estate of Lochtum. His
stronghold and revenues were plundered by the enemy. Caught in
this distressful noose, the archbishop concluded what was in truth
an ignominious but necessary alliance with his oppressor, thus
turning his enemy into his vassal. The archbishop presented him
in benefice with over a thousand hides of church lands—on the
condition, to be sure, that Magnus was without all subterfuge to

[172] Gen. 16:12.
[173] Cf. Heb. 6:16.
[174] Ps. 136:7. Cf. Isa. 53:8, 10; Jer. 11:19.
[175] The son of Ordulf, who did not become duke until after his father died,
March 28, 1072.
[176] Cf. Sallust *Catiline* xxvi.2.

revindicate and defend the rights of the Church to the counties of Frisia, of which Bernhard retained one and Egbert another against the bishop's will.[177] Thus, in fine, was the bishopric of Bremen divided into three parts. Since Udo held one part and Magnus another, barely a third remained to the archbishop. For all that, he later apportioned this third part among Eberhard[178] and other sycophants of the king, keeping almost nothing for himself. The episcopal estates and the tithes of the churches,[a] from which the clergy, the widows, and the needy ought to have been supported, all now fell to the use of laymen,[179] so that to this day courtesans and brigands live luxuriously on the goods of the Church, the while holding the bishop and all the ministers of the altar in derision. From these great gifts, as can today be seen, this alone accrued to the archbishop: Udo and Magnus refrained from expelling him from his bishopric; the others, indeed, gave him nothing by way of service except the empty title of "lord."

1 (49). This was the first calamity to overtake us in the diocese of Bremen. But great vengeance also reached across the Elbe because Prince Gottschalk was at this time slain by the pagans whom he was trying to convert to Christianity. And, indeed, the forever memorable man had turned a great part of Slavia to the divine religion. But because as yet "the iniquities of the Amorrhites are not at the full"[180] nor "the time to have mercy on them yet come,"[181] it "must needs be that scandals come,"[182] that they "also, who are approved may be made manifest."[183] Our Maccabee suffered on the seventh day before the Ides of June in the city of

---

a Schol. 78 (79). A tithe of all the bishop's living and service was, according to law, daily rendered to his chaplain for the support of the infirm and the needy and for the care of pilgrims. But the chaplain fraudulently kept back much for his own use, reserving nothing for the poor.

---

177 Cf. III.xxviii(27) above.
178 Probably count of Nellenburg.
179 Cf. Lev. 23:20.
180 Gen. 15:16.
181 Cf. Ps. 101:14.
182 Matt. 18:7.
183 I Cor. 11:19.

Lenzen with the priest Yppo, who was immolated at the altar, and many others, both lay and cleric, everywhere underwent diverse tortures for the sake of Christ. The monk Ansver[184] and with him others were stoned at Ratzeburg. Their passion took place on the Ides of July.[a]

li(50). The aged bishop John[b] was taken with other Christians in the city of Mecklenburg and held for a triumph. And because he confessed Christ he was beaten with cudgels and then was led in mockery through one city of the Slavs after another. Since he could not be turned from the profession of Christ, his hands and feet were lopped off and his body was thrown upon the road. Cutting off his head, the barbarians fixed it on a spear and offered it to their god Redigast in token of their victory. These things were done in the chief city of the Slavs, Rethra, on the fourth day before the Ides of November.[185] The daughter of the king of the Danes[186] was found with her women at Mecklenburg, the city of the Abodrites, and was sent away naked. For, as we said before, she was the wife of Prince Gottschalk, who also had a son, Henry,[187] by her. Of another woman was born Butue:[188] the two were begot to the great destruction of the Slavs.[189] When, indeed, the Slavs had achieved victory, they ravaged the whole of the region of Ham-

---

[a] Schol. 79 (80). When he went to his passion, the same Ansver is said to have implored the pagans to stone first his associates, who, he feared, would fail. When these had been crowned as martyrs he joyfully bent his knee as had Stephen.*
* Cf. Acts 7:57-59.

[b] Schol. 80 (81). This John, who had out of his love for roving come from Scotia to Saxony, was kindly received by our archbishop,† as were all, and was not long after sent by him into Slavia to the prince Gottschalk. In the days he was with Gottschalk he is said to have baptized many thousands of pagans.
† Cf. ii.xxi(20) above.

---

[184] *Boll. Acta SS.,* July IV, 97-108. Gottschalk's martyrdom took place June 7, 1066; Ansver's, July 15, 1066.

[185] John's martyrdom (November 10, 1066) is also recounted thus in northern sources. Maurer, *Bekehrung des norwegischen Stammes,* II, 584-85.

[186] Sigrid, daughter of Svein Estrithson. Cf. iii.xix(18) above.

[187] Adam must have written in a prophetic mood, because Henry fled into Denmark soon after 1066 and did not return to Slavia until 1093.

[188] Cf. *Helmold* I. xxii-xxiv,xxvi (Tschan, tr.)

[189] Cf. Luke 2:24.

burg with fire and sword.[a] Nearly all the Sturmarians were either killed or led into captivity. The stronghold of Hamburg was razed to the ground, and even crosses were mutilated by the pagans in derision of our Savior. There was fulfilled for us the prophecy which runs, "O God, the heathen are come into thy inheritance; they have defiled thy holy temple,"[190] and the other sayings which prophetically bewail the destruction of the city of Jerusalem. The perpetrator of this desolation is said to have been Blusso, who was married to Gottschalk's sister and who, on returning home, was himself murdered. And so all the Slavs, sworn to a general conspiracy, lapsed again into paganism[b] after they had killed those who persisted in the faith. In vain did our Duke Ordulf fight the Slavs time and again during the twelve years that he survived his father.[191] Never could he obtain a victory, and because he was so often beaten by the pagans even his own men derided him. The expulsion of the archbishop and the death of Gottschalk took place almost within a year, that is, the prelate's twenty-second.[192] And, unless I am mistaken, a fearful comet[193] which appeared that year about Easter time was a foretoken of the misfortunes about to come upon us.

lii (51).   At that same time also there occurred in England a memorable battle. Its importance and the fact that England had from of old been subject to the Danes do not permit us to pass over the gist of the events. When, after the death of Edward,[194] the most saintly king of the English, the princes contended for that

    [a] Schol. 81 (82). At this same time Schleswig, a city of the Transalbingian Saxons situated on the confines of the Danish kingdom, as very rich as it was very populous, was entirely destroyed by an unexpected incursion of the pagans.
    [b] Schol. 82 (83). This is the third apostasy of the Slavs, who had first been made Christians by Charles* the second time by Otto, the third time, now, by the prince Gottschalk.
    * Charles in fact did not convert the Slavs.

---

    [190] Ps. 78:1.
    [191] For language, cf. Lucan *Civil War* vii.602. Ordulf died March 28, 1072.
    [192] Gottschalk died April 15, 1066, in Adalbert's 24th year.
    [193] Later known as Halley's comet. Meyer von Knonau, *Jahrbücher,* I, 523, n. 55.
    [194] Edward the Confessor; died January 5, 1066.

realm, a certain English duke, Harold,[195] a man given to magic, usurped the scepter. And as his brother, named Tostig, set out to take it away from him, he drew to his aid Harold,[196a] the king of the Norwegians, and the king of the Scots. But Tostig himself was killed, as were the king of Hibernia[197] and Harold, together with all their army, by the king of the English.[198] Scarcely, they say, had eight days passed and, behold, William, who on account of his illegitimate descent bore the byname "the Bastard," sailed over from Gaul to England and waged war against the exhausted victor. In this war the English were at first victorious, then were defeated by the Normans and completely prostrated.[199] Harold was slain there, and besides him nearly a hundred thousand of the English. The victorious Bastard avenged God, Whom the English had offended, by expelling nearly all the clerics and monks who lived out of conformity with the rule. After doing away with these scandals, he established the philosopher Lanfranc in the Church as teacher.[200] Through his zeal, both before in Gaul and afterwards in England, many were inspired to adopt the godly way of life.

liii (52). In Sweden the most Christian king Stenkil died at that time.[201] After his passing two Erics[202b] struggled for the

a Schol. 83 (84). This Harold, king of the Norwegians, had three hundred warships, of which all were left there. In addition, a mass of gold that Harold had brought from Greece passed by this windfall into the Bastard's hands. The gold was so heavy that twelve young men could hardly lift it to their shoulders.

b Schol. 84 (85, 86). After the two Erics were killed in battle, Alstan, the son of Stenkil, was raised to the throne. When he was presently deposed, Inge* was summoned from Russia, and when he too was removed, the Swedes elected a certain Haakon.† He married the young Olaf's mother.‡

* Adam calls him Anunder, but he is the Inge of the northern sources, Alstan's brother. He was expelled between 1075 and 1080 because he refused to worship the pagan gods.

† Haakon the Red.

‡ Olaf Kyrre of Norway, son of Harold Hardrada. The matter of Haakon's marriage to Olaf's mother is confused but probably correct. Olaf Kyrre married Svein Estrithson's daughter, Ingerid, in 1068. But see Schmeidler, *Hamburg-Bremen* pp. 311-12.

195 Son of Godwin. Cf. George, *Genealogical Tables,* No. 2.
196 Harold Hardrada.
197 Perhaps the King of the Scots, who so far remains unidentified.
198 At Stamford Bridge, September 25, 1066.
199 At Hastings, October 14, 1066.

throne, and all the Swedish nobles are said to have fallen in the fighting. The two kings also perished then. In fact, with the failure of all the royal stock[203] the order of the kingdom was altered and Christianity there was seriously disturbed. The bishops whom the metropolitan had consecrated for that country stayed at home in fear of persecution. Only the bishop of Scania[204] attended the churches of the Goths, and a certain Swedish chief, Gniph, fortified the people in Christianity.

liv (53). The most illustrious king among the barbarians at that time was Svein of the Danes,[a] who held the kings of the Norwegians, Olaf and Magnus,[205][b] in leash by his great valor. Between Svein and the Bastard[206] there was continual contention over England, even though our archbishop, persuaded by William's gifts, wished to make peace between the kings. Christianity was diffused far and wide among the farther peoples by this King Svein. Distinguished though he was by many virtues, he offended only by his luxury. In the last days of the archbishop, when I came to Bremen and heard of this king's wisdom, I at once resolved to go to him. And he also received me most graciously, as he did all, and from his lips I gathered much of the material for this little book. He was well versed in the knowledge of letters and very receptive toward strangers. He personally sent his priests out as preachers into all Sweden and Norway and to the islands

---

[a] Schol. 85 (86). But the king of the Norwegians married the daughter[*] of the king of the Danes and the kings made peace with each other.

[*] Ingerid.

[b] Schol. 86 (87). They were sons of Harold.

---

[200] Lanfranc became archbishop of Canterbury in 1070.

[201] In 1066 or shortly after, since he warned his bishops not to disturb the temple at Uppsala and of the conditions that had led to the Slavic disturbances of 1066. Cf. iv.xxx(29) below.

[202]. Nothing is known about them except that Adam called them kings. They doubtless represented the old paganism which Stenkil had tried to suppress.

[203] This statement is in part corrected by Schol. 84(85) above and 140(136) below.

[204] Egino, bishop of Dalby (1060-72). Cf. iv.viii-ix below.

[205] Olaf Kyrre of Norway and Magnus II of Sweden, sons of Harold Hardrada.

[206] Svein Estrithson and William the Conqueror. Some allowance must be made in this chapter, as well as elsewhere (cf. iii.xiii(12), xviii(17) above, for Svein's account of his past doings. Relations between the two kings were strained in 1069.

that are in those parts. From his veracious and very delightsome discourse I learned that in his time many among the barbarian nations had been converted to the Christian faith, that some men had also been crowned with martyrdom in Sweden as well as in Norway. "Of them, one Eric, a pilgrim," he said, "won the martyr's crown by having his head cut off while he preached in the farther parts of Sweden. Another, named Alfward, although he long lived a holy life in obscurity among the Norwegians, could not remain hid.²⁰⁷ While, then, he was protecting an enemy, he was killed by friends. At the resting places of these men great wonders of healing are even today manifested to the people." What we have said, therefore, and what we still have to say about the barbarians, all that we have come to know from what this man related.

lv (54). Driven as they say, from court by the jealousy of the bishop of Cologne, our archbishop in the meantime stayed at Bremen privately, all in solitude, and held his peace.²⁰⁸ Would, indeed, that he had enjoyed as much mental quiet as freedom from bodily exertion. Happy, I say, would he have been if, content with the household possessions of our Church and the ancestral riches of his parents, he had either never seen or rarely visited the unhappy court. Indeed, one reads about other great men who, despising the glory of the world, fled the royal court as if it were another kind of idolatry, doubtless judging that they had to turn from the turmoil of the world and the tumult of the palace to the contemplative leisure of the solitary life as to a haven and blessed refuge. But our prelate ran a contrary course. He considered it the duty of a wise man not only to keep up his exertions at court for the welfare of his Church but even, if it should prove necessary, not to hesitate to endure dangers and death. This, unless I am mistaken, is the reason why he frequented the king's court in his early days for the purpose of exalting his Church, but toward the end, when every-

²⁰⁷ Cf. Matt. 5:14; I Tim. 5:25.
²⁰⁸ Cf. Lam. 3:28.

thing he had was lost, or rather squandered, he worked to set his bishopric free. In this respect, as the former objective was prompted by ambition for glory, so the latter was demanded by the necessities of the Church, which, continually assailed by the ill will of the dukes of this land,[a] was now at length even reduced to nothing. This calamity of his times he mournfully deplored daily, and for this reason he had special psalms[209] designated by which he might take vengeance upon the enemies of the Church.

lvi (55).   As for the fact that he showed himself so hard hearted toward his diocesans, whom he should rather have loved, even as a shepherd should look after his sheep, he himself set forth a weighty reason, and we heard it from his own lips. Other reasons we learned from other persons. The archbishop's own brother—that is, the count palatine named Dedo—was murdered by a certain priest of his diocese the same year in which Caesar also died.[210] "He was a good and a just man,"[211] who himself neither gave offense to anyone nor permitted his brother to give offense. This characteristic appeared at the memorable man's end, for, as he was dying, he entreated the bystanders for the safety of his slayer; this he also demanded of his brother. In compliance with the wishes of the deceased, the latter did, indeed, let the priest go unpunished, but from that time on hated everyone in the service of the Church. It is said that another event that kindled this hatred took place when the prelate at some time had ordered a member of his vassalage, whose name I do not know, to be apprehended for acting too haughtily. The others were thereupon moved to frenzy and, armed, sought out the archbishop's bed chamber even to do

---

[a] Schol. 87 (88). Many times, too, he declared with tears that all his predecessors had been, as it were, boiled and fried over fire in the persecution of the dukes and the malice of the diocesans. "Hence I have no doubt," he said, "that I am also to be crowned with martyrdom by these same persons for the sake of the truth."

---

[209] Cf. iii.lxx(68) below.

[210] Dedo was murdered May 4, 1056, and the emperor Conrad died the next day. Cf. *Chronicon Gozec.* i.ix(*MGH, SS,* X, 144).

[211] Luke 23:50.

him violence if he did not release the person he was detaining. And infuriated they made other threats prompted by their anger. A third cause was the fact that the bishop, to save his own fortune, stayed away from home a whole year and often two. When, after a long time, he returned to his bishopric and took account of his vassals and stewards,[212] he found all his properties and incomes no less dissipated than they would have been if he had stayed at home. For "this people," as Sallust well describes them, is "fickle and untrustworthy . . . amenable neither to kindness nor to fear."[213] Their addiction to drink, a vice peculiar to these peoples, was, furthermore, so much abominated in them by the archbishop that he often used to say of them, their "God is their belly."[214] For the contentions and brawls,[215] the maligning and blaspheming, and whatever greater sins they committed while intoxicated, they made sport of the following day. He complained, also, that even to his own times many were so steeped in the delusions of pagans that they dishonored the sixth ferial day by eating meat; that they desecrated by debauchery and fornication the vigils and feasts of the saints and the venerable season of Lent; that they thought nothing of perjury; that they held the shedding of blood in esteem. Similarly, adultery, incest, and other kinds of uncleanness contrary to nature were condemned by scarcely any one of them. Many of them had two or three, even innumerable, wives at the same time. Likewise, they used the meat of animals that had died, and blood, and strangled beasts, and the flesh of draft animals as if it were lawful.[216] In the last place, the archbishop complained in the highest degree about the ill will they bore to strangers and about their still being more faithful to the duke than they were to him and to his Church. Although the metropolitan often denounced in church these and other popular transgressions in rhetorical sermons,

---

[212] Cf. Matt. 25:19.
[213] *Jugurtha* xci.7.
[214] Phil. 3:19.
[215] Titus 3:9.
[216] Cf. Lev. 11:11, 27, 17:15; Isa. 5:25; Acts 15:20, 29.

the people regarded his paternal reproofs with disdain, nor could they be turned or moved to have any reverence for the priests or for the churches of God. This state of affairs impelled the archbishop to decide that they as a people were stiff-necked,[217] neither to be spared nor trusted, declaring, therefore, "with bit and bridle bind fast their jaws."[218] And again, I will "visit their iniquities with a rod,"[219] and other sayings. And so, when he found occasion, if anyone of them committed an offense, he forthwith ordered him thrown into prison[220] or deprived of all his goods, asserting with a laugh that afflicting the body is good for the soul, that the loss of one's goods wipes away sins. Hence, it came to pass that the administrators, to whom he committed his office, were unbridled in their seizures and afflictions. And there was fulfilled the prophecy which runs: "I was angry a little, but they helped forward the evil . . . thus saith the Lord."[221]

lvii (56). The archbishop stayed at Bremen[222] at this time and, since he had nothing left, lived off the plundering of the poor and the property of the holy congregations. A servant of his, a certain Suidger, administered the principal provostship of the bishopric. When, after the property of the brethren had been squandered, this man was deposed for the murder of a deacon and, on being again restored, had nothing with which to render service to the brethren and his lord, he fled the archbishop's wrath, smitten with fear. And so the provostship, returned into the bishop's power, was then deplorably torn to pieces by vicars who sought the "things that are their own."[223] The several communities fared in like manner. While the bishop was angry with the provosts, they raged among the people and dissipated all the property of the Church. From this destruction escaped only the xenodochium

---

[217] Cf. Exod. 32:9, 33:3; Deut. 9:13 and elsewhere.
[218] Ps. 31:9.
[219] Ps. 88:33.
[220] Cf. Sallust *Catiline* xlii.3.
[221] Zach. 1:15-16.
[222] This chapter covers the years 1066-69.
[223] Phil. 12:42; I Cor. 13:5.

which, founded by Saint Ansgar and afterwards cared for by succeeding fathers, remained whole and entire until the last days of the lord Adalbert. But then, indeed, a certain episcopal vicar of our own, as it were a "faithful and wise steward," [224] was appointed to watch over the alms of the poor. I dare not say what a sin it is to defraud the poor of their substance, for some canons call it a sacrilege, others murder. This only is it allowable to say with the good leave of all the brethren: that in all the seven years which the archbishop still lived, absolutely no alms were dispensed from that famous and opulent hospital of the Church of Bremen. And this seemed the more lamentable and inhuman because a period of famine ensued and many poor people were found dead everywhere in the streets. While our pastor was so intent upon the court, his most holy vicars ravaged the Lord's sheepfold, going through the bishopric like wolves and sparing therein only places in which they found nothing to carry away.

lviii (57). At that time one might see the deplorable tragedy at Bremen in the distress of the citizens and the knights and the storekeepers, and, what was more serious, likewise in that of the clergy and of the nuns. To the guilty, indeed, misfortune evidently came with justice, that they might be rebuked, but to others not so. In the first place, then, if a rich man was reputed innocent, he was ordered to do something nearly impossible to make him guilty. If he ignored the order, or stoutly declared compliance with it to be impossible, he was immediately stripped of all his belongings. If he presumed to murmur, he was thrown into chains. One beheld some plied with the lash, many put in prison, [225] some driven from their homes, very many sent away into exile. And, as it happened when Sulla was victorious in the civil war, [226] one of the mighty, often without the archbishop's knowledge, condemned another whom he regarded as his enemy for a private grudge, as if on the archbishop's order. Then, indeed, as if no sex or class should be

[224] Luke 12:42.
[225] Cf. II Paral. 16:10.
[226] Cf. Sallust *Jugurtha* xli.8, xcv.3, 4; *Catiline* li.32-34.

immune from such wantonness, we also beheld even frail women stripped of their gold and garments, and the perpetrators of the infamous spoliation live with priests and bishops. Again, we learned that of those who were robbed of their property or who were too severely pressed by the quaestor, some were so much affected with anguish that they lost their minds; and some, formerly rich people, went begging from door to door.[227] Although this quest for plunder reached all who were subject to the bishop, it also did not pass by the merchants who resorted to Bremen from every part of the world with the usual wares of trade. The execrable imposts levied by the episcopal vicars compelled them all to leave, often without anything. And so it is plain why to this day the city lacks citizens and the market merchandise, especially since if anything of ours remained untouched it was altogether consumed by the duke's servants. Although all these outrages had often been perpetrated before even while the archbishop was present, they became intolerable when he was away and after the day of his expulsion.

lix (58). At the expense of much effort and the lavishing of many gifts to no purpose, the metropolitan at length accomplished his wish in being restored to his former place at court after he had been expelled for a period of three years.[228] Soon also, as his affairs prospered, he attained the height of power, that is the regency, after he had been seven times consul.[229] On gaining the position of dignity in which he could display the greatness of his soul, he resolved that now he must walk circumspectly[230] with respect to the princes, in order not to offend them as he had before. On this account he desired first to be reconciled with the bishop of Cologne, then with the others against whom he had sinned—or, rather, who plainly had sinned against him. After these hindrances

---

[227] Cf. Saint Jerome Ep. lx.16 (Migne, *PL,* XXII, 594).

[228] In 1069, and to the regency in 1071. Cf. Gen. 40:13; Meyer von Knonau, *Jahrbücher,* I, 630, n. 57, II, 71-72.

[229] Cf. Cicero *Pro Plancio* xxi; Lucan *Civil War* ii.130 (for Adam's classical allusions).

[230] Cf. Eph. 5:15.

had been removed, he was not idle in behalf of his Church, for the exaltation of which he seemed to be as wanton in the lavish expenditure of money as in his intrigues at court. At this time he acquired Plisna, Duisburg, Groningen, and Sinzig.[231] Wildeshausen, a provostship in the vicinity of Bremen, he almost had in his hands; also Harsefeld, very near Hamburg. Furthermore he also designed, if he had lived longer, to subject the bishopric of Verden to our metropolis. Finally, he now worked openly to establish a patriarchate at Hamburg,[232] and to do many other great and incredible things about which more than enough has been said above.

lx (59). The prelate's renown was enhanced by the fact that in the year in which he was consul that famous conference of Caesar with the king of the Danes was held at Lüneburg to embarrass the duke.[233] Military measures against the Saxons were there agreed upon under cover of an alliance. That same year the first conspiracy formed against the king was suppressed.[234] In consequence of this insurrection Duke Otto and Magnus,[235] after devastating Saxony for a year, at length surrendered themselves into the king's power on the advice of the prelate. The king gave Otto's duchy to Guelf; our archbishop recovered the property of the Church that Magnus previously held.[236]

lxi (60). Placed thus at the very pinnacle of glory, he would still not withdraw from the business of the state though he was often afflicted with bodily ills. From the Rhine to the Danube and thence back into Saxony he would go with the king,[237] carried

[231] Cf. III.xxviii(27) above; Lappenberg, *Hamburgisches Urkundenbuch*, Vol. I, Nos. 94-97.
[232] Cf. III.xxxiii(32) above.
[233] In 1071. Cf. Meyer von Knonau, *Jahrbücher*, I, 72-76, and n.62.
[234] Before the conference at Lüneburg.
[235] Doubtless Otto of Nordheim and Magnus of Saxony. Cf. III.xxxi(30) above.
[236] Christmas, 1070. Cf. *Annalista Saxo, an.* 1071 (*MGH, SS*, VI, 698); Lambert of Hersfeld, *Annales, an.* 1071.
[237] Henry IV, accompanied by Adalbert, spent Christmas, 1071, at Worms on the Rhine and moved thence to Regensburg on the Danube by way of Lorsch. From there they went to Utrecht by way of Goslar in Saxony for the conference held on Easter, 1072. Meyer von Knonau, *Jahrbücher*, II, 88, 116-21, 151.

on a litter. Some say it had been agreed, on the solemn promise of the king, that all the desires of the archbishop's soul[238] in respect of Lorsch and Corvey and other matters were to be confirmed for him at Utrecht on the Rhine when the princes met there the following Easter. Others assert that the archbishop was led on by crafty delays on the part of the king to accept in donation to his Church twice as much, wheresoever in the realm he wished, on condition, namely, that he would forego Lorsch. But he began to be obstinate, replying that he would have nothing else. In the end he sank, his efforts frustrated, losing both his life and Lorsch, along with the rest of the property of the Church.

lxii (61). Of his imminent death there were very many signs and forebodings, so dreadful and unusual that they terrified us and, apparently, the bishop himself; so striking and plain were they that anyone who considered at all closely his stormy ways and uncertain health would say that doubtless the end was at hand. Although, indeed, the man's behavior had always been different from the deportment of ordinary mortals, toward the end—especially after the day of his expulsion and after the devastation of his diocese, which attended it—his ways seemed altogether inhuman and intolerable and alien to himself. After that day, I say, he was more perturbed by shame, indignation, and grief than is seemly for a wise man, because he found no way of recovering the property of the Church. I dare not say he was insane from overmuch anxiety about his multifarious difficulties, but his mind was affected. At a distance, some of the things he did from this time on could indicate a wandering mind or foolishness; in my opinion, "the mad Orestes himself would swear" they "were the signs of madness."[239] For example, there is the fact, to which we have referred,[240] that he spent whole nights awake and whole days asleep. Moreover, he turned away from hearing the truth to

---

[238] Cf. I Kings 23:20.
[239] Persius *Satires* III.118.
[240] Cf. III.xxxix(38) above.

fables[241] and dreams; likewise, he slighted the alms for the poor and distributed everything he could get among the rich, particularly among sycophants; and again, there is the fact that there was nothing left because, after the property of the Church had been squandered, he lived off the plunder of the wretched and the lawful income of the holy congregations. Again, in making a tenancy of a provostship and a provostship of a hospital he was not unlike one "who tears down in order to build and exchanges the square with the round;"[242] again, provoked to anger more easily than was usual, he struck some with his hand until blood came; and in exasperating many with abusive words, he dishonored himself not less than them. Toward the end he was so entirely changed from his own self and so impaired of his former virtue that none of his associates, nor he himself, could fully make out what he wished or did not wish. Still, his eloquence was to the very end such that in hearing him speak one would be very quickly persuaded that everything he did was wholly reasonable and well judged.

lxiii (62). While reports of this sinister change, or aberration, and of the very evident degeneration of this distinguished man were being spread into every country of the world on the wings of his fame, his noted brother, namely, the count palatine Frederick, came, as I recall, as far as Lesum to caution him. But since his admonitions about matters that touched the bishop's honor or welfare proved vain, the count went away sad, accusing Notebald[a] and his sort of circumventing the illustrious man with their trickeries and of disordering his mind by their counsels. These were his words, but we saw the archbishop himself at that time sink so low in repute that he was said to have given himself up to the magic arts.[243] I call to witness Jesus and His angels and all

---

[a] Schol. 88 (89). Notebald was a magician, a flatterer, and a most brazen liar.

[241] Cf. II Tim. 4:4.
[242] Horace *Epistles* I.i.100.
[243] Cf. II Paral. 33:6.

His saints that the man was free and guiltless of this crime, especially since he himself often declared that magicians and fortune tellers and men of that sort must be punished with death. But because it is written, "With the holy, thou wilt be holy; with the perverse thou wilt be perverted,"[244] I am of the opinion that at first he lapsed from the accepted state of rectitude and then broke down altogether, either because of the malice of those who he believed were true to him or because of the molestation of the enemies who were assailing his Church. Broken at length by the violence of his disordered ways and battered at the same time by reverses in his outer fortunes, he began to weaken also in body like a ship buffeted by the seas.[245] And while he was trying to recover his health with the aid of physicians, his infirmity soon became so much more serious from his repeated trials of medicaments that, as he lay in a coma at the point of death, hope was given up.[246] At that time,[247] too, he suffered a severe fall from his horse as he was on his way to court.[a] With Hezekiah,[248] then, he wept with much weeping, promising God amendment of his life. Oh, the wonted clemency of Christ! He forthwith recovered. In the three whole years during which he still lived many, but not all, the promises he had made were fulfilled.

lxiv (63).   In those days there came up a certain woman who had the power of divination.[249] She publicly declared to all the people that the archbishop would pass away suddenly within two years unless, indeed, he was converted. Physicians attested that statement. But there were with the bishop others, false prophets, who made promises of a far different kind, and in them he had

---

[a] Schol. 89 (90). From that time he abstained from the reheated salt baths which he had been used to taking almost daily and from many other practices which he noticed were objectionable to the people.

[244] Ps. 17, 26, 27; II Kings 22:26-27.
[245] Cf. Juvenal *Satires* XIV.296.
[246] Cf. Lucan *Civil War* III.747; Lambert of Hersfeld, *Annales, an.* 1072.
[247] When he returned to court in 1069. Cf. III.lix(57) above.
[248] Cf. IV Kings 20:3; Isa. 38:3.
[249] Cf. Lev. 20:27; I Kings 28:7; Acts 16:16.

greater faith. They, in truth, foretold that he would live so long as to make all his enemies his footstool,[250] and that this bodily infirmity would then be followed by perfectly good health and much success in his affairs. The most intimate of all was Notebald who had often predicted for the archbishop many things that had turned out true, but who from the first word to the last deceived his believer. At that time[251] we saw in Bremen crosses sweating tears; we saw hogs and dogs desecrating the church so boldly that they could with difficulty be driven from the very foot of the altar. We saw wolves howling in packs in the suburbs of our city, vying with horned owls in horrific contest. And although the bishop eagerly heeded dreams, everyone pointed in vain to these signs as referring to him. The dead never spoke so intimately with the living. Everything foreboded the bishop's death.[252] Now, the same year in which the metropolitan died Hamburg was burned and twice pillaged. From that time on the victorious pagans had all Nordalbingia in their power and, as the fighting men had either been killed or led into captivity, the province was reduced to a wilderness,[253] so that you might say peace also was taken from the land at the good shepherd's end. Fourteen days before his death he lay down at Goslar[254] and, as was his way, would take neither potions nor bleedings. For that reason he was seized with a very severe spell of dysentery and worn down to the very bones. Alas, he still was entirely unmindful of his own salvation! He carried on the business of the state to his very dying hour. Werinhar, the archbishop of Magdeburg, and other brethren were at hand, asking to be admitted. How they had offended him I do not know. He ordered his doors closed to them on the plea that he was unfit

---

[250] Cf. Ps. 109:1; Matt. 22:24 and elsewhere.

[251] In 1072, after Adalbert's death. Cf. Vergil *Aeneid* 1.402, IV.462, XI.243, XII.862; *Georgics* 1.486. The winter of 1071-72 was severe. Norlind, "Einige Bemerkungen über das Klima der historischen Zeit," *Lunds Universitets Aarskrift*, Vol. X (1914), No. 1, p. 24.

[252] Cf. Vergil *Aeneid* 1.91.

[253] Cf. Meyer von Knonau, *Jahrbücher*, II, 148-49, 857-69.

[254] About March 2, 1072.

to be seen by anyone on account of the uncleanness of his sickness. Visiting the sick man was conceded only to the king whom he loved devotedly to the very end. Reminding him, therefore, of his fidelity and long service, the archbishop with much sighing commended his Church and the property of the Church to him.

lxv (64). Eventually the fateful day arrived, marked by Egyptian darkness,[255] on which the great prelate Adalbert was touched by the imminent call of bitter death. Even he sensed that the dissolution of his body was at hand, as much because of his want of strength as by his premonition of the indications described. But as the physicians hesitated to make the truth known[a] and only Notebald gave assurance of life, the knowing man lay uncertain and forgetful of self between the hope of living and the dread of dying.[256] Alas, he did not take notice that "The day of the Lord shall so come, as a thief in the night," and "When they shall say, peace and security; then shall sudden destruction come,"[257] and other passages in which the Gospels enjoin us to watch, as they say, "You know not the day nor the hour."[258] In this connection I recall the observation of a certain holy man, that I cannot without tears adapt to this place. "Now," he said, "the sinner is stricken, now he is forced to depart unrepentant so that dying he forgets himself, who while he lived had forgotten God."[259] In this manner did the glorious metropolitan, still hopeful of the present life, lie alone in his agony and breathe forth his spirit on

---

[a] Schol. 90 (91). Adamatus, a physician of Salernitan origin, is said to have informed the archbishop three days in advance that the day of his death was very near at hand. But he disregarded this warning and gave heed only to Notebald, because the latter promised him that the hour for his turning point would soon come.

---

[255] Since there was no eclipse on March 16, 1072, and since no other natural phenomenon is recorded, the expression must refer to the darkness of the ninth plague of Egypt. Exod. 10:21-22.

[256] Cf. Livy *History* viii.xiii; Vergil *Aeneid* i.218, iii.629, 631.

[257] I Thess. 5:2-3.

[258] Matt. 25:13.

[259] Pseudo-Augustine *Sermons* ccxx.2, cclvii.3 (Migne, *PL*, XXXIX, 2,153, 2,221).

the sixth ferial day, at noon,[260] as his friends sat down to eat,

> and with a moan
> Life passed indignant to the shades below.[261]

Alas, that I might write better things about so famous a man who loved even me and was so illustrious in his life. But I am afraid, because it is written, "Woe to you that call evil good;" also let them perish "that put darkness for light."[262a] It seems to me hazardous for us to have to flatter either in writing or in speech a man who was undone by adulation while he lived. Nevertheless, some assert that a few spectators were at hand as he lay thus alone. In their presence he did bitter penance in his last hour for all the vexation he had caused by his deeds. He wept and wailed that he had misspent his days[263] and then at last understood how petty, in reality how miserable, is the glory of our dust, "For all flesh is as grass; and all the glory thereof as the flower of grass."[264]

lxvi (65). Oh, how false is the good fortune of mortal life! How much to be shunned the courting of honors! Of what avail to you now,[265] O venerable father Adalbert, are the things you always prized, the glory of the world, multitudes of people, exalted nobility? Forsooth, you lie alone in your high palace, abandoned by all your followers. Where now are the physicians, the sycophants, and the tricksters who used to concur with you in the desires of your heart,[266] who swore you would recover from this sickness, who reckoned you would live to a ripe old age? As I see, they were all your companions at table and did not abide in the day

---

a Schol. 91 (92). As one reads in the book of Esther: "While with crafty fraud they deceive the ears of princes that are well meaning and judge of others by their own nature. Now, this is proved both from ancient histories and by things which are done daily, how the good designs of kings are depraved by the evil suggestions of certain men." *

* Esther 16:6-7.

---

260 Friday, March 16, 1072.
261 Vergil *Aeneid* XI.831, XII.952.
262 Isa. 5:20. Cf. Juvenal *Satires* III.30.
263 Suetonius *Titus* viii.
264 I Peter 1:24. Cf. Ecclus 14:18; Jas. 1:10.
265 Cf. Lucan *Civil War* IV.799, 803.
266 Cf. Ps. 10:3; Jer. 2:24.

of distress.[267] There are left only the needy and the pilgrims, the widows and the orphans, and all the oppressed to confess that they have been desolated by your death. With them we also can truthfully affirm that no one henceforth will compare with you in benignity and generosity toward pilgrims, in the defense of the holy churches, and in reverence for all the clergy, or in withstanding so much the plundering of evildoers of might and the presumptions of the proud; and, finally, that no one may be found readier with all manner of counsel in the wise disposition of divine and human affairs. If, indeed, anything appears reprehensible in your ways, that is due to the wickedness of those in whom you trusted more than was right or to those whose enmity you bore for the sake of the truth. For by their plottings they perverted your laudable character, making of a good nature one that was bad. It behooves us, therefore, to pray the most merciful Lord to indulge you "according to the multitude of His mercies"[268] and to give you place in eternal bliss through the merits of all His saints to whose patronage you always devoutly commended yourself.

lxvii (66). Our most illustrious metropolitan Adalbert died on the seventeenth day before the Kalends of April in the tenth Indiction. That was the year of our Lord Jesus Christ one thousand and seventy-two, the eleventh of Pope Alexander, the seventeenth of King Henry the Fourth.[269][a] Except for books and relics of saints and sacred vestments, almost nothing was found in the man's treasure chest. Nevertheless, the king received all these effects and he took also the hand of Saint James the Apostle along with

[a] Schol. 92 (93). In this year also, in which he departed this life, when he went out for the last time and thereafter did not return,* he held a chapter at Bremen with the brethren, at which he deposed the deacon Liudger for a murder of which he stood accused. And on this occasion he delivered a sermon about chastity, at the end of which he made terrible threats.

* No doubt, on going to Utrecht in 1071. Cf. iii.lxi(60) above.

[267] Cf. Ecclus 6:10; Luke 8:13.
[268] Ps. 105:45; Isa. 63:7; Lam. 3:32.
[269] Correctly, the 16th year.

the documents of the Church. This hand the bishop had been given by a bishop Vitalis of the Venetians while he was in Italy.[270]

lxviii (67). Midst the great bewilderment of the whole realm the archbishop's body was borne from Goslar to Bremen, and at length on the tenth day, that is, the feast of the Annunciation of the Blessed Mary,[271] in the presence of a seemly gathering of people, it was placed in a sepulcher in the middle of the choir of the new basilica that he himself had built. Nevertheless, there are those who affirm that he had previously often asked to be entombed in the metropolitan city of Hamburg which, like his predecessors, he had with all affection always esteemed deserving of honor.[272] For while he still lived he would often spend the whole summer there and with great pomp celebrate the principal feasts. There, furthermore, he would at the proper times very often make promotions in the ecclesiastical ranks with solemn reverence throughout. There he was in the habit of appointing the time and place at which our dukes or the neighboring Slavic peoples or other legates from the arctic nations could meet him. Such esteem had he for the ruined city and such love for the exhausted mother that he said in her was fulfilled the prophecy which runs: "Rejoice thou barren that bearest not . . . for many more are the children of the desolate, more than of her that hath a husband."[273]

lxix (68). They say that he took to his bed, from which he was unable to rise, only three days before he died. So resolute of will was the man that he never would have anyone help him, never emitted a moan, when he was in a state of the uttermost bodily prostration. But as he lay at the point of death[274] and felt that the hour of his summons was at hand, he repeated with frequent sighs: "Woe is me, unfruitful and miserable one who went through so much wealth for nothing. I could have been

---

[270] Vitalis Orseolo, bishop of Torcello (1013?-1048).
[271] March 25. Lambert of Hersfeld, *Annales, an.* 1072.
[272] Cf. III.xxvii(26) above.
[273] Gal. 4:27. Cf. Isa. 54:1.
[274] Cf. Mark 5:23; Ecclus 1:13.

blessed indeed if I had distributed to the poor[275] what to my sorrow I parted with for the sake of earthly glory. However, I now call Him to witness, Whose eye considers the most hidden parts,[276] that the purpose of my heart was wholly the exaltation of my Church. Although she may appear to have been very much reduced because of my guilty demands or the overpowering hatred of my enemies, still I give thanks that more than two thousand manors have accrued to the Church from my inheritance or through my efforts." From this confession of the sage man one can discern that if in some respects he sinned as a man, he repented many times of his mistakes as a good man.

Of this characteristic I cite as one instance[277] that in the beginning of his career, when he was a very proud man, he antagonized many people because of his arrogance. For this reason, too, and because he gloried in his noble rank, he made a remark which it were better he had not uttered;[278] namely, that all the bishops who had presided before him had been obscure and ignoble persons, that he alone stood out by right of his family and wealth, worthy, then, to have been chosen for a greater see or for the apostolic chair itself. As he boasted more than once to this effect, he is said to have been terrified by an ominous vision. Because of its significance and because we gained knowledge of it from a reliable source, I do not forbear adding it here. And so in the dead of night he saw himself transported into the choir of the church where Mass was to be celebrated. His fourteen predecessors[279] stood in their places in the order of succession, so that the last, the one who had preceded him, Alebrand, carried out the rite that usage has fixed for Masses. When the Gospel had been read and the priest of God turned about to receive the oblations of the offerers, he came to the lord Adalbert, who stood in the last place of the

---

[275] Cf. Ps. 111:9.

[276] Cf. Ecclus 23:28.

[277] This story also appears in the *Historia monasterii Rastedensis xii* (*MGH, SS,* XXV, 501).

[278] Cf. Job 39:35.

[279] Correctly, fifteen.

choir. Looking upon Adalbert then with earnest eyes, he rejected
his oblation with the words, "You, a noble and distinguished man,
can have no part[280] with the lowly." And with these words he
withdrew. From that hour Adalbert was truly sorry for the remarks
he had inconsiderately made, held all his predecessors in extraordinary reverence, and with many a sigh he made it known that
he was not worthy of the company of holy men. Hence also he
soon ordained that the brethren and poor be given the amplest
meals from the income of the Bramstedt estate on the anniversary
day of each of his predecessors—something it had previously not
at all been customary for any bishop to do.[281]

lxx (68).   He left behind also many other signs of his repentance
and conversion, among them the noteworthy one that, after the
devastation of his Church and the day of his expulsion, although
he survived it for five years, he never used the baths,[282] never was
cheerful of countenance, rarely showed himself in public or at a
banquet unless he went to court or unless a feast day required it.
Oh, how often did we see[283] that face drawn by sorrow whenever
he thought of the devastation of the Church or when he saw the
devastators in person! On the feast day of the Lord's nativity
Duke Magnus[284] was present and a great multitude of guests also
was assembled. When the feast was over, the happy company, as
was the custom, voiced its applause. The archbishop, however,
was not a little displeased at this. Nodding, therefore, to our
brethren who were also present, he instructed the cantor to intone
the antiphon: "Sing ye to us a hymn."[285] And when the laymen
again broke into applause, he had the clergy begin: "We looked

---

[280] Cf. John 13:8; Ecclus 23:28.

[281] Although this document is dated 1072 in Lappenberg, *Hamburgisches Urkundenbuch,* Vol. I, No. 1072, it is of an earlier date.

[282] Cf. Schol. 89(90) below.

[283] Cf. Vergil *Georgics* I.471-72.

[284] On a Christmas after Adalbert's fall and before his restoration, 1066-1069; but
Magnus was then not yet duke. Adam doubtless was present.

[285] Ps. 136:3. The chants that follow must have been from the psalms Adam
said Adalbert had selected; III.lv(54) above.

for peace, and it did not come."[286] But when they howled in their cups still a third time, he was much irritated, ordered the table cleared, and in a loud voice announced, "Turn again our captivity, O Lord," and the choir responded, "as a stream in the south."[287] Leading the way into the chapel, with us following behind,[288] he wept bitterly.[289] "I shall not cease weeping," he said, "until 'the just judge, strong and patient,'[290] shall liberate my, or rather His, Church which He beholds, with its pastor despised, torn pitifully by wolves." Then was fulfilled the yearning of those who said: "Let us possess the sanctuary of God for an inheritance";[291] and, "Let us abolish all the festival days of God from the land";[292] and, "Let us destroy them, so that they be not a nation: and let the name of Israel be remembered no more."[293] "Arise, why sleepest thou, O Lord?" and, "Cast us not off to the end,"[294] because "the pride of them that hate thee ascendeth continually."[295] "Have mercy on us, O Lord . . . for we are greatly filled with contempt."[296] "Because they have persecuted him whom Thou hast smitten; and they have added to the grief of my wounds."[297] These and other laments of compunction we often heard from him, even that he many times longed to become a monk. Sometimes, also, he wished he might merit dying in the ministry of his legateship either in Slavia or in Sweden or in remotest Iceland.[298] Often, too, he was so willed that without hesitation he fain would even have been beheaded in the confession of Christ for the sake of the truth. Still, God who knows all the hidden things comprehends whether he was better in His

---

[286] The text is reminiscent of Jer. 8:15, 14:19.
[287] Ps. 125:4.
[288] Cf. Vergil *Aeneid* x.226 and elsewhere.
[289] Cf. IV Kings 20:3 and elsewhere.
[290] Ps. 7:12.
[291] Ps. 82:13.
[292] Ps. 73:8.
[293] Ps. 82:5.
[294] Ps. 43:23.
[295] Ps. 73:23.
[296] Ps. 122:3.
[297] Ps. 68:27.
[298] Cf. iv.xxxvi(35) below.

sight than he appeared before the eyes of men.[299] "For man seeth those things that appear, but the Lord beholdeth the heart."[300]

lxxi (70). And so I beg you, reader, to forgive me if, in putting together under various topics the complex story of so many-sided a man, I have in this part directed every effort to writing truthfully, according to the canons of certainty and probability, since I could not, as the art prescribes, have written briefly and lucidly.[301] If I have been silent on many points, it has been chiefly in order to hurry on to those which posterity will, in general, find worth knowing about or which the Church at Hamburg may in particular keep in mind to its advantage. Finally, if there is anything that displeases the hearer because it was badly done and perhaps more badly described, I warn you very earnestly and ask that in censuring the writer you correct what has been faultily said; that in reproaching him about whom I have written, you be the more cautious in the downfall of a wise man, "considering thyself, lest thou also be tempted."[302]

lxxii. Although our great archbishop Adalbert knew that all his predecessors had worked zealously in the mission which the Church at Hamburg traditionally carried on among the heathen, he extended the archiepiscopal sway far and wide over the farther nations ever more magnificently than the others had done. On this account he sedulously set about undertaking that mission himself, to see if he could bring the tidings of salvation to peoples not yet converted or impart perfection to those already converted. With his usual ostentation he began to boast about the laborious tour he would have to make: that the first evangelist had been Ansgar, then Rimbert, after that Unni; but he, the fourth evangelist, was called for because he had noticed the rest of his predecessors had

---

[299] Cf. I Kings 16:7; Dan 13:42.
[300] I Kings 16:7.
[301] Martianus Capella De Nuptiis v.551.
[302] Gal. 6:11. Adam here concluded the first draft of this book. Chapters lxxii-lxxviii contain matter relating only to the period before Adalbert's fall in 1066. This matter Adam collected after finishing the preceding chapters.

toiled at the burdensome task through their suffragans and not in person. When he was certain of going, he decided to arrange his itinerary in a manner that would enable him to cover in his travels the expanse of the north, that is, Denmark, Sweden, and Norway, and cross thence to the Orkneys and to Iceland, the farthermost land of the earth. For these peoples had in his time and by his efforts been converted to the Christian faith.[303] He was duly dissuaded from setting out on this journey, with which he already was publicly busied, by the very prudent king of the Danes, who told him that the barbarian peoples could more easily be converted by men like them in language and customs than by persons unacquainted with their ways and strange to their kind. And further, that there was nothing for him to do except by his generosity and affability to gain the good will and fidelity of those whom he found prepared to preach the Word of God to the heathen. In respect of this exhortation our metropolitan was in accord with the orthodox king and began to extend the liberality with which he treated all much more indulgently to the bishops of the heathen and to the legates of the eastern kings. Each one of them he received, entertained, and dismissed with such good cheer that, after the pope, they all sought him of their own accord as the father of many peoples, offering him extraordinary gifts and bringing back his blessing for a favor.

lxxiii. In respect of his mission the archbishop was, therefore, such as both the times and the manners of men would have him be—so affable, so munificent, so hospitable toward everyone that little Bremen was, because of his greatness, widely spoken of as the equal of Rome and sought by people in troops from all parts of the world, especially by the northern peoples. Of these the Icelanders and Greenlanders and the legates of the Goths and Orkney Islands came the farthest, entreating him to send preachers thither, as indeed he immediately did. For Denmark, Sweden, Norway,

[303] Cf. iii.lxxvii, iv.xxxvi(35) below.

and the islands of the sea he also consecrated many bishops, of whom he himself used to say joyfully: "The harvest, indeed, is great, but the laborers are few. Pray ye therefore the Lord of the harvest, that he send forth laborers into his harvest."[304]

lxxiv. Pleased with their splendid number, the archbishop finally determined, first of all, to hold a synod[305] with his suffragans in Denmark, because he considered the time opportune. That kingdom had more than a sufficient number of bishops, and many abuses were in need of correction in the new plantation. Bishops, for example, sold their blessing,[306] the people would not pay tithes, and everybody far exceeded moderation in respect of eating and of women. With the support of the authority of the pope of Rome, as regards all these matters, and with the hope of receiving the readiest aid from the king of the Danes, he planned to make, as was always his way, this council of all the northern bishops truly magnificent. However, he waited too long a time for the bishops beyond the seas. This consideration has till now delayed the synod. In confirmation of this fact there are extant letters which the pope sent to the bishops in Denmark who were opposed to the synod and letters which the archbishop himself directed to others. I considered it necessary to introduce here copies of these two letters.

lxxv. "Alexander, bishop, servant of the servants of God, to all the bishops established in the kingdom of the Danes, obedient to the Apostolic See and to our vicar, greeting and apostolic benediction. Adalbert, the venerable archbishop of Hamburg, our vicar, has by his letters and legates complained that a certain Egilbert,[307] bishop of Helgoland, who is involved in many crimes, has disdained coming to his synod even though under summons for a period of

---

[304] Matt. 9:37-38; Luke 10:12.
[305] Planned for 1062 or the two succeeding years, this synod did not meet. Cf. Dehio, *Hamburg-Bremen*, I, 241-42, Notes 1 and 4; Meyer von Knonau, *Jahrbücher*, I, 415-20.
[306] Cf. iv.xxxi(30) below.
[307] Cf. Meyer von Knonau, *Jahrbücher*, I, 415-16.

three years. Because he is said to have done this on the advice of certain of you, we demand and by virtue of apostolic authority command you to recede altogether from counsel of this kind and to admonish him to attend the hearing of our aforesaid brother, that he may after investigation be judged canonically." [308] Then follow other statements wherein they were commanded to render him obedience and subjection. Further, another letter:

lxxvi. "Adalbert, legate of the Holy Roman and Apostolic See and, besides, of all the northern nations archbishop, also unworthy provisor of the Church at Hamburg, to W., [309] bishop of Roeskilde, greeting. With grateful soul should I have noted your having attended or having sent your representative to the synod which I appointed to be held at Schleswig. But of this matter more at another time. Now, however, I do not wish to conceal from Your Fraternity what vexations have been inflicted on me by Bishop Adalward, [310] whom I consecrated bishop of the church at Sigtuna, as you may testify who were present at his consecration. Since the barbarous folk did not wish him to preside over them, he proceeded to usurp the Church at Skara. I ask you, therefore, to direct my representative, who is going thither, to the bishop of Dalby." [311] This is what I have to say about the synod, but there is also much else which I omit out of disgust.

lxxvii. Now the metropolitan consecrated many for the heathen. Their sees and names we learned from his recital. And so he constituted nine for Denmark: Rudolf for the city of Schleswig, Oddo for the city of Ribe, Christian for the city of Aarhus, Heribert for the city of Viborg, the monk Magnus and Alberic for the island of Wendsyssel,[a] the monk Egilbert for the islands of Helgoland and Fyn, Wilhelm for the island of Zealand, Egino for the province of

---

[a] Schol. 93. Alberic succeeded Magnus.

[308] Ewald, "Zu den Papstbriefen der brittischen Sammlung," *Neues Archiv,* V (1879-80), 275-414, 452-54, proves that this letter belongs to the year 1062 and had nothing to do with Adalbert's synod at Schleswig.

[309] William. Cf. Schol. 109(108) below.

[310] Cf. Schol. 136(131) below.

[311] Egino. Cf. iv.viii-ix below.

Scania. For Sweden he consecrated six: Adalward[312a] and Acilin, likewise Adalward and Tadico, as well as Simon[313] and the monk John.[314] For Norway he himself consecrated only two, Tholf and Seward. Furthermore, he graciously kept with him bishops consecrated elsewhere, provided they acknowledged obedience, and, when they left, he dismissed them cheerfully; for example, Meinhard,[315] Osmund, Bernhard, and Asgot, and many others. Besides he appointed a certain Turolf to the Orkneys. Thither also he sent John,[316] who had been consecrated in Scotland, and a certain other who bore his own name, Adalbert.[317] Islef he sent to the island Iceland. He consecrated in all twenty bishops,[b] of whom three "were born out of due time"[318] and remained idle outside the vineyard seeking "their own, not the things which are Jesus Christ's."[319] The glorious archbishop held all these bishops in becoming regard and exhorted them by counsel and reward to preach the Word of God to the barbarians. Very often, too, we saw him attended by seven or five bishops, in keeping with what we heard him say, that he could not do without a large company. And when he had dismissed them, he appeared sadder than usual on account of loneliness. Nevertheless, he would never be without at least three, of whom the most constant were: Dangward of Brandenburg, a wise man and the bishop's associate even before he attained the episcopate; another was John, a bishop of Scotland, a simple and God-fearing man,[320] who later was sent into Slavia where he

---

a Schol. 94 (94). The elder Adalward was placed in charge of the two Götalands, the younger was sent to Sigtuna and Uppsala, Simon to the Skritefingi, John was assigned to the islands of the Baltic Sea.

b Schol. 95 (94). The twentieth was Ezzo, whom he consecrated for Slavia.

---

312 An elder and a younger. Cf. III.xv(14) above and Schol. 94(94).
313 His proper name was Stenphi. Cf. IV.xxiv and Schol. 94(94).
314 His proper name was Hiltinus. Cf. *Chronicon Gozec.* I.x(*MGH, SS*, X, 145).
315 Cf. Schol. 148(142) below.
316 Probably not the John mentioned later in this chapter.
317 Cf. Schol. 148(142) below.
318 I Cor. 15:8.
319 Cf. Matt. 20:3-4, 21:39; Phil. 2:21. The reference is to Tadico, Acilin, and perhaps John (Hiltinus).
320 Job 1:1.

was slain with the prince Gottschalk; the third bore the name Bovo. Where he was born or where he was consecrated is uncertain. Still, he prided himself on having gone to Jerusalem three times because of his desire to go on pilgrimages, and on having been deported thence to Babylon by the Saracens, and on having traveled through many countries of the world when at length he was set free. Although these three were not the archbishop's suffragans, we learned that he favored them the more charitably because they did not have sees of their own.

lxxviii.   The archbishop was actuated by the same complaisant zeal toward the legates of the Roman See, whose patronage and companionship he cultivated to the highest degree of friendship. At the same time he prided himself on having only two masters, that is, the pope and the king, to whose dominion all the powers of the world and of the Church of right were subject, and he truly regarded these two with fear and honor. This was evident in the fidelity which the man observed so completely toward each that he put nothing above the apostolic authority, contended that the ancient and honorable prerogatives of the Apostolic See must be preserved in their entirety, and held that its legates were to be received with the greatest respect. Of the regard in which he held the imperial majesty his bishopric gives proof. On this account especially was he destroyed, that neither the threats nor the blandishments of the princes could swerve him from his fidelity toward the king. The royal power, however, is an object of fear for the wicked.[321] Hence it is also that many plots used to be hatched in the kingdom. With these, nevertheless, he would not even by word have anything to do. For his fidelity he was indeed rewarded by the king in being appointed chief steward in the palace. By royal gift he gained much property for the Church at Bremen, about which we have given a more detailed account above. By the pope, indeed, he was rewarded with the stately privilege of having the apostolic lord confer his

[321] Cf. Sallust *Catiline* vii.2, xix.3.

own plenary rights upon him and his successors,[322] to such an extent that he might, frequently against the will of the kings, establish bishoprics throughout the whole north in places that seemed suitable and consecrate as bishops those men from his own chapel whom he wished elected. As we have so far put off mention of their consecrations and their sees, it seems not inappropriate at the same time also to describe the location of Denmark and the nature of the rest of the countries beyond Denmark.

[322] Cf. Lappenberg, *Hamburgisches Urkundenbuch,* Vol. I, No. 75; Schmeidler, *Hamburg-Bremen,* p. 157.

Book Four

A DESCRIPTION OF THE ISLANDS
OF THE NORTH

Here, if you please, the fourth book will begin.

i (1). The country of the Danes, as one also reads in the *Gesta* of Saint Ansgar,[1] is almost all spread out over islands. Now, this Danish land is separated from our Nordalbingians by the river Eider, which rises in the densely wooded highland of the pagans, called Isarnho,[2a] which, they say, extends along the Barbarian Ocean as far as the Schlei Sea. The Eider flows into the Frisian Ocean, which the Romans in their writings call the British Ocean. The principal part of Denmark, called Jutland, extends lengthwise from the Eider River toward the north; it is a journey of three days if you turn aside in the direction of the island of Fyn. But if you measure the distance direct from Schleswig to Aalborg, it is a matter of five to seven days' travel. That is the highway of the Caesar Otto unto the farthermost sea at Wendila, which sea is to this day called the Ottinsand for the king's victory.[3] At the Eider Jutland is fairly

a Schol. 96 (95).* The wooded highland of Isarnho begins at the Danish bay called the Schlei and reaches as far as the city of the Slavs that is called Lübeck and the river Trave.

* The scholia belonging to this chapter occur only in codices of classes *B* and *C* and are not by Adam. Some are no longer legible in the MSS. No attempt has been made here to indicate words or parts of words supplied.

---

[1] Ch. xxv.

[2] The Danish Wohld—the then densely wooded expanse of eastern and north-eastern Holstein inhabited by the pagan Danes and Slavs. Kohlmann, *Adam von Bremen,* p. 109.

[3] Cf. ii.iii(3), Note 11.

wide, but thereafter it narrows little by little like a tongue to the point called Wendila, where Jutland comes to an end. Thence it is a very short passage to Norway. The soil in Jutland is sterile; except for places close to a river, nearly everything looks like a desert. It is a salt land and a vast wilderness.[4] Furthermore, if Germany as a whole is frightful for its densely wooded highlands,[5] Jutland itself is more frightful in other respects. The land is avoided because of the scarcity of crops, and the sea because it is infested by pirates. Hardly a cultivated spot is to be found anywhere, scarcely a place fit for human habitation. But wherever there is an arm of the sea it has very large cities. This region the Caesar Otto at one time subjected to tribute and divided into three bishoprics. One he established at Schleswig,[a] which also is called Haddeby[6] and is situated on the arm of the Barbarian Sea named by the inhabitants the Schlei, whence also the city derives its name. From this port ships usually proceed to Slavia or to Sweden or to Samland, even to Greece.[b] The second bishopric he founded at Ribe,[c] a city encompassed by another waterway that flows in from the ocean and over

[a] Schol. 97 (98). The first bishop in Schleswig was Hored; the second, Poppo; the third, Rudolf.*

* Ekkehard-Esico omitted here. Cf. II.xxvi(23) above.

[b] Schol. 98 (102). The first bishop in Ribe was Liafdag; the second, Odinkar;†
the third, Wal; the fourth, Odo.

† Folgbrucht omitted here. Cf. II.xxvi(23) above.

[c] Schol. 99 (96). One can sail from Ribe to Flanders at Cinkfall in two days and as many nights, from Cinkfall‡ to Prawle** in England in two days and one night. That is the farthest point of England toward the south and from Ribe thither the course is into the quarter between south and west. From Prawle to Brittany at Pointe de Saint Matthieu it is one day; thence to Capo de Vares†† near Santiago, three days and three nights; thence to Lisbon, two days and two nights, and the course is wholly in the quarter between south and west. From Lisbon to Gibraltar it is three days and three nights in the quarter between east and south. From Gibraltar to Tarragona, four days and four nights, in the quarter between north and east. From Tarragona to Barcelona it is one day, likewise between north and east. From Barcelona to Marseilles, it is one day and one night, almost directly east, but deviating a little toward the southern quarter. From Marseilles to Messina in Sicily it is four days and four nights, in the quarter between east and south. From Messina to Acre it is fourteen days and as many nights, between east and south, by going more to the east. (The notes to this scholium are on p. 188.)

[4] Cf. Deut. 32:10.

[5] Cf. Martianus Capella *De Geometria* vi.663.

[6] Cf. I.lvii(59), Note 168, for the same error.

which one sails for Frisia, of a fact, for England[a] or for our Saxony. The third bishopric he planned to fix at Aarhus,[b] separated[c] from Fyn by a very narrow channel[d] that reaches in from the Eastern Sea and extends in a long winding course[7] between Fyn and Jutland northward up to this city of Aarhus. Thence one sails to Fyn, or Zealand, or Scania, or even to Norway.

ii (2). Later, however, when this bishopric, which we set down as the third,[8] failed, Jutland until recently had only two; namely, those at Schleswig and Ribe. On the death of Wal, the bishop of Ribe, the latter diocese was with the approval of the archiepiscopal authority partitioned into four bishoprics. The archbishop presently consecrated for Ribe, Odo; for Aarhus, Christian; for Viborg, Heribert; for Wendila,[e] Magnus.[f] As the latter perished when his ship was wrecked in the Elbe on returning from his consecration, Alberic was put in his place. These four bishops were by grant of King Svein then assigned to the diocese of Ribe.[9]

iii (3). Now the archbishop consecrated from among his own clerics Rudolf for Schleswig, Wilhelm for Zealand, Egilbert for Fyn.[g] The latter, a convert from piracy, is said to have been the first to find the island Helgoland, which lies hidden in a deep recess of the ocean in the mouth of the Elbe River, and, having

‡ At the mouth of the Meuse.

** In Devon near Dartmouth and Plymouth. Lands End and Lizard Point are farther south than Prawle.

†† Or La Coruña, the port of Santiago de Compostela.

[a] Schol. 100 (97). With favorable southeast winds it is [three day's] sail to England.

[b] Schol. 101. The first bishop in Aarhus was Reginbrund; the second, Christian.

[c] Schol. 102 (99). The city halfway between Aarhus and Wendila ... Viborg ...

[d] Schol. 103 (100). Between ... Wendila ...

[e] Schol. 104 (101). Wendila ... island ... three parts ... in the mouth ... sea ... ocean ....

[f] Schol. 105 (103). The first bishop in Wendila was the monk Magnus; the second, Alberic.

[g] Schol. 106 (106). The first bishop in Fyn was Reinher; the second, the monk Egilbert.

[7] Cf. Lucan *Civil War* 1.605.

[8] Cf. ii.xlvi(44) above.

[9] C. 1057-60. Cf. ii.xxiv(23) above.

built a monastery there, to have made it habitable. This island lies
across from Hadeln. It is barely eight miles long by four miles
wide, and its people use straw and the wreckage of ships for fuel.
Report has it that whenever pirates plunder there, be the booty ever
so slight, they never return home unpunished, either perishing soon
after in shipwreck or getting killed by someone. For this reason
they are accustomed with great devotion to offer the hermits who
live there tithes of their booty. This island produces crops in the
greatest abundance and is an exceedingly rich foster mother for
birds and cattle. On it there is but one hill and not a single tree.
It is hemmed in on all sides by very precipitous crags that prohibit
access except in one place, where also the water is sweet. All
sailors hold the place in awe, especially, however, pirates. Hence
it got the name by which it is called, *Heiligland* [that is, Helgo-
land]. From the *Vita* of Saint Willebrord[a] we learned that it was
called Fosetisland and that it is situated on the boundary between
the Danes and Frisians. There also are many other islands off
Frisia and Denmark, but none of them is so noteworthy.

iv (4). Fyn is a fairly important island, lying back of that called
Wendila in the entrance of the Barbarian Gulf. It is close to the
region named Jutland, from every part of which the passage to Fyn
is very short. There is the great city of Odense. Small islands
encircle it,[10] all abounding in crops. And it is to be observed that
if you pass through Jutland into Fyn, your route is a straight way
to the north.[11] But your course faces east in going through Fyn into
Zealand. There are two passages to Zealand, one from Fyn, the
other from Aarhus; each place is an equal distance from Zealand.
The sea is naturally tempestuous and full of two kinds of danger
so that, even if you have a fair wind, you can hardly escape the
hands of pirates.

---

[a] Schol. 107 (105). In the *Vita* of Liudger ... in the time of Charles a certain
Landrich baptized ... bishop.

---

[10] Cf. IV.xvi below.

[11] Adam evidently thought Fyn lay farther north than it does.

v (5). Zealand is an island, very large in extent, situated in an inner bight of the Baltic Sea.[a][b] It is very celebrated as much for the bravery of its men as for the abundance of its crops. It is two days' journey in length and almost the same in breadth. Its largest city is Roeskilde, the seat of Danish royalty. This island, equally distant from Fyn and from Scania, may be crossed in a night. To the west of it lies Jutland, with the cities of Aarhus and Aalborg, and Wendila; to the north, where it also is a desert, is the Norwegian strait; to the south, the aforementioned Fyn and the Slavic Gulf. On the east it faces the headlands of Scania, where is situated the city of Lund.

vi (6). There is very much gold in Zealand, accumulated by the plundering of pirates. These pirates, called Vikings by the people of Zealand, by our people, Ascomanni,[12] pay tribute to the Danish king for leave to plunder the barbarians who live about this sea in great numbers. Hence it also happens that the license granted them with respect to enemies is frequently misused against their own people. So true is this that they have no faith in one another, and as soon as one of them catches another, he mercilessly sells him into slavery either to one of his fellows or to a barbarian. In many other respects, indeed, both in their laws and in their customs, do the Danes run contrary to what is fair and good. None of these points appears to me worth discussing, unless it be that they immediately sell women who have been violated and that men who have been caught betraying his royal majesty or in some other crime would rather be beheaded[c] than flogged. No kind of punishment exists

[a] Schol. 108 (107).* Between Zealand and Fyn there is a small island called Sprogoe; it is a pirate den,† a place of great terror for all who pass by.
    * The two scholia belonging to this chapter are not by Adam.
    † Cf. Matt. 21:13.
[b] Schol. 109 (108). The first bishop in Zealand was Gerbrand; the second, Avoco; the third, Wilhelm.
[c] Schol. 110 (109).‡ An ax hangs before the people in the market place, threatening the guilty with capital punishment; and, when it so happens that this is inflicted, one may see the person who is about to die go rejoicing to his execution as if to a banquet.
    ‡ This scholium is probably not by Adam.

[12] Cf. II.xxxii(30) above.

among them other than the ax and servitude, and then it is glorious for a man who is convicted to take his punishment joyfully. Tears and plaints and other forms of compunction, by us regarded as wholesome, are by the Danes so much abominated that one may weep neither over his sins nor over his beloved dead.

vii (7). From Zealand to Scania there are many routes; the shortest is that to Helsingborg, which is even within the range of vision. Scania[a] is the province of Denmark fairest to look upon—whence also its name[13]—well provided with men, opulent of crops, rich in merchandise, and now full of churches. Scania[b] is twice as large as Zealand, that is it has three hundred churches,[14] whereas Zealand is said to have half that number, and Fyn a third. Scania is the most remote part of Denmark, almost an island, for it is surrounded on all sides by sea except for one reach of land which, becoming mainland on the east, separates Sweden from Denmark. The densely wooded highlands and very rugged mountains, over which the road from Scania into Götaland necessarily runs, make one doubt whether perils by land are more easily avoided than perils by sea, and whether to prefer the former to the latter.

viii (8). No one has as yet been consecrated bishop in that region of Scania, except that prelates have come from other parts[c] and now and then served the diocese. Bishop Gerbrand of Zealand then, and after him Avoco, governed the two churches at the same time. But lately, on the death of Avoco, King Svein divided[15] the diocese of Scania into two bishoprics, giving one of them, that is

---

[a] Schol. 111 (111).* The Lombards and Goths first issued forth from this island, and the Roman historians called it Scantia or Gangavia or Scandinavia.† Its metropolitan city is Lund, and the conqueror of England, Canute, directed it to be the rival of the British London.

* The scholia belonging to this chapter are not by Adam.

† Cf. Paul the Deacon *Hist. Langobard* I.i; Jordanes *Getica* I.iii-iv (Migne, *PL*, LXIX, 1,252-54); Solinus *Collect.* xx.vii.

[b] Schol. 112 (110). The first bishop in Scania was Bernhard; the second, Henry, and Egino.

[c] Schol. 113 (112). Namely, Liafdag, Poppo, Odinkar, Gotebald, Bernhard, and . . . .

---

[13] This derivation is hardly sound.

[14] So also in the *Knytlingasaga*, Chap. xxxix (*MGH*, *SS*, XXIX, 276-77).

[15] About 1060-61. Avoco died c. 1057. Cf. iv.ix below.

Lund, to Henry,[16] the other, that is Dalby, to Egino. The archbishop, in fact, consecrated the latter; Henry had previously been bishop in the Orkneys and, it is related, the keeper of King Canute's treasure in England. Bringing this treasure over to Denmark, Henry spent his life in voluptuousness. About him it is even stated that, reveling in the pestiferous practice of drinking his belly full, he at last suffocated and burst.[17] We have learned that this was also the fate of Avoco and, likewise, that of others. But since Egino was a man who knew letters and was remarkable for his chastity, he at that very time also directed his every effort ardently to the conversion of the pagans. On this account this man won to Christ many people hitherto given to the worship of idols, especially the barbarians called Pleicani[18] and those who live near the Goths on the island of Bornholm. They all are said to have been moved to tears by his preaching and to have manifested such sorrow for their error that they immediately broke up their idols and of their own accord hastened to be baptized. Thereupon they also laid their valuables and everything they had at the bishop's feet, at the same time begging him to deign to accept their belongings. But the bishop, declining the offerings, taught them to build churches with that money, to succor the needy, and to ransom captives, of whom there are many in those parts.

ix (9). At that time in which a very great persecution of Christianity was kindled in Sweden, this same noble spirited man, Egino, is said frequently to have visited the church at Skara and the rest of the faithful, because they lacked a pastor. To those who believed in Christ he administered consolation and to the unbelievers he perseveringly announced the Word of God. There he also broke to pieces a very highly esteemed image of Frikko. For these manifestations of virtue the man of God was thereafter held in high honor by the king of the Danes. Soon after the gross Henry died, Egino received the governance of both the Scanian dioceses,

[16] Cf. Maurer, *Bekehrung des norwegischen Stammes,* II, 585-86.
[17] Cf. Acts 1:18.
[18] Their name lives in the Swedish district Blekinge.

that of Lund and that of Dalby.[a] He at once fixed his see at Lund but directed that a provostship be founded at Dalby for brethren living according to the rule. After having thus nobly spent twelve years in the priesthood,[19] the illustrious man Egino departed happily to Christ soon after he returned home from the city of Rome. His death and that of the bishop of Fyn[20][b] occurred in the same year in which our metropolitan died.

x (10). But now, since the subject provides the occasion, it seems appropriate to say something about the nature of the Baltic Sea.[c] Because I drew upon the writings of Einhard when I previously mentioned this sea in connection with the deeds of Archbishop Adaldag,[21] I shall proceed in the manner of a commentator, setting forth for our people in greater detail what he discussed in abridged form. There is a gulf, Einhard says, that stretches from the Western Ocean towards the east.[22] This gulf is by the inhabitants called the Baltic because, after the manner of a baldric,[23] it extends a long distance through the Scythian regions even to Greece. It is also named the Barbarian Sea or Scythian Lake, from the barbarous peoples whose lands it washes. But the Western Ocean[d] apparently is the one which the Romans in their writings

[a] Schol. 114 (113).* Lund, the principal city of Scania, is situated as far from . . . as from Dalby.

* This and the following scholium are not by Adam.

[b] Schol. 115 (114). . . . this Fyn . . . capital . . . suspended from office by the archbishop . . . Rome . . . died.

[c] Schol. 116 (115).† The Eastern Sea or Barbarian Sea or Scythian Sea or Baltic Sea is one and the same sea, which Martianus and the ancient Romans call the Scythian or the Maeotic marshes or the Getic waste or the Scythian strand. This sea, reaching from the Western Ocean between Denmark and Norway, stretches eastward in an unexplored length.

† The scholia belonging to this chapter are not by Adam.

[d] Schol. 117 (104). In this ocean, of which mention has been made before, there is an island of moderate size that now bears the name Farria or Helgoland. It is at three days' rowing distance from England. Still, it is in the vicinity of the land of the Frisians and of our Weser, so that it can be seen from the island which is in the mouth . . . spread sails to this island of Farria about which we have also spoken above.

---

[19] Evidently as bishop, 1060-72.
[20] Egilbert.
[21] Cf. ii.xix(16) above.
[22] Einhard *Vita Karoli* xii.
[23] More probably derived from *balta*, a swamp. ·

called the British Ocean. It is of immense breadth, terrible and dangerous, and on the west encompasses Britain to which is now given the name England. On the south it touches the Frisians[a] and the part of Saxony that belongs to our diocese of Hamburg.[b] On the east there are the Danes and the mouth of the Baltic Sea and the Norwegians, who live beyond Denmark. On the north that ocean flows by the Orkney Islands and then encircles the earth in boundless expanses. On the left there is Hibernia, the fatherland of the Scots, which now is called Ireland.[24] On the right there are the crags of Norway, and farther on the islands of Iceland and Greenland.[25] There ends the ocean called dark.[26]

xi (11). What Einhard says[27] about the unexplored length of this gulf has lately been proved by the enterprise of the highly spirited men, Ganuz Wolf, a Danish leader, and Harold,[28] the king of the Norwegians. After exploring the compass of this sea with much toilsome travel and many dangers to their associates, they finally came back, broken and overcome by the redoubled blows of the winds and pirates. But the Danes affirm that many have oftentimes explored the length of this sea. With a favorable

---

[a] Schol. 118 (3).* Frisia is a coastal region, inaccessible because of impassable swamps, and it comprises seventeen districts. Of them a third part belongs to the bishopric of Bremen. They are distinguished by the following names: Ostergau, Rüstringen, Triesmeri, Wanga, Harlingerland, Norden, and Morseti. And these seven districts comprehend about fifty churches. This part of Frisia is separated from Saxony by the marsh called Wapel and the mouth of the Weser River and from the rest of Frisia by the Emsgau marsh and the Ocean Sea.

* Cf. Schol. 3 above.

[b] Schol. 119 (4).† Of these seventeen districts, five belong to the bishopric of Münster; Saint Liudger, the first bishop of that place, received them in gift from the Emperor Charles. They are designated by these names: Hugmerchi, Hunusgau, Fivilgau, Emsgau, Federitgau, and the island Bant.‡

† This scholium is derived from the *Vita Liudgeri auctore Altfrido* I.xix (*MGH, SS*, II, 410).

‡ The island Burcana of Pliny *Natural History* IV.xcvii. It was doubtless washed away in 1362. Kretschmer, *Historische Geographie von Mitteleuropa*, p. 69.

---

[24] Often not distinguished in the earlier Middle Ages.
[25] That is, westward.
[26] The Arctic Ocean.
[27] Einhard *Vita Karoli* xii.
[28] Harold Hardrada and probably Jarl Ulf; therefore, before 1066.

wind some have reached Ostrogard[a] in Russia[29] from Denmark in the course of a month. As to its breadth, he asserts that it is "nowhere more than a hundred miles . . . and in many places much narrower."[30] This can be seen at the mouth of that sea, the entrance of which from the ocean, between Aalborg or Wendila, the headland of Denmark,[31] and the cliffs of Norway is so narrow that it is an easy trip of one night across by sail. Likewise, on leaving the bounds of Denmark, the sea stretches wide its arms,[32] which come together a second time in the region of the Goths by the side of whom live the Wilzi.[33] The farther one goes, then, the farther do its coast lines spread apart.

xii (12). Many peoples, Einhard says,[34] occupy the shores of this sea. The Danes and the Swedes, whom we call Northmen, hold both its northern shore and all the islands off it. The Slavs, the Esths, and various other peoples inhabit the eastern shore; amongst them the Welatabi, also called Wilzi, are the most important. The Danes and the Swedes and the other peoples beyond Denmark are all called Northmen by the historians of the Franks, although the Roman writers named men of this kind Hyperboreans, whom Martianus Capella extolled with many commendations.[35]

xiii (13). At the mouth of the sea mentioned before, on its southern coast facing us, there live as far as the Schlei Sea the first people, the Danes, who are called Jutes. There begins the territory

[a] Schol. 120 (116). Russia is called Ostrogard * by the barbarian Danes for the reason that, situated in the east, it is like a watered garden,† abounding in all good things. It is also called Chungard because the Huns first had their seat there.
    * Since Adam does not identify Ostrogard and Russia either in this chapter or at II.xxii(19) above, this scholium probably is not by him.
    † Cf. Isa. 58:11; Jer. 31:12.

[29] Cf. II.xxii(19) above.
[30] Cf. Einhard *Vita Karoli* xii.
[31] Vendilskagen.
[32] The reference here may be to the Bothnian arm of the Baltic. Cf. Vergil *Georgics* II.296.
[33] Since Roman and medieval charts showed the east where the north is now shown, this is the right side, the southern.
[34] Einhard *Vita Karoli* xii.
[35] Cf. *De Nuptiis* VI.664, 693.

of the diocese of Hamburg, which extends a long way through the midst of the Slavic coastal peoples as far as the Peene River. There are the limits of our diocese.[36] From that place to the Oder River the Wilzi and Leutici have their homes. Across the Oder, as we have learned, live the Pomeranians; beyond them stretches the very extensive country of the Poles, the boundary of which, they say, joins with that of the kingdom of Russia. This is the farthest and largest province of the Winuli, and it also is at the end of that sea.

xiv (14).   Returning now to the northern parts at the entrance of the Baltic Sea, first come the Norwegians; then Scania, which belongs to the Danes, juts out, and beyond it[37] live the Goths in an extensive domain reaching to Björkö. After that the Swedes rule over a spacious region extending to the land of women.[38] Beyond them,[39] as far as Russia, are said to live the Wizzi,[40] Mirri,[41] Lami,[42] Scuti,[43] and Turci.[44] In this area that sea again comes to an end. Thus, the Slavs possess the southern litoral of that sea; the Swedes, the northern.

xv (15).   Those who have a knowledge of geography also assert that some men have passed by an overland route from Sweden into Greece. But the barbarous peoples who live between make this way difficult; consequently, the risk is taken by ship.

xvi (16).   In this sea there are many islands, all of which are

---

[36] Cf. II.xxi(18), Schol. 70 (72) above.

[37] Northward.

[38] The Amazons. Cf. IV.xix below.

[39] Eastward.

[40] The Wes of Nestor, a tribe of the East Finns, also called Albani. Cf. Nestor *Chronicon* II.vii; Zeuss, *Die Deutschen und die Nachbarstämme*, pp. 688-90.

[41] Called Merja by Nestor and Merens by Jordanes, an East Finnish stock living near Rostov. Nestor *Chronicon* II.xxiv; Jordanes *Getica* xxiii (Migne, *PL*, LXIX, 1,268); Zeuss, *Die Deutschen und die Nachbarstämme*, pp. 688-90.

[42] An Estonian folk living in western Finland on the north shore of the Gulf of Finland and the east shore of the Gulf of Bothnia. Cf. Zeuss, *ibid.*

[43] An East Finnish people in Estonia, called Czjud by Nestor *Chronicon* II.xxiv. Cf. Zeuss, *Die Deutschen und die Nachbarstämme*, pp. 688-90.

[44] Called Turcu in Finnish. A Finnish folk living about Abo on the Baltic, north of the Gulf of Finland, or in Tricatia across the Dvina River. Cf. Zeuss, *ibid.*

under the dominion of the Danes and Swedes, though a few are held by the Slavs. Of these islands, at a short distance from one another, the first is Wendila, at the head of this strait, the second is Morsö,[45] the third is Thyholm.[46] The fourth, opposite the city of Aarhus, is Samsö. The fifth is Fyn, the sixth is Zealand, which lies close to it. Of these islands we have made mention before. They say that the seventh,[47] which is very near Scania and Götaland, is called Holm,[48] the most celebrated port of Denmark and a safe anchorage for the ships that are usually dispatched to the barbarians and to Greece. There are, furthermore, close to Fyn on the southeast—although Laaland reaches farther inwards to the confines of the Slavs—seven other smaller islands, which we said above[49] are rich in crops, that is, Möen, Fehmarn, Falster, Laaland, Langeland,[50] and so all the others in their vicinity.[51] These fourteen islands belong to the kingdom of the Danes, and they all are distinguished by the honor of being Christian. There also are other more distant islands that are subject to the authority of the Swedes. Of these islands the largest, the one called Courland, takes eight days to traverse. The people, exceedingly bloodthirsty because of their stubborn devotion to idolatry, are shunned by everybody. Gold is very plentiful there, the horses are of the best; all the houses are full of pagan soothsayers, diviners, and necromancers, who are even arrayed in a monastic habit. Oracular responses are sought there from all parts of the world, especially by Spaniards and Greeks. This island, we believe, is called Chori in the *Vita* of Saint Ansgar,[52] and the Swedes at that time subjected it to

---

[45] Also called Mors, in the Danish Lim Fjord.

[46] Part of western Jutland, in the Danish Lim Fjord.

[47] Codex *AC* erroneously refers to a seventh island which is unnamed. This upsets the numbering system. In the text the correct numbering of the *B* Codex is followed.

[48] Doubtless the modern Gotland, on which Wisby is located.

[49] Cf. IV.iv above.

[50] Southeast of Fyn.

[51] The two unnamed islands of the seven smaller ones are Alsen, off eastern Denmark, and Aro, south of Fyn.

[52] Chap. xxx.

tribute. A church has now been built there through the zeal of a merchant whom the king of the Danes moved to do this by many gifts. The king himself, rejoicing in the Lord, recited this canticle for me.[53]

xvii (17). We were told, moreover, that there are in this sea many other islands, of which a large one is called Estland.[54] It is not smaller than the one of which we have previously spoken. Its people, too, are utterly ignorant of the God of the Christians. They adore dragons and birds and also sacrifice to them live men whom they buy from the merchants. These men are carefully inspected all over to see that they are without a bodily defect on account of which, they say, the dragons would reject them. This island is said, indeed, to be very near the land of women, because the one referred to before is not far from Björkö of the Swedes.

xviii (18). Of the islands that lie near the Slavs, we understand that three are of considerable importance. The first of them is called Fehmarn. It is opposite the Wagiri, so it can be seen from Oldenburg,[55] like the one named Laaland. The second, opposite the Wilzi, is possessed by the Rani or Runi,[a] the most powerful of the Slavic peoples, without whose consent nothing may lawfully be done in matters of public concern; so much are they feared on account of their familiarity with the gods, or rather demons, whom this people holds in greater veneration than do the others. Both these islands, too, are infested by pirates and by very bloodthirsty robbers who spare no one who passes that way. For they kill all those whom others are accustomed to sell. The third island, that called Samland, is close to the Russians and Poles. It is inhabited by the

---

[a] Schol. 121 (117). Rügen, in the vicinity of the city of Jumne, is the island of the Runi who alone have a king.

---

[53] Cf. Phil. 3:1, 4:4.
[54] Estonia is not an island.
[55] That is, Oldenburg in Holstein

Sembi or Prussians,ª a most humane people, who go out to help those who are in peril at sea or who are attacked by pirates. Gold and silver they hold in very slight esteem. They have an abundance of strange furs, the odor of which has inoculated our world with the deadly poison of pride. But these furs they regard, indeed, as dung, to our shame, I believe, for right or wrong we hanker after a martenskin robe as much as for supreme happiness. Therefore, they offer their very precious marten furs for the woolen garments called *faldones*.[56] Many praiseworthy things could be said about these peoples with respect to their morals, if only they had the faith of Christ whose missionaries they cruelly persecute. At their hands Adalbert, the illustrious bishop of the Bohemians, was crowned with martyrdom.[57] Although they share everything else with our people, they prohibit only, to this very day indeed, access to their groves and springs which, they aver, are polluted by the entry of Christians. They take the meat of their draft animals for food and use their milk and blood as drink so freely that they are said to become intoxicated. These men are blue of color,[58] ruddy of face, and long-haired. Living, moreover, in inaccessible swamps, they will not endure a master among them.

ª Schol. 122 (118). In his lyrics Horace* thus sings in praise of these peoples:
Far better live the Scythians of the steppes
Whose wagons haul their homes from place to place,
As is their wont;

    . . . .

Far better live the Getae stern . . . .
. . . . nor
With them is tillage binding longer than a year . . . .

    . . . .

Their noble dower is their parent's worth

    . . . .

To sin is an abomination; or
If they do sin, the penalty is death.
To this day the Turci,† who are near to the Russians,
live in this way, as do other Scythian peoples.

  * *Odes* III.xxiv.9-11, 14, 21, 24.
  † Cf. IV.xiv above.

---

[56] Probably because they were folded.
[57] Cf. Thietmar *Chronicon* IV.xxviii(19); *Annales Quedlinburgenses, an.* 997 (MGH *SS*, III, 73-74).
[58] Probably through tattooing.

xix (19). In this sea there are also very many other islands, all infested by ferocious barbarians and for this reason avoided by navigators. Likewise, round about the shore of the Baltic Sea, it is said, live the Amazons[59a] in what is now called the land of women. Some declare that these women conceive by sipping water. Some, too, assert that they are made pregnant by the merchants who pass that way, or by the men whom they hold captive in their midst, or by various monsters, which are not rare there. This explanation we also believe to be more credible. And when these women come to give birth, if the offspring be of the male sex,[60] they become Cynocephali; [61] if of the feminine kind, they become most beautiful women. Living by themselves, the latter spurn consort with men and, if men do come near, even drive them manfully away. The Cynocephali are men who have their heads on their breasts. They are often seen in Russia as captives and they voice their words in barks. In that region, too, are those who are called Alani or Albani, in their language named Wizzi;[b] very hard-hearted gluttons, born with gray hair.[62] The writer Solinus mentions them. Dogs defend their country. Whenever the Alani have to fight, they draw up their dogs in battle line. Palefaced,

---

[a] Schol. 123 (119). When Emund,* the king of the Swedes, sent his son Anund into Scythia to extend his empire, the latter reached the land of women on his voyage. Thereupon they poisoned the springs, in this manner destroying the king and his army. This we also said above, and Bishop Adalward† himself told us, testifying that this and other accounts are true.

* Cf. iii.xvi(15) above.

† The Younger. Cf. iii.xxvii above.

[b] Schol. 124 (120). In their language they are called Wilzi, most cruel gluttons whom the poet calls Gelani.‡

‡ Or Geloni, as mentioned by Lucan *Civil War* iii.283; Pliny *Natural History* iii.xiv-xv; Vergil *Georgics* iii.461.

---

[59] Mentioned by Jordanes *Getica* vii-ix (Migne, *PL*, LXIX, 1,258-59); Martianus Capella *De Nuptiis* vi.665, ix.925; Solinus *Collect.* xvii.iii; x.i; Orosius *Hist. adv. Paganos* i.v (Migne, *PL*, XXXI, 724-27); and Alfred the Great's version of Orosius (Pauli *Alfred the Great*, tr. by B. Thorpe, p. 279).

[60] Cf. Num. 31:17.

[61] Martianus Capella *De Nuptiis* vi.674 tells this story about the Blemingae of interior Africa, and Solinus *Collect.* xxvii.lviii-lx, xxx.iv about certain peoples in Ethiopia.

[62] Cf. Solinus, *Collect.* xv.v, vii, ix.

green, and macrobiotic,[63] that is, long-lived men, called Husi, also live in those parts. Finally, there are those who are given the name Anthropophagi[64] and they feed on human flesh. In that territory live very many other kinds of monsters whom mariners say they have often seen, although our people think it hardly credible.

xx (20). No mention, I have learned, has been made by any of the learned men about what I have said concerning this Baltic or Barbarian Sea, save only Einhard of whom we have spoken above. But, since the names have been changed, I am of the opinion that this body of water was perhaps called by the ancient Romans the Scythian or Maeotic swamp, or "the wilds of the Getae,"[65] or the Scythian swamp, which Martian says was "full of a multifarious diversity of barbarians."[66a] There, he says, live the Getae, Dacians, Sarmatians, Alani, Neutri, Geloni, Anthropophagi, and Troglodytes. Because he deplored their delusions,[b] our metropolitan appointed Björkö as a metropolis for those peoples. This city,[c] situated in central Sweden, lies opposite Jumne, the city of the Slavs, and all the shorelines of that sea encircle it at equal distances. For this city[67] he first consecrated of our clerics the abbot Hiltinus, whom he himself wished to be named John.[68] And so, enough has been said about the islands of the Danes. Now we

---

a Schol. 125. The Amaxobii, Arimaspi, Agathyrsi.*

* These peoples and many of those noted in the text of this chapter are mentioned by Martianus Capella *De Nuptiis* VI.663. Isidore of Seville *Etymologies* IX.ii.129 (Migne, *PL,* LXXXII, 34), has the Troglodytes live in Africa. According to him, they could run faster than wild beasts.

b Schol. 126 (121). For those who sail from Scania of the Danes to Björkö it is a journey of five days; from Björkö into Russia, likewise by sea, it is a journey of five days.

c Schol. 127 (122). There is the port of Saint Ansgar and the burial mound of the holy archbishop Unni, a friendly hospice, I say, for the holy confessors of our see.

---

63 Solinus, *Collect.* XI.xxxvi, XXX.ix, xii notes such folk in Ethiopia.

64 Mentioned by Abo *Vita S. Eadmundi* v (Migne, *PL,* CXXXIX, 510); Isidore of Seville *Etymologies* IX.2, 132 (Migne, *PL,* LXXXII, 341); Juvenal *Satires* XV.xiii.

65 Cf. Schol. 134(129) below; Vergil *Georgics* III.462.

66 Cf. Martianus Capella *De Nuptiis* VI.663.

67 The location of Björkö with reference to Jumne is wrong, but it is in accord with Adam's conception of the configuration of the Baltic.

68 Cf. III.lxxvii, Schol. 94(94) above.

shall turn our discourse to the Swedish and Norwegian peoples, who are close to the Danes.

xxi (21). In going beyond the islands of the Danes there opens up another world in the direction of Sweden[a] and Norway, which are the two most extensive kingdoms of the north and until now nearly unknown to our parts. About these kingdoms the very well-informed king of the Danes[69] told me that Norway can hardly be crossed in the course of a month,[b] and Sweden is not easily traversed in two months. "I myself found this out," he said, "when a while ago I fought for twelve years in those regions under King James.[70] Both these countries are shut in by exceedingly high mountains— higher ones, however, in Norway which encircles Sweden with its alps." About Sweden, too, the ancient writers, Solinus and Orosius are not silent.[c] They say that the Swedes hold a very large part of Germany and, besides, that their highland regions extend up to the Rhiphaean Mountains.[71] There, also, is the Elbe River to which Lucan appears to have referred.[72] It rises in the alps before mentioned and courses through the midst of the Gothic peoples into the ocean; hence, also, it is called the Götaälv.[d] The Swedish country is extremely fertile; the land is rich in fruits and honey besides excelling all others in cattle raising, exceedingly happy in streams and woods, the whole region everywhere full of merchan-

---

a Schol. 128 (124). Tacitus* also calls the Swedes Sueones.

* *Germania* xliv. This scholium is not by Adam.

b Schol. 129 (123). Paul in his *Gesta* of the Lombards refers to the fecundity of the northern nations and to the seven men who lie on the coast of the ocean in the land of the Skritefingi.†

† *Hist. Langobard* I.i.4-5. For the legend of the Seven Sleepers see P. M. Huber, *Die Wanderlegende von den Siebenschläfern.* Cf. Schol. 145(141) below.

c Schol. 130 (125). The Danes, Swedes, Norwegians, and the rest of the Scythian peoples are called Hyperboreans by the Romans and they are extolled with much praise by Martian.‡

‡ *De Nuptiis* VI.664-65, 693. This scholium is almost verbatim from IV.xvi above.

d Schol. 131 (126). The river Götaälv divides Götaland from the Norwegians and is not unlike the Elbe of the Saxons in magnitude; it also takes its name from the Elbe.

---

69 Svein Estrithson.

70 Anund James, about 1028-39. Cf. II.lxxiii(71) above.

71 *Historia adv. Paganos* I.ii.53 (Migne, *PL*, XXXI, 686); Solinus *Collect.* xx.i.

72 *Civil War* II.51-52.

dise from foreign parts. Thus you may say that the Swedes are lacking in none of the riches, except the pride that we love or rather adore. For they regard as nothing every means of vainglory; that is, gold, silver, stately chargers, beaver and marten pelts, which make us lose our minds admiring them. Only in their sexual relations with women do they know no bounds;[a] a man according to his means has two or three or more wives at one time, rich men and princes an unlimited number. And they also consider the sons born of such unions legitimate. But if a man knows another man's wife, or by violence ravishes a virgin,[73] or spoils another of his goods, or does him an injury, capital punishment is inflicted on him. Although all the Hyperboreans are noted for their hospitality, our Swedes are so in particular. To deny wayfarers entertainment is to them the basest of all shameful deeds, so much so that there is strife and contention among them over who is worthy to receive a guest. They show him every courtesy for as many days as he wishes to stay, vying with one another to take him to their friends in their several houses. These good traits they have in their customs. But they also cherish with great affection preachers of the truth, if they are chaste and prudent and capable, so much so that they do not deny bishops attendance at the common assembly of the people that they call the *Warh.* There they often hear, not unwillingly, about Christ and the Christian religion. And perhaps they might readily be persuaded of our faith by preaching but for bad teachers who, in seeking "their own; not the things that are Jesus Christ's," give scandal to those whom they could save.[74]

xxii (22). There are many Swedish peoples, excelling in strength and arms, besides being the best of fighters on horse as well as on ships. This also accounts for their holding the other peoples of the North in their power. They have kings of ancient

---

a Schol. 132 (127). The Slavs also suffer from this vice, likewise the Parthians and the Mauri, as Lucan testfies about the Parthians and Sallust about the Mauri.*
* Lucan *Civil War* VIII.397-404; Sallust, *Jugurtha* lxxx.6.

73 Cf. Gen. 34:2.
74 Phil. 2:21.

lineage; nevertheless, the power of these kings depends upon the will of the people, for what all in common approve,[a] that the king must confirm, unless it be that his decision, which they sometimes reluctantly follow, seems preferable. And so they enjoy equality at home. When they go to war everyone yields perfect obedience to the king or to the one who, more skilled than the rest, is preferred by the king. Whenever in fighting they are placed in a critical situation, they invoke the aid of one of the multitude of gods they worship. Then after the victory they are devoted to him and set him above the others. By common consent, however, they now declare that the God of the Christians is the most powerful of all. Other gods often fail them, but He always stands by, a surest "helper in due time in tribulation."[75]

xxiii (23). Of these Swedish peoples, the so-called Goths[b] live nearest to us; there are other Goths known as eastern. Västergötland, indeed, borders on the Danish territory called Scania, from which they also say it takes seven days to reach Skara, the great city of the Goths. Thence Östergötland extends along the sea, the one they call the Baltic, up to Björkö. The first bishop of the Goths was Thorgaut;[c] the second was Gottschalk, a wise man and

---

[a] Schol. 133 (128). Everything of a private nature that the barbarians do is decided by taking lots; in public matters, however, they are even in the habit of seeking the responses of the demons, as can be learned from the *Gesta* of Saint Ansgar.*

* *Vita Anskarii* xviii, xix, xxvii, xxx.

[b] Schol. 134 (129). The Goths were by the Romans called Getae, of whom Vergil evidently spoke: ". . . and the keen Gelonian when he flees to Rhodope and the wilds of the Getae and there drinks milk curdled with horses' blood." † To this very day the Goths and Sembi are said to do this. Certain it is that they become inebriated on the milk of draft animals.‡

† *Georgics* iii.461-63.

‡ Cf. iv.xviii above.

[c] Schol. 135 (130-131). Although Danish and English bishops preached in Sweden before them, Thorgaut was expressly consecrated for Götaland,** to the see of Skara. On the invitation of King Harold,†† Adalward also came to Norway and because of the man's sanctity and the fame of his miracles they received him with honor. When he departed, the king gave him so much money that the bishop at once ransomed three hundred captives with it.

** Cf. ii.lviii(56) above.

†† Harold Hardrada, v.1064. Cf. ii.xxxiii(31), Schol. 67(68) above.

---

[75] Ps. 9:10.

good, as they say of him, except for the fact that he sat at home, preferring ease to toil.[76] Our metropolitan consecrated the third bishop, Adalward the elder, truly a praiseworthy man. When he thereupon came to the barbarians, he lived as he taught. For by his holy living and by his good teaching he is said to have drawn a great multitude of heathen to the Christian faith. He was renowned, too, for his miraculous powers, such as were shown when, the barbarians in their need having asked for rain, he had it fall, or again had fair weather come, and he worked other wonders that still are sought of teachers. This notable man remained in Götaland, steadfastly preaching to all the name of the Lord Jesus; and there, after many struggles, which he gladly endured for the sake of Christ, he yielded his indomitable flesh to the earth as his spirit, crowned, sought heaven.[77] After him the archbishop consecrated for those parts[a] a certain Acilin, a man in no respect worthy of bearing the episcopal title unless it was for his portly figure. He indeed loved carnal ease. In vain did the Goths send a legation, for until his death he stayed with his pleasures at Cologne.

xxiv (24). Between Norway and Sweden dwell the Wärmilani and Finns and others; who are now all Christians and belong to the Church at Skara. On the confines of the Swedes and Norwegians toward the north live the Skritefingi,[78] who, they say,

---

[a] Schol. 136 (131). The younger Adalward came at that time* into Götaland and found the bishop of the same name sick. After conducting his obsequies with sorrow, the younger Adalward hastened thence to Sigtuna. But when he was later driven out by the pagans, he came on invitation to the city of Skara. Our archbishop was not well pleased thereat and for this reason recalled him to Bremen as a violator of the canons.†

* In 1064.

† Cf. iii.lxxvi above.

---

[76] Sallust *Catiline* xxxvii.7.

[77] Probably in 1064.

[78] Laplanders. The readings following are respectively those of codices *A1.2* and *B.C2*. The latter is corrected by Adam in Schol. 137(132-133) above. Cf. Martianus Capella *De Nuptiis* vi.702 on the Troglodytes; iv.xix above.

outstrip wild beasts at running. Their largest city is Hälsing land,[a] to which the archbishop designated Stenphi[79] as the first bishop, to whom he gave the name Simon. By his preaching he won many of those heathen. There are besides countless other Swedish peoples, of whom we have learned that only the Goths, the Wärmilani, and a part of the Skritefingi, and those in their vicinity, have been converted to Christianity.

xxv (25). Let us now proceed to give a brief description of Sueonia or Sweden. On the west, Sweden has the Goths and the city of Skara; on the north, the Wärmilani with the Skritefingi, whose chief city is Hälsingland; on the south, the length of the Baltic Sea, about which we have spoken before. There is the great city of Sigtuna. On the east, Sweden touches the Rhiphaean Mountains, where there is an immense wasteland, the deepest snows, and where hordes of human monsters prevent access to what lies beyond.[80] There are Amazons, and Cynocephali, and Cyclops[81] who have one eye on their foreheads; there are those Solinus calls Himantopodes,[82] who hop on one foot, and those who delight in human flesh as food, and as they are shunned, so may they also rightfully be passed over in silence. The king of the Danes, often to be remembered, told me that a certain people[83] were in the habit of descending from the highlands into the plains. They are small of stature but hardly matched by the Swedes in strength and agility. "Whence they come is not known. They come up unexpectedly," he said, "sometimes once in the course of a year or after a three-

---

[a] Schol. 137 (132-133). Hälsingland, the land of the Skritefingi, is situated in the midst of the very high mountains that are called the Rhiphaean, on which there is perpetual snow. Men there, hardened by the cold, do not care about the shelter of their houses and make use of the flesh of wild animals for food and of their pelts for clothing. We have read that, in addition to other monsters that are there, even griffins are to be found in those Hyperborean mountains.

[79] Cf. III.lxxvii, Schol. 94(94), above.
[80] The eastern end of the Baltic. Cf. Solinus *Collect.* xxx.ix.12.
[81] Cf. *ibid.*, xxx.vi, referring to the Agriophagi of Ethiopia; Martianus Capella *De Nuptiis* vi.674.
[82] Solinus located them in interior Africa. *Collect.* xxx.vii-viii; Martianus Capella *De Nuptiis* vi.674; Pliny *Nat. Hist.* v.lxxxviii.46.
[83] The Finns or Laplanders mentioned before.

year period. Unless they are resisted with all one's might, they lay waste the whole region and then withdraw." Many other things are usually mentioned, but in my effort to be brief I have not mentioned them, letting those speak about them who declare they themselves have seen them. Now we shall say a few words about the superstitions of the Swedes.

xxvi (26). That folk has a very famous temple called Uppsala,[a] situated not far from the city of Sigtuna and Björkö.[b] In this temple, entirely decked out in gold, the people worship the statues of three gods in such wise that the mightiest of them, Thor,[84] occupies a throne in the middle of the chamber; Wotan and Frikko have places on either side. The significance of these gods is as follows: Thor, they say, presides over the air, which governs the thunder and lightning, the winds and rains, fair weather and crops. The other, Wotan—that is, the Furious—carries on war and imparts to man strength against his enemies. The third is Frikko, who bestows peace and pleasure on mortals. His likeness, too, they fashion with an immense phallus. But Wotan they chisel armed, as our people are wont to represent Mars. Thor with his scepter apparently resembles Jove. The people also worship heroes made gods, whom they endow with immortality because of their remarkable exploits, as one reads in the *Vita* of Saint Ansgar[85] they did in the case of King Eric.

xxvii (27). For all their gods there are appointed priests to offer sacrifices for the people. If plague and famine threaten, a libation is poured to the idol Thor; if war, to Wotan; if marriages

---

[a] Schol. 138 (134). Near this temple stands a very large tree with wide-spreading branches, always green winter and summer.* What kind it is nobody knows. There is also a spring at which the pagans are accustomed to make their sacrifices, and into it to plunge a live man. And if he is not found, the people's wish will be granted.

* Cf. Vergil *Georgics* II.210, 296, III.333.

[b] Schol. 139 (135). A golden chain goes round the temple. It hangs over the gable of the building and sends its glitter far off to those who approach, because the shrine stands on level ground with mountains all about it like a theater.

---

[84] This description, doubtless exaggerated, is reminiscent of that of the Temple of Redigast at Rethra. Cf. II.xxi(18), lxii(60) above.

[85] Chapter xxvi.

are to be celebrated, to Frikko. It is customary also to solemnize in Uppsala, at nine-year intervals, a general feast of all the provinces of Sweden. From attendance at this festival no one is exempted.[a] Kings and people all and singly send their gifts to Uppsala and, what is more distressing than any kind of punishment, those who have already adopted Christianity redeem themselves through these ceremonies. The sacrifice is of this nature: of every living thing that is male,[86] they offer nine heads,[b] with the blood of which it is customary to placate gods of this sort. The bodies they hang in the sacred grove that adjoins the temple. Now this grove is so sacred in the eyes of the heathen that each and every tree in it is believed divine because of the death or putrefaction of the victims. Even dogs and horses hang there with men. A Christian seventy-two years old told me that he had seen their bodies suspended promiscuously. Furthermore, the incantations customarily chanted in the ritual of a sacrifice of this kind are manifold and unseemly; therefore, it is better to keep silence about them.

xxviii (28).   In that country there took place lately an event worth remembering and widely published because it was noteworthy, and it also came to the archbishop's attention. One of the priests who was wont to serve the demons at Uppsala became blind and the help of the gods was of no avail. But as the man wisely ascribed the calamity of blindness to his worship of idols, by which

---

a Schol. 140 (136). When not long ago the most Christian king of the Swedes, Anunder,* would not offer the demons the prescribed sacrifice of the people, he is said, on being deposed, to have departed "from the presence of the council, rejoicing" that he had been "accounted worthy to suffer reproach for the name of Jesus." †

* This story is also told of King Inge in the Hervara Saga. He may be the Anunder of Adam. Cf. Schol. 84(85) above. The deposition that followed may be dated between 1076 and 1080.

† Acts 5:41.

b Schol. 141 (137). Feasts and sacrifices of this kind are solemnized for nine days. On each day they offer a man along with other living beings in such a number that in the course of the nine days they will have made offerings of seventy-two creatures. This sacrifice takes place about the time of the vernal equinox.

---

86 Cf. Gen. 7:2.

superstitious veneration he had evidently offended the almighty God of the Christians, behold, that very night a most beautiful Virgin appeared to him[87] and asked if he would believe in her Son, if to recover his sight he would put aside the images he had previously worshiped. Then he, who for the sake of this boon would refuse to undergo nothing that was hard, gladly promised he would. To this the Virgin answered: "Be completely assured that this place in which so much innocent blood is now shed is very soon to be dedicated to my honor. That there may not remain any trace of doubt in your mind about this matter, receive the light of your eyes in the name of Christ, who is my Son." As soon as the priest recovered his sight, he believed and, going to all the country about, easily persuaded the pagans of the faith so that they believed in Him who made the blind see.

xxxi (28). Impelled by these miracles, our metropolitan, forthwith obedient to the saying that runs, "Look up, and lift up . . . your eyes and see the countries; for they are white already to harvest,"[88] consecrated for those parts the younger Adalward, whom he took from the choir at Bremen, a man who shone in letters and for moral probity. Through legates of the most illustrious King Stenkil he also fixed Adalward's see in the city of Sigtuna, which is a day's journey distant from Uppsala. But the way is such that, sailing the sea from Scania of the Danes, you will arrive at Sigtuna or Björkö on the fifth day,[89] for they are close together. If, however, you go by land from Scania through the midst of the Gothic peoples and the cities Skara, Södertelge, and Björkö, it will take you a whole month to reach Sigtuna.

xxx (29). Glowing with fervor, then, Adalward entered Sweden to preach the Gospel and in a short time led to the Christian faith

[87] Cf. Gen. 24:16; II Paral. 1:7.
[88] Luke 21:28; John 4:35.
[89] Cf. Schol. 126(121) above.

all in Sigtuna[a] and round about.[90] He also secretly agreed with Egino, the most saintly bishop of Scania, that they should go together to the pagan temple called Uppsala to see if they could perhaps offer Christ some fruit of their labors there, for they would willingly undergo every kind of torture for the sake of destroying that house which was the seat of barbarous superstition. For, if it were torn down, or preferably burned, the conversion of the whole nation might follow. Observing that the people murmured about this design of the confessors of God, the most pious king Stenkil shrewdly kept them from such an undertaking, declaring that they would at once be punished with death and he be driven from the kingdom for bringing malefactors into the country, and that everyone who now believed would quickly relapse into paganism, as they could see had lately been the case in Slavia. The bishops deferred to these arguments of the king and, going through all the cities of the Goths, they broke up idols and thereafter won many thousands of pagans to Christianity. When Adalward later died in our midst, the archbishop appointed in his place a certain Tadico[91] of Ramelsloh, who out of love for his belly preferred even to starve at home rather than be an apostle abroad. Let these remarks about Sweden and its rites suffice.

xxxi (30). As Nortmannia is the farthest country of the world, so we properly place consideration of it in the last part of the book.[b] By moderns it is called Norway.[92] Of its location and extent

[a] Schol. 142 (138). Certain persons in Bishop Adalward's company told us that when he first came to Sigtuna seventy marks of silver were placed in his hands as oblations at one celebration of the Mass. So great, indeed, is the devotion of all the people of the Arctic region. At that time, also, as he was on a journey he turned aside to Björkö, which now was turned into such a wilderness* that scarcely a vestige of the city was visible. On this account the burial mound of the holy archbishop Unni could not be found.

* Cf. Gen. 47:19; Exod. 23(29).

[b] Schol. 143 (139). From these Northmen who live beyond Denmark came those Northmen who live in France, and from the latter Apulia† received a third set of Northmen a while ago.

† Cf. Schol. 40(41) above.

---

[90] But see III.lxxvi and Schol. 136(131) above.
[91] Cf. III.lxxvii above.
[92] Cf. *Gesta Cnutonis* II.vii.19.

we made some mention earlier in connection with Sweden, but this in particular must now be said, that in its length that land extends into the farthest northern zone, whence also it takes its name. It begins with towering crags at the sea commonly called the Baltic; then with its main ridge bent toward the north, after following the course of the shore line of a raging ocean, it finally has its bounds in the Rhiphaean Mountains, where the tired world also comes to an end. On account of the roughness of its mountains and the immoderate cold, Norway is the most unproductive of all countries, suited only for herds. They browse their cattle, like the Arabs, far off in the solitudes. In this way do the people make a living from their livestock by using the milk of the flocks or herds for food and the wool for clothing. Consequently, there are produced very valiant fighters who, not softened by any overindulgence in fruits, more often attack others than others trouble them. Even though they are sometimes assailed—not with impunity—by the Danes, who are just as poor, the Norwegians live in terms of amity with their neighbors, the Swedes. Poverty[93] has forced them thus to go all over the world and from piratical raids they bring home in great abundance the riches of the lands. In this way they bear up under the unfruitfulness of their own country. Since accepting Christianity, however, imbued with better teachings, they have already learned to love the truth and peace[94] and to be content with their poverty—indeed, to disperse what they had gathered, not as before to gather what had been dispersed. And whereas they had from the beginning all been given to the nefarious arts of magic, they now in simplicity confess with the Apostle, "Christ, and him crucified."[95] They also are the most continent of all mortals, with all diligence prizing frugality and modesty, both as to their food and to their morals. They have, besides, such reverence for priests and churches that he who does not daily make an offering at the Mass which he hears is hardly considered a Chris-

[93] Cf. Sallust *Catiline* v.7.
[94] Zach. 8:19.
[95] I Cor. 2:2.

tian. As a matter of fact, baptism and confirmation, the dedication of altars, and the ordination to holy orders are all dearly paid for among them and by the Danes. This, I think, proceeds from the avarice of the priests. As the barbarians still either do not know about tithes or refuse to pay them, they are fleeced for other offices that ought to be rendered for nothing. For even the visitation of the sick and the burial of the dead[a]—everything there has a price.[96] Their excellent moral character, as I have learned, is therefore corrupted only by priestly avarice.

xxxii (31). In many places in Norway and Sweden cattle herdsmen are even men of the highest station, living in the manner of patriarchs and by the work of their own hands. All, indeed, who live in Norway are thoroughly Christian, except those who are removed beyond the arctic tract along the ocean. These people, it is said, are to this day so superior in the magic arts or incantations that they profess to know what every one is doing the world over.[97] Then they also draw great sea monsters[98] to shore with a powerful mumbling of words and do much else of which one reads in the Scriptures about magicians. All this is easy for them through practice. I have heard that women grow beards in the extremely rough alps of that region and that the men live in the woods, rarely exposing themselves to sight. They use the pelts of wild beasts for clothing and in speaking to one another are said to gnash their teeth[99] rather than to utter words, so that they can

---

[a] Schol. 144 (140). Although they do not believe in the resurrection of the flesh, this is nevertheless noteworthy about the burial of the pagans that, after the manner of the ancient Romans, they conduct their cremations and obsequies with all respect. Furthermore, they bury a man's money with him and the arms and other belongings he held very dear while he lived. This also is written of the Hindus.* And this is derived from the ancient rite of the pagans in whose tombs it is still usual to find such objects, because they ordered their treasures buried with them either in amphorae or in other small vessels.

* Servius *Comment. in Virgilium Aeneidos* v.86.

---

[96] Cf. Sallust *Catiline* x.4; *Jugurtha* viii.1.
[97] Cf. Vergil *Aeneid* xi.344-45; Juvenal *Satires* vi.402.
[98] Cf. Gen. 1:21.
[99] Solinus *Collect.* xxx.iii, so describes the Troglodytes. Cf. Schol. 135(130-131) above; iv.xliv(42) below.

hardly be understood by the peoples nearest to them. That mountain region is named by Roman writers the Rhiphaean range, terrible for its perpetual snows.[100] Without these frosty snows the Skritefingi cannot live, and in their course over the deepest drifts they fly even faster than the wild beasts. In those same mountains[a] there are such large numbers of big game that the greatest part of the country subsists only on the beasts of the forest. Aurochs, buffaloes, and elk[101] are taken there as in Sweden. Bison, furthermore, are caught in Slavia and Russia. Only in Norway, however, are there black fox and hares, white martens and bears of the same color who live under water like aurochs. And since much else may there be seen that is entirely different and strange to our people, we leave it and other things to be more fully described by the inhabitants of that land.

xxxiii (32). The metropolitan city of the Norwegians is Trondhjem, which, now graced with churches, is frequented by a great multitude of peoples. In that city reposes the body of the most blessed Olaf, king and martyr.[b] At this tomb the Lord to this very day works such very great miraculous cures[102] that those who do not despair of being able to get help through

---

[a] Schol. 145 (141). Paul affirms in his *History of the Lombards** that in a cavern off the ocean in the farthest northern parts among the Skritefingi seven men lie as if asleep.† About them there are divergent opinions, including the belief that they are going to preach to those heathen about the time the world will end. Others say that some of the Eleven Thousand Virgins‡ came to this region and that their attendants and ships are buried in a mountain and that miracles are wrought there. In that place Olaf** also built a church.

* I.iv.
† Gregory of Tours *Miracula* I.xcv (Migne, *PL*, LXXI, 787-89).
‡ Of Cologne. The legend is very difficult to probe to its bases in fact. See *Catholic Encyclopedia*, "Ursula."
** Olaf the Saint of Sweden.

[b] Schol. 146 (141). The most just king Olaf first drew the Norwegians to Christianity. Magnus, his son, subjugated the Danes. Harold, the brother of the most wicked Olaf, added the Orkneys to his dominion and also extended his kingdom to the Rhiphaean Mountains and to Iceland.††
†† Cf. III.xvii(16) above. Harold did not conquer Iceland.

---

[100] Solinus *Collect.* xv.xx, xxxviii.xi-xii mentions the Rhiphaean Mountains in a chapter on the Euphrates region. Cf. Schol., 137(132-133) above.
[101] Solinus *Collect.* xx.v-vi.
[102] Cf. II.lxi(53) above.

the merits of the saint flock together there from far-off lands. But the route is of a kind that, boarding a ship, they may, in a day's journey, cross the sea from Aalborg or Wendila of the Danes to Viken,[103] a city of the Norwegians. Sailing thence toward the left along the coast of Norway, the city called Trondhjem is reached on the fifth day. But it is possible also to go another way that leads over a land road from Scania of the Danes to Trondhjem. This route, however, is slower in the mountainous country, and travelers avoid it because it is dangerous.

xxxiv (33). The first bishop, a certain John,[a][104] came from England to Norway, and he converted and baptized the king[105] with his people. He was succeeded by Bishop Grimkil, who at that time was King Olaf's legate to Archbishop Unwan. In the third place came the Sigefrid[b][106] who preached alike among the Swedes and Norwegians. And he lived to our own age along with other equally well-known priests among the people. After their deaths, on the petition of the Norwegian peoples, our metropolitan consecrated Tholf for the city of Trondhjem and Seward[107] for those same parts. Although the archbishop took it ill that Asgot and Bernhard[108] had been consecrated by the pope, he let them go laden with presents after he had taken pledges.[109] Even to this day

---

[a] Schol. 147 (142). Although Liafdag,[*] Odinkar,[†] and Poppo,[‡] of our community, preached to this people before him, it can be said that ours labored, but that the English entered into their labors.[**]

[*] Cf. ii.xxvi(23) above.

[†] The Younger. Cf. ii.xxxvi(34), xlix(47), lxiv(62) above.

[‡] Cf. Schol. 113(112) above.

[**] Cf. John 4:38.

[b] Schol. 148 (142). When this Meinhard[††] and Albert,[‡‡] who had been consecrated elsewhere, came to the bishop, he entrusted them with his authority, along with gifts, throughout Norway as well as the islands of the ocean.

[††] The Younger Sigefrid.

[‡‡] Cf. iii.lxxvii above.

---

[103] A district today called Larvik, not a town.

[104] Cf. ii.xxxvii(35) above.

[105] Olaf Tryggvason. Cf. ii.xxxiv-xxxvi above.

[106] The Younger, who met the pseudo bishop Osmund in Sweden.

[107] Cf. iii.lxxvii above.

[108] Cf. ii.lvii(55) above.

[109] Cf. Acts 17:9.

the Word of God wins through these bishops so many souls that Holy Mother Church is enjoying prosperous increase in all the provinces of Norway. On account of the newness of the Christian plantation among the Norwegians and Swedes, however, none of the bishoprics has so far been assigned definite limits, but each one of the bishops, accepted by the king or the people, cooperates in building up the Church and, going about the country,[a] draws as many as he can to Christianity and governs them without objection as long as they live.

xxxv (34). Beyond Norway, which is the farthermost northern country, you will find no human habitation,[110] nothing but ocean, terrible to look upon[111] and limitless, encircling the whole world.[112] The ocean off Norway contains many considerable islands, of which nearly all are now subject to the rule of the Norwegians and so are not to be overlooked by us because they also belong to the diocese of Hamburg. The first of them are the Orkney Islands,[113] which the barbarians call the *Organae*. Like the Cyclades, they are strewn over the ocean.[114] The Roman writers Martian and Solinus,[115] it appears, wrote about them thus: "Back of Britain,[a] where the boundless ocean begins, are the Orkney Islands, of which twenty are deserted, sixteen are inhabited.[116] The Orkney Islands, numbering nearly forty, lie close together. In their vicinity, too,

[a] Schol. 149(143) ... Pliny* says of the Hyperboreans that ... in the deep sea ..
* *Nat. Hist.* IV.xxvi.
[b] Schol. 150 (144). Sailors relate marvels about the British Ocean, which touches Denmark and Norway: that in the vicinity of the Orkneys the sea is congealed† and so thickened with salt that ships can hardly move except with the help of strong winds. For this reason also that sea is commonly called the Libersee‡ in our language.
† Cf. Martianus Capella *De Nuptiis* VI.666; Solinus *Collect* XXII.ix; Schol. 154(147) below; IV.xxxix(38) below.
‡ Cf. Schol. 150(144), 154(147) below.

110 Cf. Martianus Capella *De Nuptiis* VI.664.
111 Cf. Vergil *Aeneid* VI.277.
112 Cf. Martianus Capella *De Nuptiis* VI.603,617.
113 Cf. III.xxiv(23), lxxiii above.
114 Cf. Vergil *Aeneid* III.126-27.
115 Solinus does not mention the Orkneys. The quotation is from Orosius *Hist. adv. Paganos.* I.ii (Migne, *PL*, XXXI, 690). Cf. Martianus Capella *De Nuptiis* VI.666.
116 Orosius reads thirteen. Cf. Martianus Capella *De Nuptiis* V.666; Pliny *Nat. Hist.* IV.xvi.

are the *Electrides*,[117] on which amber originates." Situated between Norway and Britain and Ireland, the Orkneys,[a] therefore, laugh playfully at the threats of a menacing ocean.[118] It is said that one can sail to them in a day from the Norwegian city of Trondhjem. They say, too, that from the Orkneys it is just as far whether you steer toward England or set sail for Scotland. For these same Orkney Islands, although they had previously been ruled by English and Scottish bishops, our primate on the pope's order consecrated Throlf[119] bishop for the city of Birsay,[120] and he was to have the cure of all.

xxxvi (35). "The island Thule,[a] which, separated from the others by endless stretches, is situated far off in the midst of the ocean, is," they say, "barely known."[121] About it Roman writers[b] as well as barbarians report much that is worth repeating. "The farthest island of all," they say, "is Thule, in which there is no night at the summer solstice, when the sun crosses the sign of Cancer; and likewise, no day at the winter solstice.[c] This, they think, takes place every six months."[122] Bede also writes that the bright summer nights in Britain indicate without a doubt that at the solstice it is continuously day for six months and, on the con-

---

a Schol. 151 (145). It is evident here that the writer of this little book was from upper Germany, because in an effort to adapt very many words and proper nouns to his own language he corrupted them for us.*

* This scholium was probably added by the scribes of Codex *C,* who noted Adam's use of the term Libersee in the preceding scholium.

b Schol. 152 (146). Thule, situated in the ocean sea, the remotest of all the islands. Solinus relates that in the springtime its inhabitants live on the sustenance of cattle, in the summertime and after they live on milk. For they lay up the fruits of the trees for the winter.

c Schol. 153. Martian, Solinus, and . . .

d Schol. 154 (147). Britain is the largest of all the islands. From it Thule is reached by a voyage of nine days. Thence† it is a day's voyage to the frozen sea. And this sea is frozen for the reason that it is never warmed by the sun.

† Cf. Bede *De natura rerum* ix (Migne, *PL,* XC, 204); Martianus Capella *De Nuptiis* VI.666; Pliny *Nat. Hist.* IV.xvi(30).

---

117 Probably the Hebrides.
118 Cf. Vergil *Aeneid.* VI.113, X.695; Lucan *Civil War* V.578.
119 About 1050. Cf. III.xxiv(23), lxxiii above.
120 Probably on Pomona island. This identification is disputed.
121 Orosius *Hist. adv. Paganos* I.ii (Migne, *PL,* XXXI, 690).
122 Solinus *Collect.* XXII.ix.

trary, night in the wintertime, when the sun is withdrawn.[123] And
Pytheas of Marseilles writes that this happens on the island of
Thule, six days' sail distant from Britain toward the north.[124a]
This Thule is now called Iceland, from the ice which binds the
ocean. About this island they also report this remarkable fact,
that the ice on account of its age is so black and dry in appearance
that it burns when fire is set to it.[125] This island, however, is so
very large that it has on it many peoples, who make a living only
by raising cattle and who clothe themselves with their pelts. No
crops are grown there; the supply of wood is very meager. On
this account the people dwell in underground caves, glad to have
roof and food and bed in common with their cattle. Passing their
lives thus in holy simplicity, because they seek nothing more than
what nature affords, they can joyfully say with the Apostle: "But
having food, and wherewith to be covered, with these we are
content."[126] For instead of towns they have mountains and springs
as their delights. Blessed, I say, is the folk whose poverty no one
envies; and in this respect most blessed because all have now
adopted Christianity. They have many meritorious customs, especially charity, in consequence of which they have all things in
common[127] with strangers as well as with natives.[128] They hold
their bishop as king.[b] All the people respect his wishes. They hold
as law whatever he ordains as coming from God, or from the

a Schol. 155 (148). On leaving the Danish headland Aalborg, they say it is
a journey of thirty days to Iceland; less, however, if the wind is favorable.
b Schol. 156 (150). Among them there is no king, but only law: and "to sin
is an abomination; or if they sin the penalty is death." *
* Horace *Odes* iii.xxiv.24. Cf. Schol. 122(118) above.

---

123 *De temp. rat.* xxxi (Migne, *PL*, XC, 434, 436-37).
124 Cf. Pliny *Nat. Hist.* ii.lxxv; Solinus *Collect.* xxii.x(18).
125 The presence of surtarbrand escaped the observers of the phenomenon. Surtarbrand is a peatlike variety of brown coal or lignite occurring in the Pliocene
deposits and sometimes under the volcanic overflows of Iceland. The phenomenon
is also noted in the addendum on the Britannic Islands, below. Fay, *Glossary of
Mining and Mineral Industry*, s.v. "Surtarbrand."
126 I Tim. 6:8.
127 Cf. Acts 2:44; 4:32.
128 Cf. Num. 9:14; 15:29.

Scriptures, or even from the worthy practices of other peoples.ᵃ For them our metropolitan returned vast thanks to God that they had been converted in his time, even though before receiving the faith they were in what may be called their natural law, which was not much out of accord with our religion.ᵇ On their petition, therefore, the archbishop consecrated a certain most holy man named Islef.[129] And when he was sent from that region to the prelate, the latter held him in his company for a while and furthermore bestowed great honor upon him. In the meantime Islef learned in what respects peoples newly converted to Christ can salutarily be instructed. By him the archbishop transmitted letters to the people of Iceland and Greenland, reverently greeting their churches and promising them he would come to them very soon[130] that their joy may be full together.[131] From these words the high purpose which the archbishop had with regard to his legateship can be adduced as, indeed, we also learn the Apostle wished to journey to Spain in order to preach the Word of God, which intention he was unable to carry out.[132] Disregarding the fabulous, these facts about Iceland and the farthest Thule we learned are true.

xxxvii (36).   In the ocean there are very many other islands of which not the least is Greenland, situated far out in the ocean opposite the mountains of Sweden and the Rhiphaean range. To this island they say it is from five to seven days' sail from the coast of Norway, the same as to Iceland. The people there are greenish from the salt water, whence, too, that region gets its name. The people live in the same manner as the Icelanders except that they are fiercer and trouble seafarers by their piratical attacks. Report has it that Christianity of late has also winged its way to them.

ᵃ Schol. 157 (151). The largest city there is Skalholt.
ᵇ Schol. 158 (149). By Iceland the ocean is frozen and seething and foggy.

---

[129] Consecrated on Pentecost (June 4), 1055.
[130] Cf. Sallust *Catiline* xxxii.2, xliv.2.
[131] Cf. John 1:4, 12; 16:24.
[132] Cf. Rom. 15:24.

xxxviii (37). The third island is Helgeland,[133a] nearer to Norway but in extent not unequal to the rest. That island sees the sun upon the land for fourteen days continuously at the solstice in summer and, similarly, it lacks the sun for the same number of days in the winter. To the barbarians, who do not know that the difference in the length of days is due to the accession and recession of the sun, this is astounding and mysterious. For on account of the rotundity of the earth,[134] the sun in its course necessarily brings day as it approaches a place, and leaves night as it recedes from it. While the sun is approaching the summer solstice, the day is lengthened for those who live in the northern parts and the nights shortened; when it descends to the winter solstice, that is for the same reason the experience of southerners. Not knowing this, the pagans call that land holy and blessed which affords mortals such a wonder. The king of the Danes and many others have attested the occurrence of this phenomenon there, as in Sweden and in Norway and on the rest of the islands in those parts.

xxxix (38). He spoke also of yet another island of the many found in that ocean. It is called Vinland because vines producing excellent wine grow wild there. That unsown crops also abound on that island we have ascertained not from fabulous reports but from the trustworthy relation of the Danes. Beyond that island, he said, no habitable land is found in that ocean, but every place beyond it is full of impenetrable ice and intense darkness. Of this fact Martianus[135] makes mention as follows: "Beyond Thule," he says, "the sea is congealed after one day's navigation." The very

---

a Schol. 159 (152). Others say Helgeland is part of farthest Norway, lying very near the Skritefingi and inaccessible by reason of the rugged mountains and the cold.

---

[133] A district in northern Norway, not an island, as Adam learned later. Cf. Schol. 159(152) below.

[134] Adam knew that the earth is round, but could not, in his time, draw geographical conclusions from his knowledge; nor could tides have been explained before Newton came upon the theory of gravitation. Cf. Beazley, *Dawn of Modern Geography*, II, 524; Kohlmann, *Adam von Bremen*, pp. 36-37.

[135] *De Nuptiis* VI.666.

well-informed prince of the Norwegians, Harold,[136] lately attempted this sea. After he had explored the expanse of the Northern Ocean in his ships, there lay before their eyes at length the darksome bounds of a failing world, and by retracing his steps he barely escaped in safety the vast pit of the abyss.[137]

xl (39).[138]   Archbishop Adalbert of blessed memory likewise told us that in the days of his predecessor certain noble men of Frisia spread sail to the north for the purpose of ranging through the sea, because the inhabitants claimed that by a direct course toward the north from the mouth of the Weser River one meets with no land but only that sea called the Libersee. The partners pledged themselves under oath to look into this novel claim and, with a joyful call to the oarsmen, set out from the Frisian coast. Then, leaving on the one side Denmark, on the other Britain, they came to the Orkneys. And when they had left these islands to their left, while they had Norway on their right, the navigators landed after a long passage on icy Iceland. And as they furrowed the seas[139] from that place toward the farthest northern pole, after they saw behind them all the islands spoken about above, they commended their way and venture to Almighty God and the holy confessor Willehad. Of a sudden they fell into that numbing ocean's dark mist[140] which could hardly be penetrated with the eyes. And, behold, the current[141] of the fluctuating ocean whirled back[142] to its mysterious fountainhead and with most furious impetuosity drew the unhappy sailors, who in their despair now thought only of death, on to chaos; this they say is the abysmal chasm—that deep in which report has it all the back flow of the

---

[136] Harold Hardrada. The expedition must have been made some time before 1066, the year of his death. Cf. III.xvii(16) above; Beazley, *Dawn of Modern Geography*, II, 525.

[137] Cf. Vergil *Aeneid* VIII.245.

[138] The readings are respectively those of codices of the *A, C2* and *B* classes.

[139] Cf. Vergil *Aeneid* x.197.

[140] Cf. Gen. 15:17; *Vita Liudgeri* xxii (*MGH, SS,* II, 410).

[141] Cf. Lucan *Civil War* v.235.

[142] There is a dangerous whirlpool full of icebergs, called the Eis, in the ocean off the east coast of Greenland.

sea, which appears to decrease, is absorbed and in turn revomited, as the mounting fluctuation is usually described. As the partners were imploring the mercy of God to receive their souls, the backward thrust of the sea carried away some of their ships, but its forward ejection threw the rest far behind the others.[143] Freed thus by the timely help of God from the instant peril they had had before their eyes, they seconded the flood by rowing with all their might.

xli (40). No sooner had the mariners escaped the peril of darkness and the land of frost than they unexpectedly came upon an island[144] fortified like a town by very high cliffs which encircled it. When they disembarked there to explore the place, they found men lurking in underground hollows at midday. Before the entrances lay a countless number of vessels of gold and of metals of a kind considered rare and precious by mortals.[145] When they had taken as much of the treasure as they could carry away, the happy oarsmen returned quickly to their ships. Of a sudden they saw coming behind them the amazingly tall men whom our people call Cyclops. Before them ran dogs exceeding the usual size of these quadrupeds,[146] who in their attack seized one of the comrades and in a twinkling tore him to pieces before their eyes.[147] The rest, however, took to the ships and escaped the peril. The giants, as they said, followed them, with vociferations, almost out to the high sea. Attended by such good fortune, the Frisians came back to Bremen where they told Archbishop Alebrand everything as it had happened and made offerings to the blessed Christ and His holy confessor Willehad for their safe return.

[143] Philo Judaeus' statement, in his *On Dreams* II.xvii, that the Germans charged the incoming tide with drawn swords, may be the origin of the story of King Canute's ordering the sea to stop. Cf. Beazley, *Dawn of Modern Geography*, II, 525-26; Thorndike, *History of Magic and Experimental Science*, I, 351.

[144] Possibly Ireland.

[145] Cf. Sallust *Jugurtha* lxxvi.6. The men and their dogs may have appeared unusually large because of the fog. This story may have been fabricated to remove the suspicion that the Frisians turned pirate.

[146] Such dogs were noted on the Canary Islands by Martianus Capella *De Nuptiis* VI.702 and by Solinus *Collect.* LVI.xvii.

[147] Cf. Dan. 14:41.

xlii (40).　There are still other things that might not improperly be mentioned in this place about the tide of the sea which rises twice a day. This phenomenon excites all with the greatest wonder, so much so that even the natural philosophers who search out the secrets of things fall into doubt about a phenomenon of which they do not know the origin.[148] While Macrobius[149] and Bede[150] apparently have something to say about this occurrence, and Lucan[151] confesses he knows nothing,[152] various writers contend for various theories. But they all go astray with uncertain explanations. For us it is enough to declare with the prophet: "How great are Thy works, O Lord? Thou hast made all things in wisdom: the earth is filled with Thy riches."[153] And again: "Thine are the heavens, and Thine is the earth"[154] and "Thou rulest the power of the sea"[155] and "Thy judgments are a great deep,"[156] and so they rightfully call them incomprehensible.

xliii (41).　This is what we have learned about the nature of the northern regions in order to set it down to the honor of the Church at Hamburg. We behold the immensity of the blessings bestowed on it by the divine goodness that have enabled it to become the metropolitan Church of that innumerable multitude of peoples who in great part have been converted to Christianity by its preaching. There only is its preaching hushed where the world has its end. Undertaken first by the saintly Ansgar, that mission, bringing salvation to the heathen, has by prosperous increase grown continuously down to this very day, to the passing of the great Adalbert, a period of about two hundred and forty years.

xliv (42).　Behold that exceedingly fierce race of the Danes,

---

[148] Cf. IV.xxxviii, Note 134, above; Solinus. *Collect.* XXIII.xviii-xxii, XXXII.ix.
[149] *Somnium Scipionis* II.ix.3.
[150] *De Natura rerum* xxxix (Migne, *PL,* XC, 258-60).
[151] *Civil War* I.409-19, v.237, X.213-67.
[152] Cf. Vergil *Aeneid* XI.344-45.
[153] Ps. 103:24.
[154] Ps. 88:12.
[155] Ps. 88:10.
[156] Ps. 35:7.

of the Norwegians, or of the Swedes which, in the words of the Blessed Gregory, "knew nothing else but in barbarism to gnash its teeth, has long since learned to intone Alleluia in the praise of God."[157] Behold that piratical people, by which, we read, whole provinces of the Gauls and of Germany were at one time devastated and which is now content with its bounds and can say with the Apostle, "For we have not here a lasting city, but we seek one that is to come";[158] and "We believe to see the good things of the Lord in the land of the living."[159] Behold, that land of horrors, inaccessible always because of its worship of idols,

> Whose altar is no more benign
> Than that of Scythian Diana,[160]

everywhere admits eagerly, now that the native fury of its folk has been subdued, the preachers of the truth; and, since the altars of the demons have been torn down, it builds churches far and wide, and with universal acclaim everyone proclaims the name of Christ. Surely, "this is the change of the right hand of the most High,"[161] and so swiftly runs the word of the Almighty God[162] that "from the rising and from the setting of the sun, from the north and from the sea,[163] the name of the Lord is worthy of praise,"[164] and "every tongue should confess that the Lord Jesus Christ is in the glory of God the Father,"[165] with the Holy Ghost, living and reigning forever and ever. Amen.[166]

---

[157] Quoting the words attributed to him when he met English boys in the slave market in Rome. *Moralia* XXVII.xi (Migne, *PL,* LXXVI, 411).

[158] Heb. 13:14.

[159] Ps. 26:13.

[160] Lucan *Civil War* I.476.

[161] Ps. 76:11.

[162] Ps. 147:15

[163] Ps. 106:3.

[164] Ps. 112:3.

[165] Phil. 2:11.

[166] Cf. Gregory the Great *Homilia in Ezech.* II.vi (Migne, *PL,* LXXV, 59).

Epilogue

OF MASTER ADAM
TO BISHOP LIEMAR

O noble prelate, take the trifling gift
Thy servant brings to thee and to thy Church,
His heart filled full of love. Paltry it is,
Indeed,[1] and hardly worth, so do I judge,[2]
Another reading to give pleasure to
The eyes of Cato.[3] What may I suppose
These stammering words[4] will thee avail, when with
The flowers of rhetoric thou dost thy speech
Adorn, when with thy tongue thou dost the books
Of God unlock, when with thy careful search
Thou dost the Fathers' sacred tomes peruse?
But though the mighty's many gifts to God
Were pleasing, bear in mind how often praised
The widow is for her two mites.[5] I trust
Also that for this writing thou wilt have
The more esteem because naught falsely writ
Or on the surface fair wilt thou perceive
Therein, but that its every page intones

---

[1] Cf. Juvenal *Satires* VI.184.
[2] Cf. *ibid.,* VIII.188.
[3] The Censor.
[4] Cf. Horace *Satires* II.iii.274.
[5] Cf. Mark 12:42; Luke 21:2.

The Church's praise and Bremen's story true.
The Bride's fair fame is honor for her groom.
And as thou browsest countless bookish fields,
Behooves it thee to know what everywhere
Thou readest, that to others does belong :
This book is thine, is wholly wrapped in thee,
Sets forth thy predecessors' deeds to thine
Own times. Regard my wishes, then, and spare
My childish efforts.[6] Grant, I pray, that hopes
To which thy servant clings prove not in vain;[7]
To honor thee he does not blush to play
The poet. Shepherd, reverend and good,
To thee I verily confess if I
Could not write well, assuredly I wrote
Veraciously,[8] resorting to the best
Informed witnesses this subject claims.
I seek for this production neither praise
Nor recompense. Enough I reckon it,
Indeed, if my endeavor pleases thee.
Again, reflect, discredit does not come
Upon thy cloister for the least among
Its brethren to have fully wrought a work
Recording facts of vast importance. There
In writing are set forth the origins
Of our Church, the saving of the folk
In the far north, a picture of the deeds
Of those preceding thee. The time will come[9]
When someone of thy learned band,[10] or we,
Surviving thee, shall sing in loftier strains
The glories of thy celebrated deeds.

[6] Cf. Vergil *Aeneid* ii.535.
[7] Cf. Lucan *Civil War* i.469.
[8] Cf. iii.lxxi(70) above.
[9] Cf. Lucan *Civil War* viii.467, Vergil *Aeneid* ii.268.
[10] Cf. Lucan *Civil War* viii.205.

What thou hast done throughout the world, in truth,
Is fully known; without a history
Its fame would be forever[11] on the lips
Of men. Not out of mind has passed, indeed,
Thy fortunate selection. Ancient laws
The fathers held observing, thee the Ghost
Informing set before us, worthy of
A pastor's dignity, God-chosen on
The day the faithful throng to celebrate
His feast.[12] O, with what flow of tears saw we
The people win thee! Common longings pent
Before gave utterance to the prayers of all
That thou mightst prove so great, nay greater far
Than any hopes would warrant, or our faith
Deserve. By thee the people's necks were freed
Of chains oppressive, heavy burdens struck
From breaking backs. Through thee the mourning of
Afflicted people turned to joy.[13] By thee
The clergy, robber-ridden through unjust
Exactions, had their own restored; by thee
Were we from hoary superstitions freed
And sacred temples with their elegance
Redecked. Through thee the peace that, giving way
To ancient hate, had fled the churches and
The land, was summoned back; and then, when strife
A third time swelled,[14] discordant minds embraced.[15]
If aught till now remains the common joy
Disturbing, God vouchsafe thee settlement.
And may He grant thee more: that Bremen's see,

[11] Cf. Vergil *Aeneid* IX.77.
[12] Henry IV designated Liemar for the see at Magdeburg on Pentecost, May 27, 1072. Cf. Meyer von Knonau, *Jahrbücher,* II, 156-57.
[13] Cf. Jas. 4:9.
[14] Vergil, *Aeneid* XI.631, 635.
[15] Reference is to the Saxon disturbance of October, 1075, in which Liemar played a mediating role. Cf. Meyer von Knonau, *Jahrbücher,* II, 530 n. 102.

And Hamburg's freedom find through thee. The one
Beset by pagans and the other all
About by tyrants[16]—both long years have wept
Their prisonment. O Liemar, father, may
The grace of Christ incline to thee as we,
Thy flock, with heart and tongue thee venerate!

[16] Cf. iii.i above.

Appendix

THE BRITANNIC ISLANDS [1]

Norway, Helgeland. In this land the sun shines continuously for fifteen days before the feast of Saint John the Baptist[2] and for fifteen days after, and the moon a like period before the Nativity and after the Nativity of the Lord.

Scotland. A part of this land is called Morvern, where, indeed, there are Christians; but the custom has grown up among them that, when someone of common and base-born rank dies there, he is left unburied in the field or on the road. But if he was rich, they tie a stone about his neck and sink him in the sea. If, however, he was of noble rank, they tie him to a tree extended as if he were on a rack, and let him decompose there.

Götaland, Sweden, Greenland. The peoples of this land claim that they are in part Christian, even though they are without faith and without confession and without baptism. In part they even worship Jupiter and Mars, although they are likewise Christian.

Iceland. On this island the ice of the sea catches fire the moment it is broken up and, when it has taken fire, blazes like wood.[3] Here also are good Christians, but on account of the excessive cold they dare not leave their underground hollows in the wintertime. For if they go out, they are burned by the cold, which is so extreme

---

[1] This fragment was written at the end of the twelfth or early in the thirteenth century by an unknown person who made use of, and doubtless was inspired by, Adam's fourth book. He was, however, independent of Adam and for that reason this passage has been appended to Adam's work.

[2] Cf. IV.xxxvi(35) above.

[3] Cf. IV.xxxv(34) above.

that like lepers they lose their color as the swelling gradually spreads. Also, if they happen to wipe their noses, the whole nose pulls off with the mucus itself and, having come off, they throw it away.

Ireland, Inzegale. To these lands belong forty islands;[4] inhabited are Arregweite, Kentyre, Nessunt, Man.

[4] Perhaps in the North Channel between Ireland and Scotland.

Selected Bibliography

Editions and Translations of Adam's Work (in Chronological Order)

Quellen des 9. und 11. Jahrhunderts zur Geschichte der Hamburgischen Kirche und des Reiches: Fontes saeculorum noni et undecimi historiam ecclesiae Hammaburgensis necnon imperii illustrantes—Rimberti vita Anskarii, Adami Bremensis gesta Hammaburgensis ecclesiae pontificum, Wiponis gesta Chuonradi II. imperatoris, Herimanni Augiensis chronicon. Edited by Werner Trillmilch. Ausgewählte Quellen zur deutschen Geschichte des Mittelalters, 11. Darmstadt: Wissenschaftliche Buchgesellschaft, 1961. [Adam's text is pp. 137–500; the Latin text is based on Schmeidler's edition, with a German facing translation and annotation.]

Adam af Bremen, Beskrivelse af øerne i Norden. Translated by Allan A. Lund. Højbjerg: Wormianum, 1978. [Latin text following Schmeidler's edition and translation of fourth book only.]

Historien om Hamburgstiftet och dess biskopar: Adam av Bremen. Translated by Emanuel Svenberg; commentary by Carl Fredrik Hallencreutz, Kurt Johannesson, Tore Nyberg, Anders Piltz. Stockholm: Proprius Förlag, 1984. [Swedish translation of Latin text of Schmeidler's ms. A3; see bibliography for details of commentary articles.]

Hamburgische Kirchengeschichte: Geschichte der Erzbischöfe von Hamburg—Adam von Bremen. Translated by J. C. M. Laurent and Wilhelm Wattenbach; edited by Alexander Heine. Essen: Phaidon 1986. [A straightforward reprint of the nineteenth-century translation in the *Geschichtsschreiber der deutschen Vorzeit* series, from which all more recent German translations are derived.]

Storia degli arcivescovi della chiesa di Amburgo, di Adamo di Brema. Edited by Ileana Pagani. Turin: UTET, 1996. [Latin text based on Schmeidler's and Trillmilch's editions, with facing Italian translation.]

Secondary Works

Abrams, Lesley J. "Eleventh-Century Missions and the Early Stages of Ecclesiastical Organisation in Scandinavia." In Christopher Harper-Bill, ed. *Anglo-Norman Studies, XVII: Proceedings of the Battle Conference, 1994*, pp. 21–40. Woodbridge, Suffolk: Boydell and Brewer, 1995.

———. "The Anglo-Saxons and the Christianization of Scandinavia." *Anglo-Saxon England* 24 (1995): 213–49.

Ahlfeld, Richard. "Die Gozecker Chronik (Chronicon Gozecense) (1041–1135)." *Jahrbuch zur Geschichte Mittel- und Ostdeutschlands*, 16/17 (1968): 1–49.

Alkarp, Magnus. "Källen, lunden och templet—Adam av Bremens Uppsalaskildring i ny belysning." *Fornvännen* 92 (1997): 155–61.

Andermann, Ulrich. *Albert Krantz: Wissenschaft und Histographie um 1500*. Forschungen zur mittelalterlichen Geschichte 38. Weimar: Böhlau 1999.

Andersen, Per Sveeas. *Samling av Norge og kristningen av landet 800–1130*. Handbok i Norges historie 2. Oslo, Bergen, and Tromsø: Universitetsforlaget, 1977.

Anderson, Paul G. "Denmark After the Vikings: Major Developments in Danish Politics and Culture, 1042–1160." Ph.D. diss., Wayne State University, 1977.

Andrén, Anders. "Städer och kungamakt—en studie i Danmarks politiska geografi före 1230." *Scandia* 49 (1983): 31–76.

Anglert, Mats. "Den kyrkliga organisationen under äldre medeltid." In Hans Andersson and Mats Anglert, eds., *By, huvudgåd och kyrka: Studier i Ystadsområdets medeltid*, pp. 221–42. Lund Studies in Medieval Archaeology 5. Stockholm: Almqvist and Wiksell, 1989.

Bagge, Sverre. "Decline and Fall: Deterioration of Character as Described by Adam of Bremen and Sturlaþóóarson." In Jan A. Aertsen and Andreas Speer, eds., *Individuum und Individualität im Mittelalter*, pp. 530–48. Miscellanea Mediaevalia 24. Berlin: Walter de Gruyter, 1996.

———. "Kingship in Medieval Norway: Ideal and Reality." In Heinz Duchhardt, Richard A. Jackson, and David Sturdy, eds., *European Monarchy: Its Evolution and Practice from Roman Antiquity to Modern Times*, pp. 41–52. Stuttgart: Steiner, 1992.

———. "Kristendom og kongemakt." In Geir Atle Ersland, Edgar Hovland, and Ståle Dyrvik, eds., *Festskrift til Historisk institutts 40—års jubileum, 1997*, pp. 71–86. Historisk institutt, Universitetet i Bergen, Skrifter 2. Bergen: Historisk institutt, 1997.

———. "Samkongedomme og enekongedomme." *Historisk tidsskrift (Oslo)* 54 (1975): 239–74.

Bartlett, Robert. *Gerald of Wales, 1146–1223.* Oxford: Clarendon Press, 1982.

Bartlett, Robert and Angus MacKay, eds. *Medieval Frontier Societies.* Oxford: Clarendon Press, 1989

Beumann, Helmut. "Das päpstliche Schisma von 1130, Lothar III. und die Metropolitanrechte von Magdeburg und Hamburg-Bremen in Polen und Dänemark." In *Deutsche Ostsiedlung in Mittelalter und Neuzeit,* pp. 20–43. Studien zum Deutschtum im Osten 8. Cologne: Böhlau, 1971.

Birkeli, Fridjov. "The Earliest Missionary Activities from England to Norway." *Nottingham Medieval Studies* 15 (1971): 27–37.

Bjorgo, Narve. "Samkongedome kontra einekongedome." *Historisk tidsskrift (Oslo)* 49 (1970): 1–33.

———. "Samkongedome og einkongedome." *Historisk tidsskrift (Oslo)* 55 (1976): 204–21.

Blomqvist, Ragnar. "Knut den store—Lunds grundläggare." *Kulturen* (1970): 157–88.

Bohnsack, Dietrich. "Das Fundament eines steinernen Rundturmes des 11. Jahrhunderts in der Hamburger Altstadt." In *Château Gaillard: Studien zur mittelalterlichen Wehrbau- und Siedlungsforschung—2. Kolloquium Büderich bei Düsseldorf, 1964,* pp. 1–6. Bonner Jahrbücher, Beiheft 27. Cologne: Böhlau, 1967.

———. "Die Bischofsburg am Speersort in Hamburg." *Hammaburg* n.s., 7 (1986): 147–62.

Bolin, Store. "Gesta Hammaburgensis ecclesiae pontificum." *Kulturhistoriskt lexikon för nordisk medeltid* 5 (1960): 283–90.

———. "Kring Mäster Adams text." *Scandia* 5 (1932): 205–50.

———. "Zum Cod. Havniensis A. kgl. S. 2296." *Classica et Mediaevalia* 10 (1949): 131–58.

Brandt, Karl Heinz. "Erzbischofsgräber im Bremer St.-Petri-Dom (Vorbericht)." *Zeitschrift für Archäologie des Mittelalters* 4 (1976): 7–28.

———. *Ausgrabungen im Bremer St.-Petri-Dom, 1974–1976: Ein Vorbericht.* Monographien der Wittheit zu Bremen 12. Bremen: Röver, 1977.

Breengaard, Carsten. *Muren om Israels hus. Regnum og sacerdotium i Danmark 1050–1170.* Copenhagen: Gads Forlag, 1982.

Brendalsmo, A. Jan. "Kristning og politisk makt. Hovdingemakt og kirkebygging i middelalderen: hvordan gjøre seg synlig i det politiske landskapet." In Steinar Supphellen, ed., *Kultursamanhengar i Midt-Norden: Tverrfagleg symposium for doktorgradsstudentar og forskarar—Forelesingar ved eit symposium i Levanger, 1996,* pp. 69–100. Det Kongelige Norske Videnskabers Selskab, Skrifter 1/1997. Trondheim: Tapir, 1997.

Brink, Stefan. "Kristnande och kyrklig organisation i Jämtland." In Stefan

Brink, ed., *Jämtlands kristnande*, pp. 155–88. Projektet Sveriges krist-nande. Publikationer 4. Uppsala: Lunne Böcker, 1996.

Buchner, Rudolf. "Adams von Bremen geistige Anleihen bei der Antike." *Mittellateinisches Jahrbuch* 2 (1965): 96–101.

———. "Die politische Vorstellungswelt Adams von Bremen." *Archiv für Kulturgeschichte* 45 (1963): 15–59.

Busch, Ralf. "Die Stadtentstehung Hamburgs, Deutschland." In Guy De Boe and Frans Verhaeghe, eds., *Urbanism in Medieval Europe: Papers of the "Medieval Europe Brugge, 1997," Conference 1*, p. 133. I. A. P. Rap-porten 1. Zellik: Instituut voor het Archeologisch Patrimonium, Weten-schappelijke instelling van de Vlaamse Gemeenschap, 1997.

———. "Kleinfunde aus Metall von der Domplatzgrabung in Hamburg." *Die Kunde* n.s., 46 (1995): 201–9.

Christensen, Aksel E. "Denmark Between the Viking Age and the Time of the Valdemars." *Mediaeval Scandinavia* 1 (1968): 28–50.

———. "Om kronologien i Aris íslendingabok og dens laan fra Adam af Bremen." In Johs. Brondum-Nielsen, Peter Skautrup, and Allan Karker, eds., *Nordiske Studier: Festskrift til Chr. Westergård Nielsen*, pp. 23–34. Copenhagen: Rosenkilde og Bagger, 1975.

———. *Danmark, Norden og Ostersoen: Udvalgte Afhandliger—Essays by Aksel E. Christensen*. Copenhagen: Den Danske Historiske Forening, 1976.

Coupland, Simon. "From Poachers to Gamekeepers: Scandinavian War-lords and Carolingian Kings." *Early Medieval Europe* 7 (1998): 85–114.

Cowdrey, Herbert E. J. "The Gregorian Reform in the Anglo-Norman Lands and in Scandinavia." In Alfons M. Stickler et al., eds, *La Riforma Gregoriana e l'Europa, I: Congresso Internazionale, Salerno, 20–25 maggio, 1985. Relazioni*, pp. 321–52. Studi Gregoriani per la storia della "Libertas Ecclesiae" 13. Roma: Libreria Ateneo Salesiano, 1989.

———. *Pope Gregory VII, 1073–1085*. Oxford: Clarendon Press, 1998.

Danstrup, John. "Esgruserhaandskriftet, en Adam af Bremen-Afskrift af Otto Sperling den Yngre." *Det Kongelige Danske Videnskabernes Selskab: Historisk-filologiske skrifter* 1.4 (1943): 1–98.

de Anna, Luigi *Conoscenza e immagine della Finlandia e del settentrione della cultura classico-medievale*. Turku: Turun Yliopisto, 1988.

Dorum, Knut. "Romerike og rikssamlingen." *Forum Mediaevale* 1 (1998): 53–129.

Drögereit, Richard. " 'Moderne' Forschung zur Bremer Frühgeschichte." *Stader Jahrbuch* n.s., 64 (1974): 145–48.

———. "Ansgar: Missionsbischof, Bischof von Bremen, Missionserzbis-chof für Dänen und Schweden." *Jahrbuch der Gesellschaft für niedersäch-sische Kirchengeschichte* 73 (1975): 9–45.

————. "Erzbistum Hamburg, Hamburg-Bremen oder Erzbistum Bremen, Studien zur Hamburg-Bremer Frühgeschichte." *Archiv für Diplomatik, Schriftgeschichte, Siegel- und Wappenkunde* 21 (1975): 136–230.

————. "Hamburg-Bremen, Bardowiek-Verden. Frühgeschichte und Wendenmission." *Bremisches Jahrbuch* 51 (1969): 193–-208.

Fenske, Lutz. *Adelsopposition und kirchliche Reformbewegung im östlichen Sachsen: Entstehung und Wirkung des sächsischen Widerstandes gegen das salische Königtum während des Invesitturstreits.* Veröffentlichung des Max-Planck-Instituts für Geschichte 47. Göttingen: Vandenhoek and Ruprecht, 1977.

Foote, Peter G. "Historical Studies: Conversion Moment and Conversion Period." In Anthony Faulkes and Richard Perkins, eds., *Viking Revaluations: Viking Society Centenary Symposium, May 14–15, 1992*, pp. 137–44. London: Viking Society for Northern Research, 1993.

Fuhrmann, Horst. "Adalberts von Bremen Mahnung: Si non caste, tamen caute." In Werner Paravicini, Frank Lubowitz, and Henning Unverhau, eds., *Mare Balticum: Beiträge zur Geschichte des Ostseeraums in Mittelalter und Neuzeit—Festschrift zum 65. Geburtstag von Erich Hoffmann*, pp. 93–99. Kieler Historische Studien 36. Sigmaringen: Thorbecke, 1992.

————. "Provincia constat duodecim episcopatibus: Zum Patriarchatsplan Erzbischof Adalberts von Hamburg-Bremen." *Studia Gratiana* 11 (1961): 389–404.

————. "Studien zur Geschichte mittelalterlicher Patriarchate: Der Patriachatsplan Erzbischof Adalberts von Bremen." *Zeitschrift der Savigny-Stiftung für Rechtsgeschichte, Kanonistische Abteilung* 41 (1955): 120–70.

Gahrn, Lars. "Sveariket och påvebreven om ärkestiftet Hamburg-Bremen." *Historisk tidskrift (Stockholm)* 2 (1994): 189–202.

Giese, Wolfgang. *Der Stamm der Sachsen und das Reich in ottonischer und salischer Zeit.* Wiesbaden: Franz Steiner Verlag, 1979.

Glaeske, Günter. *Die Erzbischöfe von Hamburg-Bremen als Reichsfürsten (937–1258).* Quellen und Darstellungen zur Geschichte Niedersachsens 60. Hildesheim: August Lax Verlag, 1962.

Göbell, Walter. "Die Christianisierung des Nordens und die Geschichte der nordischen Kirchen bis zur Errichtung des Erzbistums Lund." In Peter Meinhold, ed., *Schleswig-Holsteinische Kirchengeschichte, 1.1: Anfänge und Ausbau I*, pp. 63–-104. Neumünster: Wachholtz, 1977.

Goetz, Hans-Werner. "Die Zeit als Ordnungsfaktor in der hochmittelalterlichen Geschichtsschreibung." In Peter Dilg, Gundolf Keil, and Dietz-Rüdiger Moser, eds., *Rhythmus und Saisonalität: Kongreßakten des 5. Symposions des Mediävistenverbandes in Göttingen, 1993*, pp. 63–74. Sigmaringen: Thorbecke, 1995.

————. "Geschichtsschreibung und Recht: Zur rechtlichen Legitimierung des Bremer Erzbistums in der Chronik Adams von Bremen." In Silke Urbanski et al., eds., *Recht und Alltag im Hanseraum: Gerhard Theuerkauf zum 60. Geburtstag*, pp. 191–205. De Sulte 4. Lüneburg: Deutsches Salzmuseum Lüneburg, 1993.

Goez, Werner. "Das Erzbistum Hamburg-Bremen im Investiturstreit." *Jahrbuch der Wittheit zu Bremen* 27 (1983): 29–47.

Göhler, Johannes. "Die Verbreitung der Heiligenverehrung zur Zeit der Christianisierung der Sachsen und ihre Schutzherrschaft über die mittelalterlichen Kirchen im Erzbistum Bremen." *Jahrbuch der Gesellschaft für niedersächsische Kirchengeschichte* 95 (1997): 9–77.

Gunnes, Erik. *Rikssamling og kritsning 800–1177*. Norges historie 2. Oslo: Cappelen, 1976.

Haas, Wolf-Dieter. "Foris apostolus intus monachus: Ansgar als Mönch und Apostel des Nordens." *Journal of Medieval History* 11 (1985): 1–30.

Hägermann, Dieter. "Heinrich der Löwe und Bremen." *Braunschweigisches Jahrbuch* 79 (1998): 47–63.

Hallencreutz, Carl F. "Adam, Sverige och trossskiftet: Det missionsvetenskapliga perspektivet." In Emanuel Svenberg, trans., *Historien om Hamburgstiftet och dess biskopar: Adam av Bremen*, pp. 355–78. Stockholm: Proprius Förlag, 1984.

———. *Adam Bremensis and Sueonia: A Fresh Look at Gesta Hammaburgensis Ecclesiae Pontificum*. Acta Universitatis Upsaliensis. Skrifter rörande Uppsala universitet C 47. Stockholm: Almqvist and Wiksell, 1984.

Hatz, Gert. "Zur Münzprägung im Erzbistum Hamburg-Bremen in der Salierzeit." In Bernd Kluge, ed., *Fernhandel und Geldwirtschaft: Beiträge zum deutschen Münzwesen in sächsischer und salischer Zeit—Ergebnisse des Dannenberg-Kolloquiums, 1990*, pp. 173–88. Römisch-Germanisches Zentralmuseum, Forschungsinstitut für Vor—und Frühgeschichte, Monographien 31; Berliner numismatische Forschungen, N.F. 1. Sigmaringen: Thorbecke, 1993.

Hauck, Karl. "Die bremische Überlieferung zur Götter-Dreiheit Altuppsalas und die bornholmischen Goldfolien aus Sorte Muld (Zur Ikonologie der Goldbrakteaten, LII)." *Frühmittelalterliche Studien* 27 (1993): 409–79.

———. "Die religionsgeographische Zweiteilung des frühmittelalterlichen Europas im Spiegel der Bilder seiner Gottheiten." *Fornvännen* 82 (1987): 161–81.

Hellström, Jan Arvid. *Vägar till Sveriges kristnande*. Stockholm: Atlantis, 1996.

———. *Biskop och landskapssamhälle i tidig svensk medeltid*. Rättshistoriskt Bibliotek 16. Stockholm: Nordiska Bokhandel, 1971.

Hoffmann, Erich. "Beiträge zur Geschichte der Beziehungen zwischen dem deutschen und dem dänischen Reich für die Zeit von 934-1035." In Christian Radtke et al., eds., *850 Jahre St.-Petri-Dom zu Schleswig: 1134–1984*, pp. 105–132. Schriften des Vereins für Schleswig-Holsteinische Kirchengeschichte. Reihe 1, 35. Schleswig: Schleswiger Druck- und Verlagshaus, 1984.

———. "Die Wechselbeziehungen der Politik Knut des Großen gegenüber Olav Haraldsson von Norwegen und dem deutschen König/Kaiser Konrad II." In Kjell Haarstad et al., eds., *Innsikt og utsyn: Festskrift til Jorn Sandnes*, pp. 59–70. Skriftserie fra Historisk institutt 12. Trondheim: Norges teknisk-naturvitenskapelige universitet, 1996.

———. "Knut der Heilige und die Wende der dänischen Geschichte im 11. Jahrhundert." *Historische Zeitschrift* 218 (1974): 529–70.

———. "Politische Heilige in Skandinavien und die Entwicklung der drei nordischen Reiche und Völker." In Jürgen Petersohn, ed., *Politik und Heiligenverehrung im Hochmittelalter*, pp. 277–324. Vorträge und Forschungen 42. Sigmaringen: Thorbecke, 1994.

Hoffmann, Hartmut. "Grafschaften im Bischofshand." *Deutsches Archiv für Erforschung des Mittelalters* 44 (1990): 375–480.

Hohmann, Michael. "Das Erzstift Bremen und die Grafschaft Stade im 12. und frühen 13. Jahrhundert." *Stader Jahrbuch* 59 (1969): 49–118.

Hultgård, A., ed. *Uppsalakulten och Adam av Bremen*. Nora: Nya Doxa, 1997.

Huschner, Wolfgang. "Über die politische Bedeutung der Kanzler für Italien in spätottonisch-frühsalischer Zeit (1009–1057)." *Archiv für Diplomatik, Schriftgeschichte, Siegel- und Wappenkunde* 41 (1995): 31–47.

Hyenstrand, Ake. "Mäster Adam i Bremen och Sveriges och Götar." *Fornvännen* 80 (1985): 285–89.

Janson, Henrik. *Templum Nobilissimum: Adam av Bremen, Uppsalatemplet och konfliktinnjerna i Europa kring år 1075*. Avhandlingar från Historiska institutionen i Göteborg 21. Göteborg: Historical Institute, 1998.

Jenal, Georg. *Erzbischof Anno II. von Köln (1056–1075) und sein politisches Wirken: ein Beitrag zur Geschichte der Reichs- und Territorialpolitik im 11. Jahrhundert*. 2 vols; Monographien zur Geschichte des Mittelalters 8. Stuttgart: Hiersemann, 1974–1975.

Johanek, Peter. "Die Erzbischöfe von Hamburg-Bremen und ihre Kirche im Reich der Salierzeit." In Stefan Weinfurter and Frank Martin Siefarth, ed., *Die Salier und das Reich, 2. Die Reichskirche in der Salierzeit*, pp. 79–112. Sigmaringen: Thorbecke, 1991.

Johannesson, Kurt. "Adam och hednatemplet i Uppsala." In Emanuel Svenberg, trans., *Historien om Hamburgstiftet och dess biskopar. Adam av Bremen*, pp. 379–407. Stockholm: Proprius Förlag, 1984.

Johnsen, Arne Odd. "Om misjonsbiskopen Grimkellus." *Historisk tidsskrift (Oslo)* 54 (1975): 22–34.

Jordan, Karl. "Heinrich der Löwe und Bremen." In Klaus Friedland, ed., *Stadt und Land in der Geschichte des Ostseeraums: Festschrift für Professor Dr. Phil. Wilhelm Koppe zum 65. Geburtstag überreicht von Freunden und Schülern*, pp. 11–22. Lübeck: Verlag Max Schmidt-Römhild, 1973.

Katholische Akademie, Hamburg, ed. *Mit Ansgar beginnt Hamburg*. Publikationen der Katholischen Akademie Hamburg 2. Hamburg: EB-Verlag, 1986.

Knöpp, Friedrich. "Adalbert, Erzbischof von Hamburg-Bremen 1043–1072." In Friedrich Knöpp, ed., *Die Reichsabtei Lorsch. Festschrift zum Gedenken an ihre Stiftung 764, 1*, pp. 335–46. Darmstadt: Hessische Historische Kommission, 1973.

Körner, Sten. "Schweden in frühmittelalterlichen Quellen." In Werner Paravicini, Frank Lubowitz, and Henning Unverhau, ed., *Mare Balticum: Beiträge zur Geschichte des Ostseeraums in Mittelalter und Neuzeit. Festschrift zum 65. Geburtstag von Erich Hoffmann*, pp. 53–59. Kieler Historische Studien 36. Sigmaringen: Thorbecke, 1992.

Kristensen, Anne K. G. *Studien zur Adam von Bremen Überlieferung*. Skrifter utgivet af det historiske institut vde Københavns universitet 5. Copenhagen: Kobenhavns Universitet, Historisk Institut, 1975.

Kulturhistorisk Leksikon for nordisk midelalder: Fra vikingetid til reformationstid, 22 vols., Oslo, Gyldendal Nordisk Forlag, 1956-1978.

Lammers, Walther. "Formen der Mission bei Sachsen Schweden und Abotriten." *Blätter für deutsche Landesgeschichte* 106 (1970): 23–46.

Leyser, Karl. "From Saxon Freedoms to the Freedom of Saxony: The Crisis of the Eleventh Century." In Timothy Reuter, ed., *Communications and Power in Medieval Europe: The Gregorian Revolution and Beyond*, pp. 51–67. London: Hambledon, 1994.

———. "The Crisis of Medieval Germany." In Timothy Reuter, ed., *Communications and Power in Medieval Europe: The Gregorian Revolution and Beyond*, pp. 21–49. London: Hambledon, 1994.

Lobbedey, Uwe. "Der romanische Dom in Bremen: Ein Werk Erzbischof Liemars (1072–1101)." *Frühmittelalterliche Studien* 19 (1985): 312–29.

Löfstedt, Bengt. "Einige Notizen zur Sprache des Adam von Bremen." *Acta Classica* 22 (1979): 162–64.

Lund, Niels. *Harald Blåtands død*. Roskilde: Museums Forlag, 1998

Misch, Georg. "Das Bild des Erzbischofs Adalbert in der Hamburgischen Kirchengeschichte des Domscholasters Adam von Bremen." In Misch, *Geschichte der Autobiographie*, 3.1, pp. 168–214. Frankfurt: Schulte-Bulmke, 1959.

Morrison, Karl F. *History as a Visual Art in the Twelfth-Century Renaissance*. Princeton, N.J.: Princeton University Press, 1990.

Müller, Gunter. "Harald Gormssons Königsschicksal in heidnischer und christlicher Deutung." *Frühmittelalterliche Studien* 7 (1973): 118–42.

Mundal, Else. "Íslendingabók vurdert som bispestolskronike." *Alvíssmál* 3 (1994): 63–72.

Näsman, Ulf. "Från region till rike—Från stam till stat: Om danernas etnogenes och om denu danska riksbildningen." In Jens Flemming Kroger, ed., *Rikssamlingen—hovdingmakt og kongemakt: Karmoyseminaret, 1996*, pp. 46—65. Stavanger: Dreyer, 1997.

Nass, Klaus. *Die Reichschronik des Annalista Saxo und die sächsische Geschichtsschreibung im 12. Jahrhundert*, pp. 122–31. Schriften der Monumenta Germaniae Historica 41. Hannover: Hahnsche Buchhandlung, 1996.

Nilsson, Bertil, ed. *Kristnandet i Sverige: Gamla källor och nya perspektiv.* Projektet Sveriges kristnande. Publikationer 5. Uppsala: Lunne Böcker, 1996.

Nowak, Johannes. *Untersuchungen zum Gebrauch der Begriffe populus, gens und natio bei Adam von Bremen und Helmold von Bosau.* Reprographically published diss., University of Münster, 1971.

Nyberg, Tore S. "Adam av Bremen och Florenslistan." *Scandia* 57 (1991): 153–89.

———. "Adam av Bremen och terminologi." *Fornvännen* 82 (1987): 115–26.

———. "Grenzen erzählen Geschichte: Zum Konzept der frühen Mission in den Ländern und Gebieten Skandinaviens." *Zeitschrift der Gesellschaft für Schleswig-Holsteinische Geschichte* 107 (1982): 15–36.

———. "Skt. Peters efterfolgere i brydningstider: Omkring pavedommets historie Rom og Noreuropa 750–1200." *Odense University Studies in History and Social Sciences* 58 (1979): 1–188.

———. "Stad, skrift och stift: Några historiska inledningsfrågor." In Emanuel Svenberg, trans., *Historien om Hamburgstiftet och dess biskopar. Adam av Bremen*, pp. 295–339. Stockholm: Proprius Förlag, 1984.

———. *Die Kirche in Skandinavien: Mitteleuropäischer und englischer Einfluss im 11. und 12. Jahrhundert.* Beiträge zur Geschichte und Quellenkunde des Mittelalters 10. Sigmaringen: Thorbecke, 1986.

Ostergaard, Bent. "Sven Estridsens og Adams Danmarkshistorie om kong Gorm og hans forgængere." In *Vejle Amts Aarbog*, pp. 38–49, 1995.

Otto, Eberhard. "Beiträge zur Textgeschichte des Adams von Bremen." *Neues Archiv der Gesellschaft für ältere deutsche Geschichtskunde* 49 (1930): 10–55.

Padberg, Lutz E. von. "Geschichtsschreibung und kulturelles Gedächtnis: Formen der Vergangenheitswahrnehmung in der hochmittelalterlichen Historiographie am Beispiel von Thietmar von Merseburg, Adam von Bremen und Helmold von Bosau." *Zeitschrift für Kirchengeschichte* 105 (1994): 156–77.

Petersohn, Jürgen. *Der südliche Ostseeraum im kirchlich-politischen Kräftespiel des Reichs, Polens und Dänemarks vom 10. bis 13. Jahrhundert: Mission—Kirchenorganisation—Kultpolitik.* Ostmitteleuropa in Vergangenheit und Gegenwart 17. Cologne/Vienna: Böhlau, 1979.

Petri, Franz, ed. *Bischofs- und Kathedralstädte des Mittelalters und der frühen Neuzeit.* Städteforschung. Reihe A. Darstellungen, 1 Cologne: Böhlau, 1976.

Piltz, Anders. "Adam, Bibeln och auctores: En studie i litterär teknik." In Emanuel Svenberg, trans., *Historien om Hamburgstiftet och dess biskopar: Adam av Bremen,* pp. 341–54. Stockholm: Proprius Förlag, 1984.

Postel, Rainer. "Hamburg–Bremen, 1974–1989." *Blätter für deutsche Landesgeschichte* 126 (1990): 625–83.

Pulsiano, P. (ed.). *Medieval Scandinavia: An Encyclopedia.* New York: Garland Press, 1993.

Randsborg, Klaus. "The Viking Age State Formation in Denmark." *Offa* 38 (1982): 259–76.

Rech, Manfred. "Mittelalterliche Knochenkämme aus der Bremer Altstadt." *Bremisches Jahrbuch* 73 (1994): 9–11.

Reinecke, Karl. "Adalbert von Bremen als Kanzler für Italien." *Bremisches Jahrbuch* 51 (1969): 285–87.

———. "Bischofsumsetzung und Bistumsvereinigung: Ansgar und Hamburg-Bremen 845–864." *Archiv für Diplomatik, Schriftgeschichte, Siegel- und Wappenkunde* 33 (1987): 1–53.

———. "Das Erzbistum Hamburg-Bremen und Köln 890–893." *Stader Jahrbuch* 63 (1973): 59–76.

———. "Hammaburgensis sive Bremensis ecclesia (Hamburg-Bremen)." In Stefan Weinfurter and Odilo Engels, eds., *Archiepiscopatus Hammaburgensis sive Bremensis,* pp. 4–52. Series episcoporum ecclesiae catholicae occidentalis ab initio usque ad annum MCXCVIII 5.2. Stuttgart: Anton Hiersemann Verlag, 1984.

Rindal, Magnus, ed. *Fra hedendom til kristendom: Perspektiver på religionsskiftet i Norge.* Oslo: Ad Notam Gyldendal, 1996.

Robinson, Charles H., trans. *Anskar: The Apostle of the North, 801–865: The Vita Anskarii by Bishop Rimbert, His Fellow Missionary and Successor.* London: The Society for the Propagation of the Gospel in Foreign Parts, 1921.

Robinson, Ian S. "*Periculosus homo*: Pope Gregory VII and Episcopal Authority." *Viator* 9 (1978): 103–31.

———. *Henry IV of Germany, 1056–1106.* Cambridge: Cambridge University Press, 1999.

Rothe, Gunnhild. "Kristningskongene og religionsskiftet i Norge." *Middelalderforum* 1 (1996): 36–53.

Sandnes, Jorn. "Germanisches Widerstandsrecht und die Schlacht bei Stiklestad 1030." In Werner Paravicini, Frank Lubowitz, and Henning Unverhau, eds., *Mare Balticum: Beiträge zur Geschichte des Ostseeraums in Mittelalter und Neuzeit—Festschrift zum 65. Geburtstag von Erich Hoffmann*, pp. 61–66. Kieler Historische Studien 36. Sigmaringen: Thorbecke, 1992.

Sawyer, Birgit. "Scandinavian Conversion Histories." *Harvard Ukrainian Studies* 12–13 (1988–89): 46–60.

Sawyer, Birgit and Peter H. Sawyer. *Medieval Scandinavia: From Conversion to Reformation, ca. 800–1500.* The Nordic Series 17. Minneapolis: University of Minnesota Press, 1993.

——. "Adam and the Eve of Scandinavian history." In Paul Magdalino, ed., *The Perception of the Past in Twelfth-Century Europe*, pp. 37–51. London: Hambledon, 1992.

Sawyer, Birgit, Peter H. Sawyer, and Ian Wood. *The Christianization of Scandinavia: Report of a Symposium Held at Kungälv, Sweden, August 4–9, 1985.* Alingsås: Viktoria Bokförlag, 1987.

Sawyer, Peter H. "Dioceses and Parishes in Twelfth-Century Scandinavia." In Barbara E. Crawford, ed., *St. Magnus Cathedral and Orkney's Twelfth-Century Renaissance*, pp. 36–45. Aberdeen: Aberdeen University Press, 1988.

——. *Kings and Vikings: Scandinavia and Europe AD, 700–1100.* London and New York: Methuen, 1982.

——. *The Making of Sweden.* Occasional papers on medieval topics 3. Alingsås: Viktoria, 1988.

——, ed. *The Oxford Illustrated History of the Vikings.* Oxford: Oxford University Press, 1997.

Schieffer, Theodor. "Adnotationes zur Germania Pontificia und zur Echtheitskritik überhaupt." *Archiv für Diplomatik, Schriftgeschichte, Siegel- und Wappenkunde 32* (1986): 503–45.

Schmale, Franz-Josef. "Adam von Bremen." In Kurt Ruh et al., eds., *Die deutsche Literatur des Mittelalters: Verfasserlexikon*, Vol. 1. Second edition, pp. 50–54. Berlin and New York: Walter de Gruyter, 1978.

Schmeidler, Bernhard. "Zur Entstehung und zum Plane der Hamburgischen Kirchengeschichte Adams von Bremen." *Neues Archiv der Gesellschaft für ältere deutsche Geschichtskunde* 50 (1933): 221–28.

Schulz, Caroline. "Die Befestigungen auf dem Hamburger Domplatz." In Manfred Gläser, ed., *Archäologie des Mittelalters und Bauforschung im Hanseraum: Eine Festschrift für Günter P. Fehring*, pp. 175–80. Rostock: Reich, 1993.

Schumacher, Franz and Karl Heinz Brandt. *Der Dom zu Bremen: Wiederherstellung und Ausgrabung.* Schriften der Wittheit zu Bremen, N.F. 8. Bremen: Döll, 1982.

Schwebel, Marianne. "Die Glocke am Bremer St. Petri Dom." *Bremisches Jahrbuch* 77 (1998): 266–76.

Seegrün, Wolfgang. *Das Erzbistum Hamburg in seinen älteren Papsturkunden*. Studien und Vorarbeiten zur Germania pontificia 5. Cologne and Vienna: Böhlau, 1976.

———. "Das Erzbistum Hamburg—eine Fiktion?" *Zeitschrift des Vereins für hamburgische Geschichte* 60 (1974): 1–16.

———. *Das Papsttum und Skandinavien bis zur Vollendung der nordischen Kirchenorganisation*. Quellen und Forschungen zur Geschichte Schleswig-Holsteins 51. Neumünster: Wachholtz, 1967.

———. *Provincia Hammaburgo-Bremensis*. Germania pontificia 6. Göttingen: Vandenhoeck and Ruprecht, 1981.

Skre, Dagfinn. "Kirken for sognet: Den tidligste kirkeordningen i Norge." In Hans-Emil Lidén, ed., *Motet mellom kristendom og hedendom i Norge*, pp. 170–233. Oslo: Universitetsforlaget, 1995.

———. "Missionary Activity in Early Medieval Norway: Strategy, Organization and the Course of Events." *Scandinavian Journal of History* 23 (1998): 1–19.

Solli, Brit. "Narratives of Encountering Religions: On the Christianization of the Norse Around AD 900–1000." *Norwegian Archaeological Review* 29 (1996): 89–114.

Sot, Michel. *Gesta episcoporum: Gesta abbatum*. Typologie des sources du moyen âge occidental 37. Turnhout: Brepols, 1981.

Staecker, Jörn. "Bremen—Canterbury—Kiev—Konstantinopel? Auf Spurensuche nach Missionierenden und Missionierten in Altdänemark und Schweden." *Akademie der Wissenschaften und der Literatur (Mainz). Abhandlungen der geistes- und sozialwissenschaftlichen Klasse* 3 (1997): 59–81.

Starke, H. D. "Die Pfalzgrafen von Sachsen bis zum Jahre 1088" *Braunschweiger Jahrbuch* 36 (1955): 24–52.

Steinsland, Gro. "The Change of Religion in the Nordic countries: A Confrontation Between Two Living Religions." *Collegium Medievale* 3 (1990): 123–35.

Theuerkauf, Gerhard. "Die Hamburgische Kirchengeschichte Adams von Bremen: Über Gesellschaftsformen und Weltbilder im 11. Jahrhundert." In Dieter Berg and Hans-Werner Goetz, eds., *Historiographia Mediaevalis: Studien zur Geschichtsschreibung und Quellenkunde des Mittelalters—Festschrift für Franz-Josef Schmale zum 65. Geburtstag*, pp. 118–37. Darmstadt: Wissenschaftliche Buchgesellschaft, 1988.

———. "Urkundenfälschungen des Erzbistums Hamburg-Bremen vom 9.-11. Jahrhundert." *Niedersächsisches Jahrbuch für Landesgeschichte* 60 (1988): 71–140.

Trommer, Aage. "Komposition und Tendenz in der Hamburgischen Kirchengeschichte Adam von Bremens." *Classica et Mediaevalia* 18 (1957): 207–57.

Vollrath, Hanna. "Konfliktwahrnehmung und Konfliktdarstellung in erzählenden Quellen des 11. Jahrhunderts." In Stefan Weinfurter and Hubertus Seibert, eds., *Die Salier und das Reich, 3. Gesellschaftlicher und ideengeschichtlicher Wandel im Reich der Salier*, pp. 279–96. Sigmaringen: Thorbecke, 1991.

Walberg, Oystein, ed. *For og etter Stiklestad 1030: Religionsskifte, kulturforhold, politisk makt. Seminar på Stiklestad, 1994*. Verdal: Stiklestad nasjonale kultursenter, 1996.

Warner, David, ed. and trans. *Ottonian Germany: Thietmar's Chronicon*. Manchester: Manchester University Press, 2001.

Wavra, Brigitte. *Salzburg und Hamburg: Erzbistumsgründung und Missionspolitik in karolingischer Zeit*. Giessener Abhandlungen zur Agrar- und Wirtschaftsforschung des europäischen Ostens 179. Berlin: Duncker and Humblot 1991.

Weibezahn, Ingrid. "Lag im sog: 'Bezelin-Grab' wirklich Erzbischof Bezelin? Zur Identifizierung eines Grabes im Bremer St. Petri Dom." *Bremisches Jahrbuch* 76 (1997): 83–100.

Wolter, Heinz. "Die Synodaltätigkeit der Erzbischöfe von Hamburg-Bremen bis zum Jahre 1223." *Annuarium historiae conciliorum* 22 (1990): 1–30.

Index

Aachen, 114; destruction of palace, 38

Aalborg, 190

Aarhus, 190; bishopric, 188; church burned, 124; diocese discontinued, 86; transfer of bishopric, 62n

Abhelin, bishop of Oldenburg, 106, 131

Abingdon, abbey, 94n

Abrodites, xix, 9, 65, 130, 157

Acilin, bishop, 183, 205

Adalbert, bishop of the Bohemians, martyred, 78n, 199

Adalbert, archbishop of Hamburg-Bremen, xiii, 114-85; acquaintance with Adam, xiv, xx; bishops consecrated by, 179 ff.; character, xxi f., 115 ff., 134; Christmas service, 177 f.; conflict with nobles, 116 ff.; consecration, 114; as imperial consul, xxiii, 142, 166; death, xxiii f., 172 ff.; decline of power, xxiii f., 155 f., 161 f.; driven from court, 154 f.; enmity toward the clergy for murder of his brother, 162 f. entombment, 175; faults, xxii; final degeneration, 168 ff.; forged document, xiv, 15; good deeds, 174; and Gottschalk, 132; and Henry II, 119 ff.; and King Harold, 128 f.; relations with Henry III, 137 f.; influence with Leo IX and Henry III, 139; and Henry IV, 150 f.; and legates of the Apostolic See, 184; letter to bishop of Roeskilde, 182; living habits, 147; missionary endeavors, 122 ff., 222; monasteries founded by, 121 f.; and Odinkar the younger, 79; omens of death, 168, 171 f.; plan for a patriarchate in Hamburg, 140 f.; plans for Hamburg-Bremen, xxii f.; policy toward women, 138 f.; projected missionary journey, 179 f.; projected synod in Denmark, 181; as provost at Halberstadt, 115; relations with nobles, 148 ff.; as regent, 166; repentance, 175 ff.; return to power, 166 f.; services held at Hamburg, 136 f.; as subdeacon of Hermann, 102; superstitions, 146 f.; and Svein

Estrithson, 123 f., 129 f., 132; sycophants, 145 f.; and Turholz monastery, 28n; unstable temperament, 145, 168 ff.; vainglory, xxiii, 137 f., 143 ff., 154 ff., 173 f.; vision of the Mass, 176 f.; wealth, 152

Adalbert, archbishop of Magdeburg, consecration of, 62; death, 69

Adalbert, bishop of the Orkneys, 183, 214n

Adalbert, son of Berengar, 59n

Adaldag, archbishop of Hamburg-Bremen, 46, 54-74, 79, 118, 193; consecration of bishops for Denmark, 71; death and entombment, 73 f.; imperial favor, 69; royal chancellor, 55n

Adalgar, archbishop of Hamburg-Bremen, 42-46; assistant of Rimbert, 42 f.; death and entombment, 46; remains transferred, 103

Adalgar, abbot of Corvey, 35

Adalward, bishop of Verden, 54

Adalward the Elder, bishop of Götaland, 183; as legate in Sweden, 126 f.; miraculous powers, 205; in Norway, 127n, 204n; and pirate corpse, 77, 127n; vision, 127

Adalward the Younger, bishop of Sigtuna, xx, 182, 183, 205n, 209 f.; story of the Amazons, 200n

Adam of Bremen, arrival in Bremen, 118; attitude toward his writing, 4; career, xiii; death, xvi; superstitions, xx; and Svein Estrithson, 160 f.; writings, xvii

—Gesta, xiii; analysis of, xx f., xxiv ff.; borrowings from, xxxi; codices, xxvii f.; conclusion of first draft, 179; content of work, xviii f.; critical editions, xxxii; date of, xv f.; geographical sources, xix; manuscripts and printings, xxvi ff.; scholia, xxvii f.; sources, xvi f., 4 f., 20n; sources for expressions in the prologue, 3n; test of authenticity of texts, xxx; translations, xxxii f.; writing of, xiv f., xv f.